# MOBILIA

# *Sourcebook* ™

## First Edition

Published by

MOBILIA

M A G A Z I N E

MOBILIA® Sourcebook™

ISBN: 0-9656249-9-4

Copyright © 1997 Hyatt Research Corp.

Publishers:
MOBILIA® Magazine
(ISSN: 1068-7793)
P.O. Box 575, Middlebury, VT 05753

TEL 802-388-3071
FAX 802-388-2215
e-mail: mobilia@aol.com
Website: http://www.mobilia.com

## Bulk Copies

Wholesale accounts for bulk purchases of the MOBILIA Sourcebook should call our exclusive distributors:

Motorbooks International
TEL 1-800-458-0454
FAX 715-294-4448
729 Prospect Ave., P.O. Box 1, Osceola, WI 54020 • USA

# MOBILIA Sourcebook

## From the Publisher—

The *MOBILIA Sourcebook* is finally here, and I hope that it helps you make better connections in the automobilia hobby. This first edition includes 600 main listings, 2,000 cross-references,—indexed by more than 50 unique collecting categories. It's a hobby first, and we're proud of the results!

If your particular interest is gas-powered miniature racers, you'll find a special section devoted to the many active suppliers in that market. Interested in petroliana? We've got it covered with two sections: one for pumps and globes, and another for general interest. Toys and models figure largely in the *Sourcebook,* too, so you can quickly zero in on particular suppliers. We tried to include all the automobilia categories you'd be interested in: Signs, Art, Literature, Mascots, Plates, Racing, Promos, Pedal Cars, Hot Rod Memorabilia, even Motorcycle collectibles, to name just a few! The *Sourcebook* additionally lists services such as Auction Companies, Museums, Appraisers, and many more.

A directory such as the *Sourcebook* is only as good as its indexing. We worked hard to ensure you can find key contacts without a fuss. Please refer to the Table of Contents and, at the rear, the comprehensive indexes for quick access to all the listings.

The contents of the *Sourcebook* were obtained by mailing several thousand Free Listing forms to every world automobilia specialist we could find (we made many personal reminder calls, too). Future new listers who wish to be in our next edition should either fill out the Free Listing form or use the Request form (both are included at the rear of this directory). *Existing listers must also renew their listing for the next edition—don't forget!*

I'd like to thank one and all for participating in the *Sourcebook.* As a bonus, this first edition of the *Sourcebook* also includes our popular annual look at the "Automobilia Top 10." This full-color section begins on page 65.

I hope that you find the *MOBILIA Sourcebook* a valuable resource, and your comments to make it better are always welcome. By the way, if you'd like even more news and information on the automobilia hobby, please consider subscribing to our monthly magazine, *MOBILIA*. Subscriptions are just $29 for 12 issues by calling 1-800-967-8068.

Eric H. Killorin
*Sourcebook* Publisher

## From the Editor—

This is my uncle's fault. A longtime editor of *Mustang Monthly* magazine, he got me started on car magazines when I was young. I read them with interest through the years, but had no idea until recently that such a gem existed in my own hometown.

I have been preparing the book you are now holding since starting at *MOBILIA*. My tasks ran the gamut: from developing the database and entering listing information to chatting with many of the business owners and arranging all of this into a form that we hope you like. Without the wonders of desktop publishing, I don't think that our small staff could have managed such an effort and in such a short period of time!

All of the *MOBILIA* team have been integral parts to this project. I owe a special debt to our data entry folks for helping me rebuild lost data near the end of the process. I also must thank Cyndie Klopfenstein of The World-Wide Power Company for her invaluable assistance with developing the index and table of contents.

As my first encounter with *MOBILIA* readers, compiling this *Sourcebook* has been both fun and instructive. I read all of your comments with interest, and remain impressed at the commitment you have to automobile collectibles. (I'm fascinated that some of you collect spark plugs—now I wonder less about how others view my Lego collection!)

An example of this dedication is Ron Van Oeveren of Blast From the Past. He called me in December and asked for a category called "Neon." We agreed that if Ron could find four friends (for a total of five listings), we'd create the category. Within two weeks I had commitments from Ron and several other *Sourcebook* listers, all requesting a separate Neon section. You will find the Neon listings on page 61, thanks to Ron's legwork.

Thanks to you all, and good luck! Keep your eyes open for next year's *Sourcebook* Free Listing forms (a copy is also included in this edition on pages 142-143). The deadline to provide us with your completed listing is November 30, 1997.

While this first edition of the *MOBILIA Sourcebook* is likely to be collected just like any other valuable ephemera, please let us know how we can improve it in the coming years. Your comments are always welcome!

Jeff Inglis
*Sourcebook* Editor

# Table of Contents
## Alphabetical by Collecting Category
### *See also Indexes beginning on p. 129*

# APPRAISAL SERVICE

## AVM Automotive Consulting

Box 338
Montvale, NJ 07645 USA
TEL: 201-391-5194
FAX: 201-782-0663
Email: avm/tony@aol.com

Appraisals & consulting for individuals, insurers, attorneys for insurance, financial, legal & estate purposes. In person or by mail. Member of the International Automotive Appraisers Association. Call weekdays 9-5 or Email.

## Abbott & Hast Ltd. Auto Promos & Kits

See our main listing under "Models, Kits"

## C. Sherman Allen, Auctioneer & Associates

See our main listing under "Auction Firm"

## Antiques by Doug

Douglas Ross
4600 N. Portland
Oklahoma City, OK 73112 USA
TEL: 405-947-8570

Antique cars, slot machines, gas-powered race cars.

## Automobilia International

See our main listing under "Auction Firm"

## Car-ARDS Literature

Dennis Wandass
18 Nagel Dr.
Buffalo, NY 14225 USA
TEL: 716-681-8483

Have 3,800 contacts worldwide. Auto sales literature; postcards; trading cards; shop, parts, body, owner's manuals. Can provide information on most auto-related interests. Nominal fee for services to contact these sources. Personal library collection 1892 to present. Also have coins, stamps, advertisements. 37 years' hobby/business interest.

*Other categories: Literature; Books; Cards, Postal*

## Collector Auto Appraisal Co.

Carl Bomstead
PO Box 1083
Lake Stevens, WA 98258 USA
TEL: 206-334-5215
FAX: 206-334-7812

Appraise collector automobiles & automobilia for insurance & estate settlement. Buy, sell, & trade gas & oil collectibles, advertising signs, & automotive-related mascots & badges. Will purchase complete collections.

*Other categories: Petroliana, Other; Signs; Mascots/Badges/Emblems*

## Curtis Equipment Co.

Ken Curtis
421 Eby St. PO Box 506
Raleigh, NC 27602 USA
TEL: 919-832-7422
FAX: 919-775-1095

I am a licensed NC auto dealer with 46 years' experience buying/selling vehicles with special interest in Chrysler products. All signs, pins, toys, etc. are welcome. Life member of AACA, HCCA,

Current Airflow Club. Call me on any item or your need for an appraisal.

*Other categories: Marque Specific; Signs; Specialized Automobilia*

## Don's Body Shop

Don Montgomery
2030 South St.
Long Beach, CA 90805 USA
TEL: 310-634-9672

Appraiser & consultant specializing in automobiles, automotive collectibles, old automotive toys, race cars, racing memorabilia, advertising signs, automotive general store, etc., guitars, mandolins, etc. Will also purchase above items. Buy, sell, trade.

*Other categories: Gas-Powered Racers; Petroliana, Other; Mixed Automobilia*

## Elevenparts AG

See our main listing under "Literature"

## Ellerson Auction Co.

See our main listing under "Auction Firm"

## Hudson Motor Car Company Memorabilia

See our main listing under "Specialized Automobilia"

## International Automotive Appraisers Association

Box 338
Montvale, NJ 07645 USA
TEL: 201-391-3251
Email: avm/tony@aol.com

IAAA is an association open to recognized automotive appraisers which provides a service to the community who are in need of locating a qualified IAAA member appraiser in their area.

## J & E Spindizzie

See our main listing under "Gas-Powered Racers"

## J & J Models

See our main listing under "Toys, General"

## S.L. Jaffe, Inc.

Sam Jaffe
226C Palmetto Dr.
Ft. Myers, FL 33908 USA
TEL: 941-454-7863

Appraisal services. Sam Jaffe Auto, division of S.L. Jaffe, Inc.: antique & collectible cars, automobilia & petroliana. January through March: 226C Palmetto Dr., Ft. Myers, FL 33908, 941-454-7863; April through December: 32 Woodcrest Dr., Scotia, NY 12302, 518-399-5910.

*Other categories: Mixed Automobilia; Specialized Automobilia; Petroliana, Other*

## Ted Knorr

See our main listing under "Racing Artifacts"

## Dan Kruse Classic Car Productions

See our main listing under "Auction Firm"

## Legendary Collectibles

See our main listing under "Models, Precision"

## License Plates, Etc.

See our main listing under "License Plates, Tags, etc."

## Lust Auction Services

See our main listing under "Auction Firm"

## M&M Automobilia Appraisers

Mike Grippo
4349 WN Peotone Rd.
Beecher, IL 60401-9757 USA
TEL: 708-258-6662
FAX: 708-258-9675

Appraises special interest, collectible, & antique automobiles & automobile collectibles for insurance coverage, loan valuation, marriage or business dissolutions & value disputes.

*Other categories: Literature; Mixed Automobilia; Showroom Items*

## New Era Toys

See our main listing under "Restoration Service"

## The Oil Barron

See our main listing under "Art, Prints & Posters"

## Arthur Price

See our main listing under "Racing Artifacts"

## Stephen J. Raiche

See our main listing under "License Plates, Tags, etc."

## Frank R. Righetti

See our main listing under "Signs"

## Ron's Relics

See our main listing under "Pedal Cars"

## James T. Sandoro

24 Myrtle Ave.
Buffalo, NY 14204 USA
TEL: 716-855-1931

For 34 years appraiser-consultant auctioneer collector car parts, memorabilia for insurance, estates, divorce, restoration problems, etc. Collector of Pierce-Arrow, Thomas Flyer, & all Buffalo-made auto, motorcycle, bicycle, truck & accessory items, signs, displays, literature, parts. No tools or ads. For permanent museum to open in Buffalo.

*Other categories: Specialized Automobilia; Showroom Items; Museum*

## Sotheby's

See our main listing under "Auction Firm"

## SpeedArt Enterprises

See our main listing under "Mascots/Badges/Emblems"

## Tiger Automotive

See our main listing under "Promos"

## Vintage Jag Works

See our main listing under "Marque Specific"

## Winner's Circle Racing Collectibles

See our main listing under "Hot Wheels"

## Wyoming Vintage Tin

Rick Eccli
PO Box 1553
Cheyenne, WY 82003 USA
TEL: 307-634-3231

Buy, sell, trade. Petroliana, old & new toys, antique auto/street rod parts. Toy gas stations are a specialty. Antique auto appraisals, unrestored or restored gas pumps for sale.

*Other categories: Petroliana, Pumps & Globes; Hot Wheels*

## John J. Zolomij, Inc.

John J. Zolomij
1725 Elmhurst Dr.
Whitehall, PA 18052 USA
TEL: 610-821-0111
FAX: 610-821-9070
Email: rehac@aol.com

Automotive art & memorabilia consultant, focusing on all aspects of collection design, presentation, & management. Capable of researching items, doing computerized inventory, preparation of articles, pamphlets, & books on your art. Serves as private broker for sale of individual items or entire collections globally. Conduct assessment, appraisals, & other services needed by hobbyist/collectors.

*Other categories: Art, Original; Specialized Automobilia; Museum*

# ART, ORIGINAL

## Mats Alfvag

See our main listing under "Art, Prints & Posters"

## The Automobile Art Studio

Bill Harbort
805 7th St. NW
Minot, ND 58703 USA
TEL: 701-838-1808

The finest in original automotive art. The finest in quality limited edition art prints. Call or write for additional info.

*Other categories: Art, Prints & Posters; Art, Other; General Interest*

## Automobilia International

See our main listing under "Auction Firm"

## Automotive Fine Art

See our main listing under "Art, Prints & Posters"

## British Only Motorcycles & Parts, Inc.

See our main listing under "Motorcycle Collectibles"

## Kenneth R. Chane

See our main listing under "Toys, General"

## DXR Automotive

See our main listing under "Signs"

## Getz Grafiks

Don Getz
2245 Major Rd.
Peninsula, OH 44264-9626 USA
TEL: 216-657-2807
FAX: 216-657-2311

Specialize in dramatic, large-scale acrylic paintings of sports car, hot rod, classic & racing engines. Posters & note cards available. Custom T-shirt designs produced. Commissions accepted. Works in numerous corporate collec-

tions, including Goodyear, Firestone, Miller Brewing, Butler Art Museum. 40 years of experience. Collect diecast & tin race cars.

*Other categories: Art, Prints & Posters; Hot Rod Memorabilia; Art, Other*

## Glassmobiles

See our main listing under "Art, Other"

## Dan Kirchner

See our main listing under "Literature"

## The Klemantaski Collection

See our main listing under "Photographs"

## Dave Kurz, Artist

See our main listing under "Art, Prints & Posters"

## The Loved Ones Gallery

See our main listing under "Art, Prints & Posters"

## Buz McKim Racing Art

See our main listing under "Art, Prints & Posters"

## Edward E. Moberg, Jr.

2554 Lincoln Blvd. #255
Marina Del Rey, CA 90291
TEL: 805-297-2955

Von Dutch, the legendary custom car cultural icon of the 1950s & 1960s. It's a

two-sided airbrushed sweater dated 1958 & twice signed, on exhibit at museums across America for a year in 1993-1994. Only one known to exist. Call or write – serious inquiries only, please.

*Other categories: Art, Other; Specialized Automobilia; Museum*

## Mobil & Morgans

See our main listing under "Petroliana, Other"

## Mysteries & Motorcars

See our main listing under "Books"

## Racy Thangs, Inc.

Bill Neale
12308 Brittany Cir.
Dallas, TX 75230 USA
TEL: 972-701-0172
FAX: 972-701-0172

Automobile art for the collector. Original paintings, limited edition, signed, & numbered prints of racing cars. Vintage & present. Award-winning member of the Automotive Fine Arts Society (AFAS).

*Other categories: Art, Prints & Posters; Art, Other*

## Remember Woodward, Inc.

See our main listing under "Mixed Automobilia"

## Charles Schalebaum

1545 W. Fairmont St.
Allentown, PA 18102 USA
TEL: 610-435-4440
FAX: 610-435-3388

The finest automobilia, US & foreign: art, sculpture, antique, mascots, toys, racing. Buy, sell, trade.

*Other categories: Specialized Automobilia; Toys, General; Mascots/Badges/Emblems*

## Wheels Art & Memorabilia

Jerry L. Avey
958 Cherryvale Rd.
Boulder, CO 80303 USA
TEL: 303-494-7896
FAX: 303-494-5402

We have a new line of bronzes. First series will be pedal car related, second series will be classic cars, hot rods, gas

& oil. These bronzes will be limited editions & a very fine quality. We handle all types of automobilia art. Buy now, low numbers.

*Other categories: Art, Prints & Posters; Art, Other; Pedal Cars*

## Yosemite Sam's Auto Art

Sam Radoff
3623 Springer
Delaware, Ontario N0L 1E0 Canada
TEL: 519-652-6956

Original sculptures, paintings, model cars, fine art by Hall of Famer Yosemite Sam. Pinstripe panels on painted aluminum sculptures & paintings using car, motorcycle etc. parts. Original customized 1/24 plastic model cars turn your favorite part into a work of art. Commissions available. Also fine art sculptures & paintings.

*Other categories: Hot Rod Memorabilia; Mixed Automobilia; General Interest*

## John J. Zolomij, Inc.

See our main listing under "Appraisal Service"

# ART, PRINTS & POSTERS

## AiLE bv

Gies Pluim
De Gaullesingel 117
Ede, Netherlands 6716 LG
TEL: +31 318 64 34 17
FAX: +31 318 64 28 68
Email: Gies@user.diva.nl

I own about 1,400 original negatives of GP Racing 1902-1914 of which I can make prints for collectors at cost. See my site
http://www.bitpress.nl/aile/carprints

*Other category: Photographs*

## Mats Alfvag

Skutuddsvagen 7
Saltsjobaden, Sweden 133 38
TEL: +46-8-717-63-06
FAX: +46-8-660-02-62

Specialize in all kinds of automobilia posters. Showroom posters, racing, motorcycles, & airlines. Always 500-600

items in stock. Buy, sell, trade. Send $5 for current catalog.

*Other categories: Art, Original; Racing Artifacts; Literature*

## Auto-Cycle Publications

See our main listing under "Literature"

## The Automobile Art Studio

See our main listing under "Art, Original"

## Automobile Quarterly

See our main listing under "Publications, Current"

## Automobilia

See our main listing under "Retail Store"

## Automobilia Cycles Trucks (ACT)

See our main listing under "Specialized Automobilia"

## Automotive Fine Art

Dick Deam
1020 Wrencoe Hills Rd.
Sandpoint, ID 83864 USA
TEL: 208-263-0932

Renowned automotive artist offers limited edition lithographs of original oil paintings: 57 Thunderbird, 54 Cadillac, 32 Ford, 50 Chevrolet pickup, Indian motorcycle, Vol 1. Hot Rod magazine in color, Wurlitzer juke box 1015 w/ 49 Mercury. Send SASE & $1 refundable for color brochure. Commissions are accepted, call for information.

*Other categories: Art, Original; Hot Rod Memorabilia; Motorcycle Collectibles*

## Autosaurus

Bob Luther
600 North Henry St.
Alexandria, VA 22320 USA
TEL: 703-519-0742
FAX: 703-549-0758
Email: rjluther@aol.com

Autosaurus gallery, artwork, old prints, books, globes, signs, photographs, notepads, sculptures, desktop items, vintage toys, racing memorabilia, & artifacts. Access on the Internet at www.qualityservices.com or write or call for catalog. Visit by appointment.

Other categories: Art, Other; Mixed Automobilia; Online Service

## Back Issue Car Magazines

See our main listing under "Literature"

## Alan Bowden

See our main listing under "Models, Kits"

## Bullivant Gallery

Robert Bullivant
1100 Lami St.
St. Louis, MO 63104 USA
TEL: 888-767-8375
FAX: 314-865-0078
Email: bullivant@stlnet.com

Bullivant Gallery has just released a stunning motorcycle art print entitled "DaVinci's Dream: To Fly Without Wings." The print features the Ducati 916 motorcycle in Leonardo's 15th-century studio. Museum-quality 8-color printing on premium archival paper. Visit our website at http://home.stlnet.com/~bullivant/

Other categories: Motorcycle Collectibles; Online Service; Clothing

## Harry Burnstine

See our main listing under "Specialized Automobilia"

## C.S.P. Calendars

See our main listing under "Specialized Automobilia"

## Car Crazy, Inc.

See our main listing under "Retail Store"

## Kenneth R. Chane

See our main listing under "Toys, General"

## Chelsea Motoring Literature

See our main listing under "Literature"

## Christie's

See our main listing under "Auction Firm"

## The Classic Motorist

See our main listing under "Books"

## Collector's Studio Motorsport Gallery

See our main listing under "Racing Artifacts"

## DKC & Company

See our main listing under "Models, Precision"

## Dragster Australia

John Baremans
PO Box 6225
Baulkham Hills, NSW 2153 Australia
TEL: +61-2-9894-7499
FAX: +61-2-9894-7790

Dragster Australia is Australia's longest-running drag racing publication. It comes out every two weeks & covers both local & overseas news. We market a lot of merchandise on drag racing, including T-shirts, videos, books, diecast, plastic models, & art prints, including Youngblood, Peters, Ibusuki, & more.

Other categories: Models, Kits; Books; Clothing

## Elevenparts AG

See our main listing under "Literature"

## Enterprise Cars

See our main listing under "Signs"

## Fast Art

Kevin Parks
3506 Chancellor Dr.
Ft. Wayne, IN 46815 USA
TEL: 219-483-4374

Specializing in racing art, prints, & posters. Original event posters from LeMans, Monaco, & others. Also racing models, kits, photographs, & other racing artifacts. Send SASE for current list. Call after 5pm.

Other categories: Models, Kits; Photographs; Racing Artifacts

## Fast Times Automobilia

Darla Gustaitis
445C E. Cheyenne Mnt. Blvd Ste 319
Colorado Springs, CO 80906 USA
TEL: 719-579-8545
FAX: 719-579-8545

Nostalgic drag racing & hot rod prints, posters, videos, & T-shirts. Mazmanian, K.S. Pittman, S-W-C, Jungle Jim, Wild Willy Borsch, & others. Posters by Dennis McPhaig. Art by Ibusuki, Fredericks, & Seitz.

Other categories: Hot Rod Memorabilia; Clothing; Specialized Automobilia

## Gallery Automania

Bill Michalak
308 East Street
Rochester, MI 48307 USA
TEL: 810-656-8571

Specializing in automotive art & collectibles. Original art & prints by Fearnley, Dennis Brown, Koka, Watts, Tom Fritz, AFAS artists, & many more. Event & historic posters. Ad & studio art. New & used books. Sculpture by Larry Braun, Hossack, & Alex Buchan. Serving the collector for over ten years.

Other categories: Mixed Automobilia; Books; Art, Other

## Getz Grafiks

See our main listing under "Art, Original"

## Pablo Gudino

See our main listing under "Photographs"

## Rick Hale

See our main listing under "Books"

## Hiway 79 Classic Collectibles

See our main listing under "Mixed Automobilia"

## Hot Rod Art

Wayne Bloechl
PO Box 1934
Freedom, CA 95019 USA
TEL: 408-722-1934
FAX: 408-722-7952

Specializing in prints, sculpture, & collectible hot rod, custom & 1950s/60s cars. Representing over 30 artists' works showing 1950s/60s drive-in scenes, gas stations, & junkyard settings. Collector edition diecast cars in stock. Call or write for listings.

Other categories: Hot Wheels; Petroliana, Other; Specialized Automobilia

## Alan J. Isselhard

See our main listing under "Racing Artifacts"

## Anthony Jackson

34 Camden Rd.
Bexley, Kent DA5 3NR UK
TEL: +44-1322522197
FAX: +44-1322522197

Racing automobilia, including autographs, posters, programs, bought & sold.

*Other categories: Racing Artifacts; Photographs; Books*

## Dale Klee

25345 Eureka Ave.
Wyoming, MN 55092 USA
TEL: 612-464-2200
FAX: 612-464-7688

Limited edition art prints of favorite American automobiles in rustic settings. Prices range from $35 to $85. For color brochures & free future mailings call or fax.

*Other category: General Interest*

## Dave Kurz, Artist

Dave Kurz
2450 S. Dudley St.
Lakewood, CO 80227 USA
TEL: 303-980-9227
Email: dav3kurz@ecentral

Limited edition automotive prints from original pastel paintings on sandpaper. Free color catalog upon request.

*Other categories: Art, Original; Art, Other*

## LMG Enterprises/Gallery L'Automobile

See our main listing under "Books"

## L'art et l'automobile

Jacques Vaucher
PO Box 1071, 16 Alexis Ct.
Amagansett, NY 11930 USA
TEL: 516-267-3378
FAX: 516-267-3379
Email: jvautoart@aol.com

Large selection of paintings, prints, posters, photographs, sculptures, mascots, objects, badges, trophies, signs, books, literature, programs, toys, pedal & motorized cars, models, automobilia, etc. from 1895 to 1997; 8500 items. In business since 1975. By appointment, mail order auctions, & catalog. Buy, sell, trade, appraisal, consultant. Ship worldwide.

*Other categories: Books; Mixed Automobilia; Toys, General*

## The Loved Ones Gallery

Gale Armstrong
P.O. Box 710
Searsport, ME 04974 USA
TEL: 902-798-0886
FAX: 902-798-0886
Email: lovedone@glinx.com

Fine art originals & prints of the classic makes (e.g., Jaguar, Rolls, Thunderbird); commissioned auto portraits.

*Other category: Art, Original*

## Mail Order Service

See our main listing under "Literature"

## Malone Design Works

Barry Malone
11350 McCormick Rd. Suite 1001
Hunt Valley, MD 21031 USA
TEL: 410-584-9040
FAX: 410-584-9042
Email: barry@malonedesign.com

Offering a collection of limited edition museum quality automotive art prints, carefully selected for their rarity & design significance. The collection consists of both American classics & European sports/racing automobiles.

## Tony Marchitto

See our main listing under "Slot Cars"

## Buz McKim Racing Art

Buz McKim
PO Box 10500
Daytona Beach, FL 32120-0500 USA
TEL: 888-RACE-500
FAX: 904-822-9109

Daytona legend Buz McKim has released a "Famous Firsts" limited edition art prints numbered & signed by the driver & Buz. Available direct for only $99.95 each, these NASCAR collectibles are quickly becoming scarce. Measuring 18x24, they contain a historical description under artwork. Special attention to the 1950s & 1960s.

*Other categories: Art, Original; Art, Other*

## Ken Miller Specialties

See our main listing under "Literature"

## Edmund F. Molloy, Jr.

See our main listing under "Literature"

## Morris Manor Collectables

See our main listing under "Toys, General"

## Motoring Memories

See our main listing under "General Interest"

## Mysteries & Motorcars

See our main listing under "Books"

## Nighthorse Inc.

See our main listing under "Motorcycle Collectibles"

## Thomas Novinsky

See our main listing under "Petroliana, Other"

## The Oil Barron

Scott G. Peterson
316 West Wabasha St.
Duluth, MN 55803 USA
TEL: 218-728-5678

Posters, reproduced from originals, auto, motorcycle, lube, gasoline. Only limited runs will be made & will be numbered. Always buying & selling rough petroleum, auto, & motorcycle signs; tin & porcelain. Call or write for availability.

*Other categories: Petroliana, Other; Petroliana, Pumps & Globes; Appraisal Service*

## Pedal Car Guys

See our main listing under "Pedal Cars"

## Arthur Price

See our main listing under "Racing Artifacts"

## The Printer's Stone, Ltd.

See our main listing under "Art, Other"

## Pro Drop

See our main listing under "Mixed Automobilia"

## Pro Line Sports Art

PO Box 642, Dept. MMB
Ottumwa, IA 52501
TEL: 888-776-2788

Fine art prints from America's top auto-motive artists. Satisfaction guaranteed!

## Racy Thangs, Inc.

See our main listing under "Art, Original"

## Rally Enterprises

See our main listing under "Models, Kits"

## Richard's

See our main listing under "Personalities"

## Rick's Gallery

447 99th Ave. N.
Naples, FL 34108 USA
TEL: 941-332-5990

Metal plus porcelain signs, posters, neon clocks, framed pictures, old time LED light scenes, trays, straw & napkin holders, Rt. 66 items, street signs, tins, thermometers, bar lights, beer taps. Red #57 at Fleamasters, Fort Myers, Florida, Fri-Sun 8-4.

*Other category: Neon*

## SABAR International

See our main listing under "Motoring Accessories"

## Skyline Design

Rich Olsavsky
315 Mapledale Place
Bridgeport, CT 06610 USA
TEL: 203-371-5820
Email: rdesign@localnet.com

Limited edition art prints, featuring muscle cars, cars of the 1950's & 60s. New additions monthly. Online catalog/gallery with online ordering.

*Other category: General Interest*

## Spyder Enterprises

See our main listing under "Specialized Automobilia"

## Vanished Roadside America Art

Warren H. Anderson, Artist
6802 N. Longfellow Dr.
Tucson, AZ 85718 USA
TEL: 520-299-1006

Full-color, hand-signed art prints depicting old gasoline signs, pumps, vintage motel & diner neon signs in realistic detail. 2 sizes: 11x7 ins. mounted on 16x12 in. matboard & 7x4.5 ins. (avg.) on 10x8 in. matboard. 97 in all! (Some original prismacolor drawings also available.) "Catalog" showing 97 precise color images: $3, from artist.

*Other categories: Rt. 66 & Roadside; Petroliana, Other; Signs*

## Marnix Verkest

See our main listing under "General Interest"

## Vintage Autos & Automobilia

See our main listing under "Mixed Automobilia"

## Wheels Art & Memorabilia

See our main listing under "Art, Original"

## Wizard's

See our main listing under "Racing Artifacts"

## Wizzy's Collector Car Parts

See our main listing under "Mixed Automobilia"

# ART, OTHER

## The Automobile Art Studio

See our main listing under "Art, Original"

## Autosaurus

See our main listing under "Art, Prints & Posters"

## Barnett Design Inc.

See our main listing under "Models, Precision"

## Classic Services

See our main listing under "Specialized Automobilia"

## Finesse Fine Art

See our main listing under "Mascots/Badges/Emblems"

## Wm. P. Fornwalt, Jr.

See our main listing under "Models, Precision"

## Gallery Automania

See our main listing under "Art, Prints & Posters"

## Getz Grafiks

See our main listing under "Art, Original"

## Glassmobiles

Jim Harrington
17 Winsor Ave
Johnston, RI 02919-1119 USA
TEL: 401-949-3060

From side-view color photograph an exact replica of automobile is created in matching hand-cut stained glass on oak base or in custom window for home or office. Most work completed in one month. Send photo & SASE for quote. Free color brochure.

*Other categories: Art, Original; Displays/Fixtures; Lamps*

## Dwayne L. Gordon

See our main listing under "Mixed Automobilia"

## Kirk's Ghetto Garage

See our main listing under "Mixed Automobilia"

## Dave Kurz, Artist

See our main listing under "Art, Prints & Posters"

## Lost Highway Art Co.

See our main listing under "Rt. 66 & Roadside"

## Max Neon Design Group

See our main listing under "Manufacturer"

## Buz McKim Racing Art

See our main listing under "Art, Prints & Posters"

## Edward E. Moberg, Jr.

See our main listing under "Art, Original"

## Motoring Memories

See our main listing under "General Interest"

## Nostalgia Productions, Inc.

Edward K. Reavie
268 Hillcrest Blvd.
St. Ignace, MI 49781 USA
TEL: 906-643-8087
FAX: 906-643-9784
Email: EdReavie@nostalgaprod.com

Automotive art show & model car contest June 26-28, 1997. Toy show & swap meet with pedal car competition Sept 12-14, 1997. Call for details.

*Other categories: Models, Kits; Pedal Cars*

## The Printer's Stone, Ltd.

Arthur H. Groten, MD
PO Box 30
Fishkill, NY 12524 USA
TEL: 914-471-4179
FAX: 914-471-3829
Email: imagenest@earthlink.net

Specialize in small-format graphics, particularly posters, stamps & Matchbox labels, both US & foreign: automakers, parts, services, safety, trucks & motorcycles, motor shows. Most date from 1915 to 1940. Specific want lists solicited.

*Other categories: Art, Prints & Posters; Specialized Automobilia; Promos*

## Racy Thangs, Inc.

See our main listing under "Art, Original"

## Remember Woodward, Inc.

See our main listing under "Mixed Automobilia"

## Roadkill Decorators Supply Company

See our main listing under "Signs"

## Scale Autoworks

See our main listing under "Models, Precision"

## Wheels Art & Memorabilia

See our main listing under "Art, Original"

# AUCTION FIRM

## C. Sherman Allen, Auctioneer & Associates

C. Sherman Allen
11367 State Hwy 285
Conneaut Lake, PA 16316 USA
TEL: 800-282-2922
FAX: 814-382-2923

Complete auction marketing services. Selling or buying one or thousands of: antique, collectible, classic, muscle, unique vehicles or automobilia related & antique/collectible farm tractors & toys. We bring buyer & seller together. Call today for details how we can help you buy or sell. Call anytime.

*Other categories: General Interest; Appraisal Service*

## Automobilia Auctions, Inc.

Gerry Lettieri
Box 2183
Manchester Center, VT 05255 USA
TEL: 860-529-7177
FAX: 860-257-3621

Annual no-reserve consignment auction of automotive literature, books, toys, models, pedal cars, signs, petroliana, lamps, artwork, prints, photos, sculpture, racing material & fine collector-grade automobilia. Appraisals, consultation, estate liquidations undertaken. Low commission rates. Over 50 years' combined automobilia experience.

*Other categories: Mixed Automobilia; Specialized Automobilia*

## Automobilia International

Robert C. Auten
PO Box 606
Peapack, NJ 07977 USA
TEL: 908-469-9666
FAX: 908-781-5447

Automotive auction company with April & October sales. Consignments accepted year-round. Wholesale out-of-print book dealer. European automotive artists' representative. Automotive collectibles appraisal service. Buyer of high-quality automobilia.

*Other categories: Appraisal Service; Art, Original; Books*

## Autopia Advertising Auctions

Win W. Maynard
15209 NE 90th St.
Redmond, WA 98052 USA
TEL: 206-883-7653
FAX: 206-867-5568

Autopia is your absentee catalog auction source for advertising memorabilia & transportation toys. Two sales held yearly featuring wide arrays of lines in our 100% color format, including automobilia, petroliana, soda, motorcycle, transportation toys, & advertising. Country store, tobacco, & brewery. Always seeking quality consignments. Join our mailing list today.

*Other categories: Mixed Automobilia; Petroliana, Other; Toys, General*

## Christie's

David Gooding
342 N. Rodeo Drive
Beverly Hills, CA 90210 USA
TEL: 310-275-4102
FAX: 310-275-2218

Specialist fine art auctioneers, focusing on exceptional motoring automobilia. Auctions are held annually worldwide in association with our collectors' car sales. Venues include California, New York, London, & Geneva. Specialist transport memorabilia & model auctions are also held at Christie's South Kensington, London. Please write to us with/for details.

*Other categories: Art, Prints & Posters; Specialized Automobilia; Motoring Accessories*

## Collectors Auction Services

Mark Anderton
RR 2 Box 431 Oakwood Rd.
Oil City, PA 16301 USA
TEL: 814-677-6070
FAX: 814-677-6166
Email: manderton@usachoice.net

Our auction house specializes in the sale of high-quality oil, gas, & automotive memorabilia through a full-color catalog format. We have set & hold several world records in the sale of these types of collectibles. "When great oil & gas memorabilia is sold, CAS sells it!" See our ad on the back cover of this *Sourcebook*.

*Other categories: Petroliana, Other; Petroliana, Pumps & Globes; General Interest*

## Dunbar's Gallery

See our main listing under "Motorcycle Collectibles"

## Ellerson Auction Co.

H.W. Ellerson
PO Box 1080
Orange, VA 22960 USA
TEL: 540-672-2109
Email: soowee@aol.com

We provide auction services & legal services throughout Virginia. Appraisals done on request. Auto restoration databases available for Buick, Pontiac, & Cadillac. Signs & other collectibles for sale. Will purchase items on occasion. Legal practice limited to tax & business consultations.

*Other categories: Legal Service; Appraisal Service*

## Jaguar Automobilia Collector

See our main listing under "Marque Specific"

## Dan Kruse Classic Car Productions

Bruce Knox
11202 Disco Drive
San Antonio, TX 78216 USA
TEL: 210-495-4777
FAX: 210-499-4217
Email: jaguillard@saami.com

Auction company specializing in collector cars, memorabilia, & art auctions.

Auctioneers Daniel Kruse & Jim Richie rated as one of the top auction teams in the world. Appraisal service available for estate settlements, financing, & insurance valuations. In addition, DKCCP will purchase entire collections. Please call for a confidential proposal.

*Other categories: Shows & Events; Appraisal Service; Mixed Automobilia*

## Kruse International

PO Box 190
Auburn, IN 46706
TEL: 800-968-4444

The world's largest collector car auction organization. Worldwide mailing list and customer base.

## Lust Auction Services

Richard O. Lust, CAI
7552 Pioneer Place - RR 13
Verona, WI 53593-9669 USA
TEL: 608-833-2001
FAX: 608-833-9593
Email: rolust@aol.com

Wisconsin auctioneer will accept your quality automobilia items for sale at our bimonthly general auction sales in Madison, Wisconsin, area. 22+ years' experience as one of Wisconsin's foremost auction firms. Auctioning any & all types of automobilia & related collectibles.

*Other categories: General Interest; Toys, General; Appraisal Service*

## Sotheby's

Toby Wilson
34-35 New Bond St.
London, England W1A 2AA UK
TEL: +44-171-408-5491
FAX: +44-171-408-5958
Email: http://www.sotheby's.com

Sotheby's veteran, vintage, & classic vehicle auctioneers can assist you in all matters relating to automobilia, motoring art, motor vehicles, motorcycles, & bicycles. For further details regarding saleroom valuations, estimates, reserves, valuations for probate, insurance or family division, please contact our expert staff.

*Other categories: Appraisal Service; Specialized Automobilia*

# BOOKS

## AMWP

See our main listing under "Publications, Current"

## David T. Alexander

See our main listing under "Literature"

## Frank Ashley

See our main listing under "Literature"

## Autographics

David Greeney
19 Hazelmere Rd.
Auckland, New Zealand
TEL: +64-9-630-1675
FAX: +64-9-630-1674

Out-of-print motor racing books & related motor racing ephemera with emphasis on autographed material.

*Other categories: Racing Artifacts; Mixed Automobilia; Specialized Automobilia*

## Automobile Quarterly

See our main listing under "Publications, Current"

## Automobilia International

See our main listing under "Auction Firm"

## Autophile Car Books

Richard Stafferton
1685 Bayview Ave.
Toronto, Ontario M46 361 Canada
TEL: 416-483-8898
FAX: 416-483-8898

New & used car books, videos, diecast 1/43-scale model cars. Retail store open Tuesday through Sunday. No catalog.

*Other categories: Toys, General; Literature; Publications, Current*

## Bare Necessities

See our main listing under "General Interest"

## Binder Books

See our main listing under "Literature"

## Blaser's Auto

See our main listing under "Specialized Automobilia"

## C & N Reproductions, Inc.

See our main listing under "Pedal Cars"

## Cadillac Motorbooks

Roy A. Schneider
PO Box 7
Temple City, CA 91780 USA
TEL: 818-445-1618
Email: cadbooks@earthlink.net

Cadillac Motorbooks, an imprint of Royco Publishing, specializes in hardcover books on Cadillac exclusively. Popular titles currently in print: *Cadillacs of the Sixties, Cadillac 1950-1959 Motor Cars, Cadillacs of the Forties*. Will purchase or trade for Cadillac factory dealership photos, literature, jewelry, etc. Free brochure sent on request.

*Other categories: Marque Specific; Publications, Current; Photographs*

## Car-ARDS Literature

See our main listing under "Appraisal Service"

## Casey's Collectibles

Casey Hayes
5350 E. 66th Way
Commerce City, CO 80022 USA
TEL: 303-288-5869

Automobile quarterlies & many other automotive-related books, especially Henry Ford. Also many custom-made hat tacs, especially flathead Ford items.

*Other category: Mascots/Badges/Emblems*

## Chelsea Motoring Literature

See our main listing under "Literature"

## Classic Motorbooks

Tim Parker, President & CEO
729 Prospect Ave. PO Box 1
Osceola, WI 54020 USA
TEL: 800-826-6600
FAX: 715-294-4448
Email: mbibks@win.bright.net

World's largest selection of automobile books & videos. Classic Motorbooks' catalog is mailed worldwide, featuring books & videos on automobiles, racing, restoration, street rods, motorcycles, trucks, tractors, & many other related automobilia, memorabilia, petroliana, etc. subjects. Motorbooks International

is the world's foremost automotive book publishers & wholesaler.

## The Classic Motorist

PO Box 363
Rotterdam Jct., NY 12150-0363 USA

Specializing in classic-era books, art, literature, magazines, aftermarket catalogs, & motoring accessories. Interested in formal car, chauffeur, & coachbuilding memorabilia. Early auto radio signs. Packard enthusiast desiring marque, club, & CCCA publications. Packard parts – buy, sell, trade.

*Other categories: Chauffeur/Taxi Items; Club/Organization; Art, Prints & Posters*

## Bob Crisler

See our main listing under "License Plates, Tags, etc."

## DKC & Company

See our main listing under "Models, Precision"

## Demarest Motorbooks

Creighton Demarest
17 Lake Dr.
Darien, CT 06820-3122 USA
TEL: 203-324-7639

Out-of-print auto & motorcycle books & ephemera. GP, F-1, sports car, annuals, auto art, cycle/sidecar road racing, marque, personalities. Bridgehampton, Imola, IOM-TT, Le Mans, Lime Rock, Monza, Nurburgring, Spa. Buy & sell, send $0.96 postage for 600+ item catalog.

*Other categories: Literature; Racing Artifacts; Motorcycle Collectibles*

## Diecast Toy Collectors Association

See our main listing under "Club/Organization"

## Dragster Australia

See our main listing under "Art, Prints & Posters"

## David Ellnor

31 Swinnate Rd.
Arnside, Carnforth, Lancashire
LA5 0HR England
TEL: +44-1524-762271

Motoring literature bought & sold. Cars, motorcycles, commercial, bicycles, caravans. Books mainly.

*Other categories: Literature; Mixed Automobilia; General Interest*

## Fast Toys, Inc.

See our main listing under "Marque Specific"

## Gallery Automania

See our main listing under "Art, Prints & Posters"

## Rick Hale

10309 Trestlewood
Boise, ID 83709 USA
TEL: 208-362-4146

Rare & out-of-print automotive books bought, sold, found. Large sales literature collection, posters, & dealer promo items. Many Indy 500 items & autographs. Automotive videos, including over 600 hours of movies, TV specials, & car show videos, including 22 hours of Hot August Nights. Send SASE your list.

*Other categories: Literature; Racing Artifacts; Art, Prints & Posters*

## Haven Books & Collectibles

See our main listing under "Retail Store"

## Todd P. Helms

See our main listing under "Petroliana, Other"

## Hosking Cycle Works

See our main listing under "Motorcycle Collectibles"

## Hot Rods

See our main listing under "Hot Rod Memorabilia"

## ICPM Automotive Books

Steve Fields
7944 Clover Hill
Fair Oaks, CA 95628 USA
TEL: 916-863-5513
FAX: 916-863-5519
Email: jsfields@earthlink.net

Out-of-print car books. Histories, bios, marque books. Specializing in racing, sports cars, exotic & classic cars. Also race programs & sales literature for the above-type cars. Mail order, or by appointment. Send $1 for 50-page catalog.

*Other categories: Literature; Racing Artifacts*

## Imperial Palace Auto Collection

See our main listing under "Museum"

## J & J Models

See our main listing under "Toys, General"

## Anthony Jackson

See our main listing under "Art, Prints & Posters"

## Howard Johansen

See our main listing under "Slot Cars"

## Keith's Hobby Shop

See our main listing under "Models, Kits"

## David M. King Automotive Books

David M. King
5 Brouwer Lane
Rockville Centre, NY 11570 USA
TEL: 516-766-1561
FAX: 516-766-7502

Always interested in buying books on automotive history, racing, biography, & travel. Send me your price lists. Mail order only.

*Other categories: Literature; Photographs; Cards, Postal*

## Dan Kirchner

See our main listing under "Literature"

## LMG Enterprises/Gallery L'Automobile

Dave McClure
9006 Foxland Drive
San Antonio, TX 78230 USA
TEL: 210-979-6098
FAX: 210-979-6098
Email: 102341.142@compuserve.com

Dealing in all kinds of automotive & racing books, new & used, current & out-of-print. Specializing in Rolls-Royce & Bentley publications & automobilia. Also dealing in automotive prints, original art, racing posters, mascots, & general automobilia. SASE for book list. Visa/MasterCard. Satisfaction guaranteed. We buy collections!
http://www.specialcar.com/lmg

*Other categories: Art, Prints & Posters; Mixed Automobilia; Online Service*

## L'art et l'automobile

See our main listing under "Art, Prints & Posters"

## Dave Leopard

See our main listing under "Toys, General"

## Magazine Man

B. Coleman Castellaw
3935 Manhattan Dr.
Kennesaw, GA 30144 USA
TEL: 710-926-6800

Automotive magazines of all types, 1940s to present. Buy & sell, mail order or swap meets.

*Other categories: Hot Rod Memorabilia; Toys, Truck; Mixed Automobilia*

## Tony Marchitto

See our main listing under "Slot Cars"

## Mike Martin

See our main listing under "Racing Artifacts"

## McLellan's Automotive History

See our main listing under "Literature"

## Walter Miller

See our main listing under "Literature"

## Don Montgomery's Hot Rod Books

See our main listing under "Hot Rod Memorabilia"

---

**Buy Online at the MOBILIA Website:**
http://www.mobilia.com

---

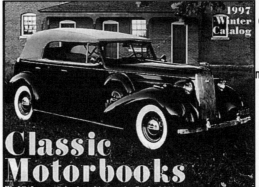

## MotoMedia

Stephen W. White
PO Box 489
Lansdowne, PA 19050-0489 USA
TEL: 610-623-6930
FAX: 610-623-6930

MotoMedia is your best source for automotive magazines, books, & sales literature. Our 3 lists of magazines, books, & auto miscellanea are updated monthly & cost $2.50 for all 3. We also buy. Send your lists of magazines, books, & literature for our fast, fair offer.

*Other categories: Hot Rod Memorabilia; Literature; Racing Artifacts*

## Mysteries & Motorcars

Gary Schmidt
PO Box 3006
Florence, OR 97439 USA
TEL: 541-997-1023
FAX: 541-902-0215

We offer a wide variety of memorabilia with an emphasis on Italian, European cars. We have art, posters, books, models, magazines, club publications, many items back to first publication.

*Other categories: Art, Original; Art, Prints & Posters; Literature*

## Donroy Ober

See our main listing under "Toys, General"

## Original Auto Literature

See our main listing under "Literature"

## Paper Race

David Reininger
13532 Brightfield Lane
Herndon, VA 22071 USA
TEL: 703-689-0160
FAX: 703-437-3319
Email: cv806@cleveland.freenet.edu

The Paper Race offers a selection of old, rare, & out-of-print automotive books. Our complete inventory is listed on the Internet at http://www.motor-sport.com/paper-race.

*Other category: Cards, Postal*

## Rick Pease

See our main listing under "Petroliana, Other"

## Paul Politis Automotive Literature

See our main listing under "Literature"

## Portrayal Press

See our main listing under "Literature"

## Russell S. Rein

See our main listing under "Rt. 66 & Roadside"

## Gunnar Söderblom

See our main listing under "Literature"

## SpeedWay MotorBooks

Bob Westinicky
TEL: 602-969-7290
Email: bobwest@primenet.com

Out-of-print auto books & memorabilia. Browse our online Web catalog at www.primenet.com/~komet/speed/speedway.html

*Other categories: Literature; Racing Artifacts; Mixed Automobilia*

## TMC Publications

See our main listing under "Literature"

## Tavares Motorsport

See our main listing under "Specialized Automobilia"

## Russell Taylor

See our main listing under "License Plates, Tags, etc."

## Edward Tilley Automotive Collectibles

See our main listing under "Promos"

## Vintage Autos & Automobilia

See our main listing under "Mixed Automobilia"

## Vintage Motorbooks

Dean Newton
42 NW Wallula
Gresham, OR 97030-6814 USA
TEL: 503-661-1482
FAX: 503-661-1482
Email: vintage-moto@worldnet.att.net

Dealing in out-of-print, rare, collectible books on motoring history. Autos, motorcycles, racing, general history, travel, adventure, people, annuals, quarterlies. Over 15 years' experience serving collectors all over the world. Buy, sell, trade. Visa/MC accepted. Mail order only.

*Other category: Racing Artifacts*

## T. E. Warth Esq. Automotive Books

Lumberyard Shops
Marine on St. Croix, MN 55047 USA
TEL: 612-433-5744
FAX: 612-433-5012

Largest inventory of rare & out-of-print automotive, motorcycle, truck, tractor, model, etc. books in world. Search service available. Publisher of *TE Warth OP Book Price Guide*. Discount OP & secondhand books available at Stillwater, Minn. book center. Keen buyer of book collections.

## Zwart Design Group, Inc.

R. L. Zwart
1900 E. Warner, Suite E
Santa Ana, CA 92705-5549 USA
TEL: 714-261-1112
FAX: 714-261-2251

MG vintage car restoration & research. T series cars & earlier.

*Other categories: Marque Specific; Mascots/Badges/Emblems*

# CARDS, POSTAL

## Tom Adams

See our main listing under "Literature"

## American Automobile Sales Literature of Lancaster, PA

See our main listing under "Petroliana, Other"

## Frank Ashley

See our main listing under "Literature"

## Auto Racing

See our main listing under "Racing Artifacts"

## Bare Necessities

See our main listing under "General Interest"

**Car-ARDS Literature**

See our main listing under "Appraisal Service"

**Clark's Historic Rt. 99 General Store**

See our main listing under "Mixed Automobilia"

**Le Cramer**

See our main listing under "Showroom Items"

**Pablo Gudino**

See our main listing under "Photographs"

**Jim Jones**

17011 Oketo
Tinley Park, IL 60477 USA
TEL: 708-532-3285
Email: indylover@msn.com

Indy racing postcards, 1911 through present day. Postals & promo cards, all sizes, black & white, color.

*Other categories: Promos; Specialized Automobilia; General Interest*

**David M. King Automotive Books**

See our main listing under "Books"

**George Koyt**

See our main listing under "Racing Artifacts"

**Morris Manor Collectables**

See our main listing under "Toys, General"

**Paper Race**

See our main listing under "Books"

**Pedal Car Guys**

See our main listing under "Pedal Cars"

**Paul Politis Automotive Literature**

See our main listing under "Literature"

**Russell S. Rein**

See our main listing under "Rt. 66 & Roadside"

**Bill Sandy**

See our main listing under "Marque Specific"

**Thomas Stone**

See our main listing under "Hot Wheels"

**Taxi Toys & Memorabilia**

See our main listing under "Chauffeur/Taxi Items"

**Michael Wojtowicz**

See our main listing under "Racing Artifacts"

## CARDS, TRADING

**Bill Behlman**

See our main listing under "Racing Artifacts"

**Flashback**

See our main listing under "Racing Artifacts"

**Milwaukee Miniature Motors**

See our main listing under "Models, Kits"

**Thomas Novinsky**

See our main listing under "Petroliana, Other"

**San Remo Hobby and Toy**

See our main listing under "Promos"

## CHAUFFEUR/TAXI

**Checker USA**

See our main listing under "Literature"

**The Classic Motorist**

See our main listing under "Books"

**Bob English**

See our main listing under "Signs"

**Dr. Edward H. Miles**

888 - 8th Ave
New York, NY 10019 USA
TEL: 212-684-4708

Chauffeur badges, taxi, hack, driver badges. Disabled veterans keychain tags. B.F. Goodrich keychain tags. Registration & inspection windshield stickers. Paper automobile licenses & registrations. License plates. Have many duplicates for sale or trade. I buy collections. Call evenings, EST, or write.

*Other category: License Plates, Tags, etc.*

**Taxi Toys & Memorabilia**

Nathan Willensky
5 E 22 St. #24C
New York, NY 10010 USA
TEL: 212-982-2156
FAX: 212-995-1065

Taxi toys & memorabilia. Anything taxi-cab.

*Other categories: Toys, General; Literature; Cards, Postal*

**Clifford Weese**

See our main listing under "License Plates, Tags, etc."

## CLOTHING

**Automobile Sportswear Inc.**

Tom Laurito
3 Brandywine Dr.
Deer Park, NY 11729 USA
TEL: 516-242-8400
FAX: 516-242-8443
Email: cbruschi@aol.com

Specializing in automotive sportswear & promotional wear for your club or special event. Jackets, caps, T-shirts, sweatshirts, & denim shirts & jackets. Screenprinting, custom embroidery & an in-house art department to develop your concepts. Call for a full-color catalog.

*Other categories: Club/Organization; General Interest; Marque Specific*

**Bullivant Gallery**

See our main listing under "Art, Prints & Posters"

**Classic Performance**

See our main listing under "Hot Rod Memorabilia"

**Dragster Australia**

See our main listing under "Art, Prints & Posters"

## Fast Times Automobilia

See our main listing under "Art, Prints & Posters"

## Meow

Kathleen Schaaf
2210 E. 4th St.
Long Beach, CA 90814 USA
TEL: 562-438-8990
FAX: 562-434-1252

A full-service vintage department store featuring original, never worn 1940s through 1970s clothing & accessories. Car club & motorcycle jackets, denim, sneakers, Japan souvenir jackets. Always buying quality vintage & "dead stock" apparel & accessories.

*Other categories: Retail Store; Hot Rod Memorabilia; Motorcycle Collectibles*

## Tim Moe

See our main listing under "Racing Artifacts"

## Muffler Time Exhaust & Memorabilia

See our main listing under "Hot Rod Memorabilia"

## Railfan Specialties

See our main listing under "Specialized Automobilia"

## Thunder Road

See our main listing under "Retail Store"

## Wizard's

See our main listing under "Racing Artifacts"

# CLUB, ORGANIZATION

## AMRCC

Kurt Ritthaler
3411 Woodward Rd.
Huntingdon Valley, PA 19006-4053
USA
TEL: 215-947-1380

Antique Miniature Race Car Collectors. This organization, currently active, caters to collectors of tether & rail racers of all sizes & shapes.

## AMWP

See our main listing under "Publications, Current"

## Automobile Sportswear Inc.

See our main listing under "Clothing"

## Capitol Miniature Auto Collectors Club

Charles F. Wilding
10207 Greenacres Dr.
Silver Spring, MD 20903-1402 USA
TEL: 301-434-6209
FAX: 301-445-1732

The Capitol Miniature Auto Collectors Club has been in existence since 1968. It meets on a monthly basis at the home of one of its members. Two shows are held each year at the Dunn Loring Fire Hall in Virginia.

*Other categories: Toys, Truck; Shows & Events*

## The Classic Motorist

See our main listing under "Books"

## Cole Motor Car Club

Leroy Cole, President
201 W. Rising St.
Davison, MI 48423 USA
TEL: 810-658-5373
FAX: 810-653-9419
Email: ldcole58@aol.com

The Cole Motor Car Club is open to membership to all Cole admirers. The Cole Bulletin is published twice a year & features present owners' cars as well as a running history of the Cole. We now know of 72 Cole autos. Dues are $12 yearly.

*Other categories: Marque Specific; Publications, Current*

## Diecast Toy Collectors Association

Dana Johnson Enterprises
PO Box 1824
Bend, OR 97709-1824 USA
TEL: 541-382-8410
Email: toynutz@teleport.com

Join the DTCA & receive the monthly newsletter *Diecast Toy Collector*. Rates as indicated (US funds, please): 1 year – $15 USA, $18 Canada, $24 International. 2 years – $26 USA, $32 Canada, $44 International. 3 yrs. – $37 USA, $46 Canada, $64 International. Send LSASE for more info.

*Other categories: Toys, General; Books; Publications, Current*

## Greater Dakota Classics

Stan Orness
PO Box 314
Devils Lake, ND 58301 USA
TEL: 701-662-7222
FAX: 701-662-8671
Email: My24@aol.com

Interested in memorabilia of all sorts, mostly dealing with autos & gas stations. We are a car club in North Dakota & buy, sell, & trade anything dealing with classic cars & hot rods.

*Other categories: Shows & Events; Mixed Automobilia*

## Horseless Carriage Club of America

Garyl Turley
128 S. Cypress St.
Orange, CA 92666-1314 USA
TEL: 714-538-HCCA
FAX: 714-538-5764

The preservation of early automobiles, their history, & related artifacts is a fascinating hobby. The Horseless Carriage Club of America is a nonprofit organization founded in 1937 by a group of enthusiasts dedicated to the preservation of automotive history. Anyone with an interest in early automobiles & their history is invited to join.

*Other categories: Mixed Automobilia; Publications, Current; Shows & Events*

## Jaguar Drivers Club of South Australia

Sharon Munchenberg
17 Westcliff Court
Marino, South Australia 5049
Australia
TEL: +61-8-3770778
FAX: +61-8-3771353
Email: mosm@dove.mtx.net.au

The Jaguar Drivers Club of South Australia conducts its own club wares shop. We carry a comprehensive range of clothing, badges, mugs, glasses, key rings, etc. Also in our range is the

Jaguar Fragrance Collection. We will make gift baskets or packs for special occasions, e.g., Valentine's Day.

*Other category: Marque Specific*

## Michael Knittel
See our main listing under "Literature"

## Model A Ford Cabriolet Club
Larry Machacek
PO Box 515
Porter, TX 77365 USA
TEL: 281-429-2505

Membership 400, dues $12 USA & Canada, $14 overseas. Quarterly publication. Club formed to provide a way to exchange information & parts among owners & enthusiasts of the cabriolet (a rare body style of the Model A Fords), manufactured from 1929 to 1931.

*Other categories: Marque Specific; Publications, Current; General Interest*

## Northwest Hot Rod & Custom Car Council
Walt Kaplin
4106 101st St Ct NW
Gig Harbor, WA 98332 USA
TEL: 206-858-8739
Email: wkaplin@harbornet.com

1997 Can-Am Nationals, a North American "Hot Rod Happening" URL http://204.188.39.233/events/can-am/cahome.htm

*Other category: Shows & Events*

## PL8MAN
See our main listing under "License Plates, Tags, etc."

## SRE Industries
See our main listing under "Mascots/Badges/Emblems"

## San Francisco Bay Brooklin Club
See our main listing under "Models, Precision"

## Wheel Goods Trader Magazine
See our main listing under "Pedal Cars"

# DINER MEMORABILIA

## Blast from the Past, Inc.
See our main listing under "Retail Store"

## City Classics
See our main listing under "Models, Kits"

## Paul Furlinger
See our main listing under "Petroliana, Other"

## Max Neon Design Group
See our main listing under "Manufacturer"

## Moonlight Peddler
See our main listing under "Pedal Cars"

## The Old Road
See our main listing under "Signs"

## Russell S. Rein
See our main listing under "Rt. 66 & Roadside"

## Sign of the Times
See our main listing under "Signs"

## Steve's Service Station Stuff
See our main listing under "Petroliana, Other"

# DISPLAYS, FIXTURES

## Ron Berkheimer Designs
Ron Berkheimer
1801 Briggs Chaney Rd.
Silver Spring, MD 20905 USA
TEL: 301-384-5070
FAX: 301-384-3348

Model car displays. Miniature showroom-style buildings with turntables, lights, etc. Several designs & scales. Lighted shadowboxes, some enclosed. Identification plaques & easels. Call, fax, write.

## Carney Plastics Inc.
Paul Carney
1295 Crescent St.
Youngstown, OH 44502 USA
TEL: 300-743-2300
FAX: 300-743-2344

Manufacturers of lightweight, crystal clear acrylic display cases with mirror back & hinged front cover to keep your collection as dust-free as possible. Call for a list & prices of standard cases to fit most diecast, promos, models, haulers, banks, etc. Custom cases available. Dealer inquiries invited.

*Other categories: Models, Kits; Toys, Truck; Promos*

## Craco Showcase Sales Gallery
94 Lawrence Rd.
Randolph, NJ 07869 USA
TEL: 800-361-0027
FAX: 201-361-4982

Glass showcases delivered worldwide. Display & protect your valued collectibles in the finest quality showcases available. Many sizes & styles to choose from for home, office, or business.

*Other categories: Showroom Items; Models, Precision; Toys, General*

## 4 Tek
Garland Rush
Box 1221
Glen Ellen, CA 95442 USA
TEL: 707-935-3411
FAX: 707-935-5876
Email: 4tek@vom.com

Manufacturer of vacuum-formed clear plastic display cases with dustcovers for diecast cars, etc. Collect VW toys & memorabilia.

*Other categories: Showroom Items; Manufacturer; Marque Specific*

## GameRoomAntiques
See our main listing under "Games"

## Glassmobiles
See our main listing under "Art, Other"

## Joseph Herr
See our main listing under "Toys, General"

## Holliday Canopies

Wes Holliday
141 Woodbridge Dr.
Charleston, WV 25311 USA
TEL: 800-788-3969
FAX: 304-343-CARS

Tents: Vendor tents, economical prices, custom colors & sizes available. Call for a price quote. Trade for gas globes & signs.

*Other categories: Retail Store; Promos; Shows & Events*

## Holly's Miniatures

See our main listing under "Specialized Automobilia"

## Hot Stuff By Tri-C

See our main listing under "Hot Wheels"

## Jamar Company

J. Ensign
5015 State Rd.
Medina, OH 44256 USA
TEL: 330-239-2889
FAX: 330-239-2889
Email: jmdisplays@aol.com

Acrylic display cabinets & cases for models, toys, & collectibles. Best quality & selection available. Cabinets for 1/64 through 1/18 scale. Custom cases available. Send $2 for catalog.

*Other categories: Models, Kits; Toys, Truck; General Interest*

## Jimmy Lightning

See our main listing under "Hot Wheels"

## Seebee Enterprises

Buddy Seeberg
PO Box 197
Oakland, FL 34760-0197 USA
TEL: 407-877-9139

Specializing in revolving display cases for: Matchbox (up to 1/16-scale model cars), Motometers, oil cans, spark plugs, radiator emblems, & mascot collections. Dust-free cases revolve manually or by remote control. Send SASE for free information on our product line, or call after 6pm. No collect calls, please.

*Other categories: Models, Precision; Spark Plugs; Mascots/Badges/Emblems*

## Specto

233 N. 12th St.
Allentown, PA 18102
TEL: 800-662-0656
FAX: 610-820-8201
Email: specto@fast.net

Advanced displays for miniatures. Highest quality protection. Many styles available.

# GAMES

## EWJ Marketing

See our main listing under "Racing Artifacts"

## GameRoomAntiques

Ken Durham
909 26th St. NW
Washington, DC 20037 USA
Email: http://www.gameroomantiques.com

World Wide Web site for game room collectors, buy & sell, articles, books, resources, updates each week.

*Other categories: Displays/Fixtures; Online Service; General Interest*

## George Koyt

See our main listing under "Racing Artifacts"

## Snyder's Oil & Gas Collectibles

See our main listing under "Mixed Automobilia"

## Yankee Trader

See our main listing under "Toys, General"

# GAS-POWERED RACERS

## Antique Toys

See our main listing under "Toys, General"

## Bob Barnes

See our main listing under "Toys, Truck"

## Gabriel Bogdonoff

46 Porter Rd
Howell, NJ 07731 USA
TEL: 908-363-4064

Buying old model gasoline-powered race cars. Also broken cars & parts such as chassis, bodies, motors, flywheels, rear ends, wheels. Also old magazines related to gas-powered race cars.

*Other categories: Racing Artifacts; Toys, General*

## Don's Body Shop

See our main listing under "Appraisal Service"

## EinSteins

Mike Ludwig
1301 Manhattan Ave
Hermosa Beach, CA 90254 USA
TEL: 310-379-8933
FAX: 310-379-6535

Gas-powered racers, all original or restored. Cars only – no parts. Buy & sell.

*Other category: Toys, General*

## Flashback

See our main listing under "Racing Artifacts"

## J & E Spindizzie

Jerry Bryant
17337 Aspenglow Lane
Yorba-Linda, CA 92886 USA
TEL: 714-993-5482
FAX: 714-572-8696

Specializing in vintage miniature gas-powered race cars from 1940s & 1950s. Will purchase or trade for important prewar or history cars with provenance, whole collections, or memorabilia connected to this hobby. We also provide free professional appraisals. Will trade, buy, or sell some cars.

*Other categories: Appraisal Service; Specialized Automobilia; Hot Rod Memorabilia*

## George Koyt

See our main listing under "Racing Artifacts"

## John Lorenz

8165 Shady Brook Ln.
Flushing, MI 48433-3007 USA
TEL: 810-659-1452
FAX: 810-762-9836
Email: jlorenz@nova.gmi.edu

Collector seeking gas-powered miniature race cars from 1930s, 40s, 50s; especially mite cars designed specifically for racing.

## Pacific Restoration

See our main listing under "Slot Cars"

## US Toy Collector Magazine

See our main listing under "Toys, Truck"

## Wee Wheels Restoration

See our main listing under "Pedal Cars"

## Kirk F. White

Box 999
New Smyrna Beach, FL 32170 USA
TEL: 904-427-6660
FAX: 904-427-7801

Collector buying, selling, & trading the finest in authentic gas-engined racers. Spanning the period from 1937-1960s. Always a good selection for sale. Inventory listing available. As it has been for over 20 years, the highest prices paid for top examples of full-size racers & metal mite cars.

*Other categories: Models, Precision; Racing Artifacts; Slot Cars*

# HORNS

## The Horn Shop

Bill Randall
7129 Oriskany Rd.
Rome, NY 13440 USA
TEL: 315-336-8841

Horn(s) won't toot? We give a hoot! We specialize in the complete mechanical & electrical restoration of your "antique" auto, truck, or M/C horn. Send the horn, a large SASE, plus $10 to cover inspection, written estimate, & return shipping.

## Roy Lassen

See our main listing under "Motoring Accessories"

## Wolo Manufacturing Corp.

Stan Solow
1 Saxwood St
Deer Park, NY 11729 USA
TEL: 516-242-0333
FAX: 516-242-0720
Email: wolo@worldnet.att.net

The automotive aftermarket's source for security; alarms & steering wheel locks. Also the most complete line of horns (electric & air), lighting, & safety products.

*Other categories: License Plates, Tags, etc.; Manufacturer; Motoring Accessories*

# HOT ROD

## American Eagle Racing

John Shoemaker
3305 Horseshoe Dr.
Sacramento, CA 95821 USA
TEL: 916-483-6503
FAX: 916-575-2352

Manufacturers of authentic polished aluminum drag racing top fuel rod piston clocks with American-made quartz clock fit-ups. Great for the automobilia enthusiast. Also available collage picture frames shaped like nostalgia front-engine dragster, current rear-engine dragster, & funny car, walnut grain, holds 10-12 snapshots - 36 in. long.

*Other categories: Racing Artifacts; Specialized Automobilia; General Interest*

## Automobilia & Collectibles

See our main listing under "Mixed Automobilia"

## Automotive Fine Art

See our main listing under "Art, Prints & Posters"

## Back Issue Car Magazines

See our main listing under "Literature"

## Barnett Design Inc.

See our main listing under "Models, Precision"

## Bill's Garage

See our main listing under "Models, Kits"

## Joseph Camp

See our main listing under "Mixed Automobilia"

## Car Crazy

Michael & Cheryl Goyda
Box 192
E. Petersburg, PA 17520 USA
TEL: 717-569-7149
FAX: 717-569-0909

We carry an extensive inventory of hot rod & drag racing material in the following categories: hot rod movie posters, toys, games, photos, programs, magazines, handouts, trophies, jackets, club plaques, etc. Everything original: no repros or reprints. We buy what we sell.

*Other categories: Racing Artifacts; Models, Kits; Specialized Automobilia*

## Classic Performance

Stan Fairfax
PO Box 7283
Loveland, CO 80537-0283 USA
TEL: 970-667-4171

Hot rod, muscle car, racing apparel, books, manuals, decals, jewelry, more. American-British motorcycle pins. Show vendor & mail order business. Call or write for details.

*Other categories: Clothing; Motorcycle Collectibles; Racing Artifacts*

## Classic Transportation

See our main listing under "Pedal Cars"

## Cotton Candy Classics

Glenn Thomson
2 Verbeke Court
Saskatoon, Saskatchewan S7K 6L8
Canada
TEL: 306-934-5830
FAX: 306-242-0600
Email: cottonclass@sk.sympatico.ca

1950s & 60s accessories, decals, toys, club plaques. Sell at shows & swap meets. Small but happy.

*Other categories: Mixed Automobilia; Toys, General*

## D & K Collectables

See our main listing under "Petroliana, Other"

## Doo-Wop Props

Jack Koffron
8600 N. 53rd St.
Brown Deer, WI 53223 USA
TEL: 414-354-4850
FAX: 414-765-1207

Woodie skateboards wanted from 1950s-70s. Also buying hot rod LPs, videos, 1950s/60s car club jackets & patches, older racing trophies, 1966-74 CAN-AM programs & McLaren models. Call after 5pm, fax anytime.

*Other categories: Specialized Automobilia; Racing Artifacts; Toys, General*

## Fast Times Automobilia

See our main listing under "Art, Prints & Posters"

## Getz Grafiks

See our main listing under "Art, Original"

## Half-Pint Motors

See our main listing under "Pedal Cars"

## HO Motoring & Racing

See our main listing under "Slot Cars"

## Hot Rod Coffee

Tony Leopardo
1314 Rollins Rd.
Burlingame, CA 94010 USA
TEL: 415-348-8269
FAX: 415-340-9473
Email: www.motorville.com

Hot Rod Coffee makes the perfect gift for your motorhead friend: each 3-lb. gift pack of "Hot Rod Coffee" has our premium gourmet roasted decaffeinated, special blend, & dark roast! We accept Visa & MasterCard.
Send/fax/mail us $34.50 for each gift pack ordered & we'll do the rest!

## Hot Rods

Frank Glover
244 Lakeview Dr.
Cross Junction, VA 22625 USA
TEL: 540-888-3066

Buy, sell, trade. Anything to do with 1940s-70s hot-rodding, including toys, photos, advertising, books, magazines, hot rod & custom car equipment or accessories. Also interested in buying an original 1940s-50s hot rod or custom car needing restoration.

*Other categories: Toys, General; Books; Racing Artifacts*

## Inside Only

See our main listing under "Toys, General"

## J & E Spindizzie

See our main listing under "Gas-Powered Racers"

## Magazine Man

See our main listing under "Books"

## Mega-Zines

See our main listing under "General Interest"

## Meow

See our main listing under "Clothing"

## Tim Moe

See our main listing under "Racing Artifacts"

## Don Montgomery's Hot Rod Books

Don Montgomery
636 Morro Hills Rd.
Fallbrook, CA 92028 USA
TEL: 614-728-5557

Hot rod history books, author & publisher. Available mail order & autographed, four books on early hot-rodding 1930s to 1950s. Two books on 1960s drag racing: *Supercharged Gas Coupes & Those Wild Fuel Altereds*. Send SASE for information.

*Other category: Books*

## MotoMedia

See our main listing under "Books"

## Moviecraft Inc.

See our main listing under "Manufacturer"

### Muffler Time Exhaust & Memorabilia

Ed Chamberlain
575 Dawson Dr. #9
Camarillo, CA 93012 USA
TEL: 805-482-9950

Collector of hot rod, racing, & car club memorabilia. I mainly collect car club, drag strip, & hot rod jackets, plaques, & posters. NHRA, AHRA, SCTA, or NDBA. Looking to buy or trade for car club jackets, or racing memorabilia, posters, club plaques. Send list or pictures. Call 9-6 PST Mon-Sat.

*Other categories: Racing Artifacts; Clothing; Specialized Automobilia*

### Frank A. Poll

See our main listing under "Models, Kits"

### Smith Automotive Group

Ken Smith
PO Box 85
Fremont, OH 43420-0085 USA
TEL: 419-332-3654

Specializing in hand-built hot rod & custom car models in various scales. We also deal in unbuilt model car kits, promotional models, & the "Ken's Kustom Kar Supply" line of detailing items, including mirror dice, & Ken's Kustom Fuzzi-Fur detail flocking. Write or call for current list.

*Other categories: Models, Precision; Models, Kits; Promos*

### Squat Rods

See our main listing under "Pedal Cars"

### Supercar Collectibles

See our main listing under "Toys, General"

### VIP Ltd.

See our main listing under "Models, Kits"

### Yosemite Sam's Auto Art

See our main listing under "Art, Original"

## HOT WHEELS

### The Auto Collectibles Co.

See our main listing under "Retail Store"

### Auto Futura

Harold Tanenbaum
7775 SW 130 St.
Miami, FL 33156 USA
TEL: 305-662-7551
Email: htbomb@aol.com

Buy, sell, trade Redlines, Treasure Hunts, & variation cars. Top dollar paid for Redlines in package. Seeking 95 TH Camaro. Also need Corgi Batmobiles, James Bond, Monkee Mobile, Yellow Submarine, & Chitty Chitty Bang Bang. Will purchase complete collections.

*Other categories: Toys, General; General Interest*

### Paul Garnand Sales

See our main listing under "Models, Kits"

### Joseph R. Golabiewski

See our main listing under "Toys, Truck"

### David L. Gray

See our main listing under "Mixed Automobilia"

### Hot Rod Art

See our main listing under "Art, Prints & Posters"

### Hot Stuff By Tri-C

Sue Cresse
27820 Fremont Court, #3
Valencia, CA 91355 USA
TEL: 805-295-1550
FAX: 805-295-1597
Email: peggesu@scvnet.com

Custom collectors display stand. Hang & display your mint on card toys, Hot Wheels, Matchbox, Star Wars figures, Micro Machines, Racing Champs, Johnny Lightning, etc. Holds 128 Hot Wheels. All-steel construction, black powder-coated finish. 5-1/2 in. tall & 14 in. wide. Only $125. Dealer inquiries welcome. Visa/MC accepted.

*Other categories: Displays/Fixtures; Mixed Automobilia; Toys, General*

### The Hunt

See our main listing under "Toys, General"

### Jimmy Lightning

James Svehla
4536 Forest Ave.
Brookfield, IL 60513 USA
TEL: 708-485-9270

Specialize in original Johnny Lightning cards & racetracks from 1969 to 1971. Buy, sell, trade – single pieces or complete collections purchased. Also collect original Johnny Lightning toy ads, display, & old store stock.

*Other categories: Toys, General; Literature; Displays/Fixtures*

### Junkyard Dog

See our main listing under "Petroliana, Other"

### Milwaukee Miniature Motors

See our main listing under "Models, Kits"

### Bob Neubauer

See our main listing under "Models, Kits"

### Pro Drop

See our main listing under "Mixed Automobilia"

### Race Place Collectables

See our main listing under "Retail Store"

### San Remo Hobby and Toy

See our main listing under "Promos"

### Thomas Stone

29 White Oak Lane
Waterbury, CT 06705 USA
TEL: 203-756-5808

Recent Hot Wheels, Matchbox, Maisto, & Johnny Lightning cars & trucks are my specialty. Also, beautiful postcards of old autos (1898-1937) priced very low. New listing of diecast vehicles twice a year. SASE brings free list & collector card.

*Other category: Cards, Postal*

### Clifford D. Stubbs

1200 2nd St. SE
Minot, ND 58701-5910 USA
TEL: 701-838-0164

Like to exchange Hot Wheels or exchange information on varieties of the same models. Note: Hard of hearing; can't hear some people on the phone.

*Other categories: Models, Precision; Toys, Tractor*

## Toy Time

Suzanne Rufiange
121 Laurel Street
Fitchburg, MA 01420
TEL: 508-827-5261
FAX: 508-827-3175

Specialty diecast vehicles. Johnny Lightning, Matchbox, Hot Wheels.

## Transportation Station

See our main listing under "Retail Store"

## Wheels of Fun, Inc.

See our main listing under "Slot Cars"

## Winner's Circle Racing Collectibles

Phil Anderson
6238 S. Castleford Drive
West Jordan, UT 84084 USA
TEL: 801-294-5645
Email: nascar@vii.com

Racing Collectibles of all kinds. Everything from sheetmetal to diecasts. Best prices guaranteed on most items. If we don't have it, we'll get it! Fans serving fans.

*Other categories: Appraisal Service; Promos; Racing Artifacts*

## Wyoming Vintage Tin

See our main listing under "Appraisal Service"

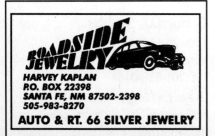

# JEWELRY

## BJM

See our main listing under "Mascots/Badges/Emblems"

## Classic Services

See our main listing under "Specialized Automobilia"

## GM Studios, Inc.

Thomas McGinnity
405 Tarrytown Rd, Suite 534
White Plains, NY 10607-1349 USA
TEL: 914-946-9545
FAX: 914-948-5228
Email: GM597@aol.com

Jewelry handcrafted in America. V8 badge design in 14kt gold or silver. Available as a pin or pendant with chain. Teardrop taillights with "Blue-Dots." Silver bezel in center. Pin/tie-tack, pendant, earrings. Call, write, fax, Email for info.

*Other categories: Manufacturer; Mascots/Badges/Emblems; Promos*

## Innovative Ideas

Kris Gainey
91 Redwood Road
San Anselmo, CA 94960 USA
Email: MORGYDOLL2@AOL.COM

Antiques, war memorabilia, & beautiful clocks.

*Other categories: Manufacturer; Motoring Accessories; Museum*

## Legendary Collectibles

See our main listing under "Models, Precision"

## Lights Up

See our main listing under "Specialized Automobilia"

## Oniell's Collectibles

See our main listing under "Petroliana, Other"

## Railfan Specialties

See our main listing under "Specialized Automobilia"

## Roadside Jewelry

Harvey Kaplan
PO Box 22398
Santa Fe, NM 87502-2398
TEL: 505-983-8270

Auto & Rt. 66 silver jewelry.

# LAMPS

## Finesse Fine Art

See our main listing under "Mascots/Badges/Emblems"

## Glassmobiles

See our main listing under "Art, Other"

## Roy Lassen

See our main listing under "Motoring Accessories"

## Te Amo J

Judie Miller
408 W. Indiana St.
New Buffalo, MI 49117 USA
TEL: 616-469-5036

Collectible diecast cars sitting on classic hubcaps or porcelain Rt. 66 signs, crafted into nostalgic lamps. Plus other collectibles & lamp creations available. Catalog $2.

*Other categories: Rt. 66 & Roadside; Specialized Automobilia; Mixed Automobilia*

# LEGAL SERVICE

## Ellerson Auction Co.

See our main listing under "Auction Firm"

## Unocal 76 Products

See our main listing under "Petroliana, Other"

# LICENSE PLATES, TAGS, ETC.

## Antique & Vintage Motorcycle

See our main listing under "Motorcycle Collectibles"

## Bob Bennett

PO Box 616
East Greenwich, RI 02818 USA
TEL: 401-294-1430

License plates, tags, etc. Want to buy license plates. Any year or state or type, especially Rhode Island porcelains or unusual types. Also any Rhode Island badges or plate toppers.

## Andy Bernstein

43-60 Douglaston Pkwy. #524
Douglaston, NY 11363 USA
TEL: 718-279-1890

Avid collector of all types of license plates from anywhere, early porcelains, tins, & graphics. Will purchase an entire collection, individual plate, or trade. Will gladly help with appraisal of plates or collections. Hablo Español. Je parle français.

*Other categories: Mixed Automobilia; Specialized Automobilia; Motorcycle Collectibles*

## Greg Bowden

See our main listing under "Motorcycle Collectibles"

## Classic Chassis

Ken Letzring
3157 7th Ave. No.
St. Petersburg, FL 33713-6617 USA
TEL: 813-323-3384

Specialize in Florida auto & cycle plates, also crests. Collect pre-1915 motorcycle memorabilia & chauffeur badges.

## Bob Crisler

109-D Alyene Dr.
Lafayette, LA 70506 USA
TEL: 318-984-9460

Specialize in US & Canadian license plates. Buy, sell, trade. Publish *License Plate Values: A Guide to Relative Prices of Collectible US Auto License Plates & Their Grading*. $19.95 postpaid in US & Canada.

*Other categories: Books; Publications, Current*

## Norman D'Amico

44 Middle Rd.
Clarksburg, MA 01247 USA
TEL: 413-663-6886

License plates. All states, years, types, countries. Also driving licenses, registrations, plate color & data information charts, etc. Miscellaneous license plate frames.

## Dave's Tag Barn

Dave Lincoln
Box 331
Yorklyn, DE 19736 USA
TEL: 610-444-4144

American & foreign license plates bought, sold, swapped. Active collector offering extras - thousands available, modern graphics to early porcelains; USA sets; vanities; cycles; recent bulk; Y.O.M. Send stamp with your specific wants. Always interested in purchasing collections, accumulations from anywhere, any vintage, any quantity. I'll travel to buy your plates!

*Other categories: Specialized Automobilia; Mixed Automobilia; Motorcycle Collectibles*

## Cliff Douglas

Box 149
Vergennes, VT 05491 USA
TEL: 802-759-2186

License plates, model Fords, literature. Your porcelain headquarters for Vermont license plates. Singles, pairs, all for sale or trade.

*Other categories: Models, Kits; Literature; Promos*

## Bob English

See our main listing under "Signs"

## Enthusiast's Specialties

Kenneth Lemoine
14 Aberdeen Rd.
Framingham, MA 01702 USA
TEL: 800-718-3999
FAX: 508-872-4914

Manufacturer of "MagTags®", the magnetic country of origin tags. 30+ countries in black on white & special edition gold on black. Custom orders on 100+ pcs. Fine quality English picnic hampers with wool rugs, crystal, bone china, stainless. Valve logo caps, car grille badges, 1/18-scale models, & misc. automobilia.

*Other categories: Luggage/Picnic Sets; Mascots/Badges/Emblems; Mixed Automobilia*

## Fifth Avenue Graphics

Randy Rundle
415 Court
Clay Center, KS 67432 USA
TEL: 913-632-3450
FAX: 913-632-6154

Tag Toppers are back! Fifth Avenue Graphics has reintroduced one of the most popular forms of advertising from the 1940s & 50s. Two sizes available. Custom-imprinted Tag Toppers are available using your colors & logo. Dealer inquiries are welcome.

## Georgian Olympic Plates

4989 Mercer University Drive
Macon, GA 31210
TEL: 912-471-6325

Brand new, never issued, Georgia Olympic license plates.

## Gregory Gibson

14028 North Rd.
Fenton, MI 48430 USA
TEL: 810-629-6628

Buying, selling, & trading license plates from all states. In particular, older plates including auto, motorcycle, & dealer plates.

*Other categories: Photographs; Publications, Current; Signs*

## William Goetzmann

See our main listing under "Motorcycle Collectibles"

## Ralph A. Herbst

Box 174
Moorhead, MN 56561-0174 USA
TEL: 218-236-6209

Specialize in license plates, esp. Minnesota, North Dakota, South Dakota. Also collect gasoline collectibles, Skelly Tybol-Veedol, Pure, Cities Service, Fyre-Drop, & Gulf brands for display in 1925 gas station I have restored. Mascots, hubcaps, badges, road maps, auto & gas signs, tag attachments, AAA badges, & tire ashtrays. Buy, sell, trade. Call after 6pm.

*Other categories: Petroliana, Other; Mixed Automobilia; Mascots/Badges/Emblems*

## Richard Hurlburt

27 West St.
Greenfield, MA 01301 USA
TEL: 413-773-3235

Advertising signs, especially vehicle, aircraft, cycle, boat-related. License plates, toys, vehicle literature, vehicle accessories. Buy, sell, trade. Also willing to swap from my collection for musical instruments. Also interested in pedal cars, planes, tractors, & old bike items.

*Other categories: Mixed Automobilia; Signs; Toys, General*

## Jaguar Automobilia Collector

See our main listing under "Marque Specific"

## Legendary Collectibles

See our main listing under "Models, Precision"

## License Plates, Etc.

Peter W. North
Tuttle Rd.
Woodbury, CT 06978 USA
TEL: 203-266-0550

Specialize in license plates. Buy, sell, trade. Complete collections or individual plates. Appraisals for insurance or estate settlement.

*Other categories: Signs; Mixed Automobilia; Appraisal Service*

## Bob Lint Motor Shop

See our main listing under "Mixed Automobilia"

## Larry Machacek

PO Box 515
Porter, TX 77365 USA
TEL: 281-429-2505

Deal in vinyl decal reproductions of 1951-73 Texas safety inspection stickers, $20 each, plus original Texas license plates (1925-75) at various prices. Also sell reproduction WWII gasoline windshield ration stickers & posters of vintage-era photographs. Mail orders accepted.

*Other categories: Mixed Automobilia; General Interest; Photographs*

## Marchbanks Ltd.

See our main listing under "Pedal Cars"

## Jamie McGuire

See our main listing under "Specialized Automobilia"

## McLong Tags & Ads

Donald G. Long
14 Sunrise Point Court
Lake Wylie, SC 29710 USA
TEL: 803-831-2455
FAX: 803-831-2455
Email: ccmdon@aol.com

Specialize in license plates, political & other license plate attachments, & Model A Ford advertising items. Buy, sell, trade. Send description & price of items for sale. Also collect all of the above items.

*Other categories: Specialized Automobilia; Mixed Automobilia; General Interest*

## Dr. Edward H. Miles

See our main listing under "Chauffeur/Taxi Items"

## Motoring Memories

Jim Miller
202 So. Main St.
Balta, ND 58313 USA
TEL: 701-542-3870

License plates: buy, sell, trade. Also collect gasoline everything, signs, & Coca-Cola memorabilia.

*Other categories: Petroliana, Other; Petroliana, Pumps & Globes; Signs*

## Pat's Parts

See our main listing under "General Interest"

## PL8MAN

Rick Morrison
4322 Wood Bridge Rd.
Wheeler, MI 48662 USA
TEL: 517-842-5679
FAX: 517-793-0157

Specialize in old Michigan license plates, pre-1950. Buy, sell, trade. Such as leather, porcelain, dealers, schools, fire dept., road comm., motorcycle, etc. Also collect Michigan registrations & driver's licenses pre-1940 & pictures that clearly show Michigan plates pre-1920. (Prefer originals.) Call after 6pm or fax anytime.

*Other categories: Motorcycle Collectibles; Club/Organization; Photographs*

## Stephen J. Raiche

Box 50087
Washington, DC 20091 USA
TEL: 202-363-2414

Expert will help you appraise your old auto tags. Always buying, selling, trading for early license plates. Best prices paid for early plates. Write or call with your wants, or to have your questions answered. All phone calls returned promptly. Information provided, no charge. As a hobbyist, glad to help!

*Other categories: Appraisal Service; Specialized Automobilia; General Interest*

## Railfan Specialties

See our main listing under "Specialized Automobilia"

## Frank R. Righetti

See our main listing under "Signs"

## Joseph Russell

See our main listing under "Mixed Automobilia"

## Russell Taylor

PO Box 16664
San Diego, CA 92716-6664 USA

License plates, mostly newer "graphics." All states, many types, also many Australia. No "bulks." Collector specializes in antique auto, horseless carriage plates. Also buy old pre-1920 plates. Please send large SASE for updated listing. Special: 10 different US graphics, my choice, $30 postpaid USA & Canada, limit 1.

*Other categories: Mixed Automobilia; Books; Literature*

## Wayne Tyler

14548 Mill Creek Dr.
Montpelier, VA 23192 USA
TEL: 804-749-4641

License plates: specializing in Virginia, Maryland, North Carolina, West Virginia. Matching sets, singles. Car, truck, cycle, misc. Also buying or trading on above.

## David Wasserman

See our main listing under "Motorcycle Collectibles"

## Clifford Weese

Rt 2 Box 58A
Harrisville, WV 26362 USA
TEL: 304-643-4227

West Virginia license plates, chauffeur badges, DAV, BF Goodrich, all types, all years. Buy, sell, trade. Paper chauffeur, operator licenses, registration cards, wagon, bicycle, city plates. Collect Sterling, Penn Seal, Gold Seal, Pavania, Duplex, globes, signs, oil cans, maps, advertisements. If it is Sterling, Quaker State, gas or oil related, I want it.

*Other categories: Chauffeur/Taxi Items; Petroliana, Other; Petroliana, Pumps & Globes*

## Wolo Manufacturing Corp.

See our main listing under "Horns"

## Woody's Garage

Stephanie Heering
121 Walnut Hill Road
Bethel, CT 06801 USA
TEL: 800-868-2538
FAX: 203-790-5880
Email: TheHTeam@eci.com

Woody's Garage manufactures the finest quality custom novelty vanity state license plates. We produce plates for all 50 states. These full-size replica license plates are made from multi-ply laminated exterior UV-rated sign plastic, custom engraved with anything you want...up to 11 characters. Only $19.95 each. Special club deals, logo plates, etc. available.

*Other categories: Showroom Items; Specialized Automobilia; General Interest*

# LITERATURE

## Tom Adams

9153 W. Utopia Rd.
Peoria, AZ 85382 USA
TEL: 602-566-8777

Mustang original sales brochures, postcards, promos 1964-1/2 through 1975. Mail order only. Also sell NOS parts & accessories 1964-67.

*Other categories: Mixed Automobilia; Promos; Cards, Postal*

## David T. Alexander

PO Box 273086 - Dept. M
Tampa, FL 33618 USA
TEL: 813-968-1805
FAX: 813-264-6226
Email: dtacoll@tampa.mindspring.com

Auto racing publications & memorabilia for sale: 1920s-1990s: programs, yearbooks, magazines, annuals, books, media guides, press kits, photos, posters, postcards, speed age, stock car racing, NASCAR, Indy 500, midgets, sprint cars, sports cars, F1, motorcycle racing. We specialize in obscure material. Want lists welcome. Send $1 for catalog.

*Other categories: Books; Racing Artifacts; Models, Kits*

## Mats Alfvag

See our main listing under "Art, Prints & Posters"

## American Automobile Sales Literature of Lancaster, PA

See our main listing under "Petroliana, Other"

## Antique & Vintage Motorcycle

See our main listing under "Motorcycle Collectibles"

## Frank Ashley

Box 79
Spickard, MO 64679-0079 USA
TEL: 816-485-6648

Dealer exclusively specializing in automobile racing literature. Books, programs, yearbooks, media guides, magazines, photos, postcards, etc. Entire collections purchased at fair prices. Send SASE with wants or for latest price lists. No manuals or models. Dealer since 1985. Call noon-9pm CST.

*Other categories: Books; Cards, Postal; Photographs*

## Auto Literature & Collectibles

John Hambrock
PO Box 99
Grapevine, TX 76099 USA
TEL: 817-488-3458
FAX: 817-488-3458

Original auto literature, catalogs, mailers, promotional models, old kits, postcards, & showroom items. Always searching for the unusual. We buy, sell, & trade with collectors worldwide. Phone, fax, or send for a copy of our monthly lists.

*Other categories: Promos; Showroom Items; Mixed Automobilia*

## Auto World Books

John Ziemer
Box 562
Camarillo, CA 93011 USA
TEL: 805-987-5570

Car & truck literature, manuals, & magazines. US & foreign. Free research service.

## Auto-Cycle Publications

Ted Essig
104 Cherokee Ln.
Noblesville, IN 46060 USA
TEL: 317-773-5302
FAX: 317-773-1992
Email: auto-cycle@aol.com

Specialize in 1929-1970 foreign & domestic auto sales literature. Extensive inventory of press kits, owner's manuals, books & magazines, some older motorcycle & scooter collectibles. Buy, sell, trade. Everything original, no reproductions or reprints. Send SASE with your wants.

*Other categories: Art, Prints & Posters; Motorcycle Collectibles; Mixed Automobilia*

## Automotive Magazines

Russell Schaller
80 Cone Rd.
Hebron, CT 06248 USA
TEL: 860-228-1110

Specialize in automotive-related magazines from *Hot Rod* to *Motor Trend*, Drag Racing to Cartoons. Also, gasoline collectibles: oil cans, maps, signs, & toy pumps. Always looking for Richfield items. Buy, sell, trade. Send your want list with SASE or call.

*Other categories: Petroliana, Other; Specialized Automobilia*

## Autophile Car Books

See our main listing under "Books"

## Back Issue Car Magazines

Del Fisher
PO Box 170243
Arlington, TX 76003 USA
TEL: 817-472-9480

100,000 back issue car magazines, 1948-present, all titles. Computer indexed by road tests, major races, top personalities. Also annuals, Fawcett,

Trend, specials, research service, bags with unique index labels, posters, & collectibles from 160 Hollywood auto-related movies. 16 years of providing service around the world. Catalog $3.

*Other categories: Hot Rod Memorabilia; Art, Prints & Posters; Personalities*

## Binder Books

Scott Satterlund
PO Box 230269
Tigard, OR 97281-0269 USA
TEL: 503-684-2024
FAX: 503-684-3990
Email: ssatter@ix.netcom.com

Specialize in manuals & literature relating to International Harvester products. Specifically trucks, scouts, & tractors. Buy, sell, & collect. Call 9-8 Monday through Saturday.

*Other category: Books*

## Bob's British Car Parts

See our main listing under "Marque Specific"

## Jerry Bougher

3628 Union St. SE
Albany, OR 97321 USA
TEL: 541-928-6919

Largest selection of clean, reasonably priced car ads, plus magazines & automobilia of all kinds. Call or write.

## Alan Bowden

See our main listing under "Models, Kits"

## Greg Bowden

See our main listing under "Motorcycle Collectibles"

## British Only Motorcycles & Parts, Inc.

See our main listing under "Motorcycle Collectibles"

## Gary Brunsch

PO Box 510088
New Berlin, WI 53151 USA
TEL: 414-786-4222

Buying & selling automotive literature; specializing in sales brochures. Also owner & shop manuals. Small or large collections purchased.

## Harry Burnstine

See our main listing under "Specialized Automobilia"

## Car-ARDS Literature

See our main listing under "Appraisal Service"

## Kenneth R. Chane

See our main listing under "Toys, General"

## Checker USA

Terry Vaught
3401 Congress Ct.
Jeffersonville, IN 47130 USA
TEL: 812-283-6134

Specialize in factory-issued sales brochures on all Checker Motors Corp. taxicabs, limousines, & Marathon-Superba passenger cars. Collect everything Checker. Buy - sell - trade. Send SASE for detailed free list. Call before noon, EST.

*Other categories: Marque Specific; Showroom Items; Chauffeur/Taxi Items*

## Chelsea Motoring Literature

David Kayser
34 Jonesdale
Metuchen, NJ 08840 USA
TEL: 908-321-0146
FAX: 908-548-0696

Original sales literature. Specializing in postwar British & European sports & classics, including many specialist racing marques of the 1950s & 60s. Also European microcars & American high-performance & muscle cars. Literature research service. Your want lists wanted! We travel worldwide to buy literature collections.

*Other categories: Books; Art, Prints & Posters; Photographs*

## Le Cramer

See our main listing under "Showroom Items"

## Demarest Motorbooks

See our main listing under "Books"

## Doc & Jesse's Auto Parts

See our main listing under "Models, Kits"

## Cliff Douglas

See our main listing under "License Plates, Tags, etc."

## Elevenparts AG

M. Marinello
PO Box 107
Zurich, Switzerland 8046
TEL: +41-137-21785
FAX: +41-137-15368

Specialize in Porsche collectibles. Sell literature, posters, books, old toys, pins. Buy, sell, trade.

*Other categories: Toys, General; Art, Prints & Posters; Appraisal Service*

## David Ellnor

See our main listing under "Books"

## Dick Farnsworth

See our main listing under "Marque Specific"

## Frost International Enterprises

George Frost
Woods Rd.
Cold Spring, NY 10516 USA
TEL: 914-265-4049
FAX: 914-265-2860

Specialize in precision models, old toy cars & trucks (Dinky, Corgi, etc.), automobile & truck literature. Buy, sell, trade. Also do appraisals on collections. Call or fax anytime.

*Other categories: Models, Precision; Toys, Truck; Mixed Automobilia*

## Gus Garton Auto

Gus Garton
401 North 5th
Millville, NJ 08332 USA
TEL: 609-825-3618

Buy & sell auto & classic bicycle sales literature; also auto showroom collectibles: Ford blotters, original postcards, dealer albums, showroom pictures, auto memorabilia of all types; stock NOS Ford, Mercury 1932-85 fenders, grilles, radiators, chrome, mechanical parts. We pay for leads! Always buying NOS Ford & other makes from dealerships. Call us!

*Other categories: Mixed Automobilia; Showroom Items; Signs*

## Get It On Paper

See our main listing under "Retail Store"

## William Goetzmann

See our main listing under "Motorcycle Collectibles"

## Philip R. Goldberg

See our main listing under "Mascots/Badges/Emblems"

## Dwayne L. Gordon

See our main listing under "Mixed Automobilia"

## Rick Hale

See our main listing under "Books"

## Haven Books & Collectibles

See our main listing under "Retail Store"

## Paul Helmbach

104 Canal Way
Hackettstown, NJ 07840 USA
TEL: 908-813-0581
Email: helmbach@world2u.com

Automobiles sales catalogs - Buy, sell, but prefer to trade original showroom sales brochures of modern collectible cars from 1976-1996.

## Peter E. Hoyt

See our main listing under "Models, Kits"

## Stan Hurd Auto Literature

Stan Hurd
W3008 Palmer Rd.
Rio, WI 53960 USA
TEL: 414-992-5260
FAX: 414-992-3889

We buy & sell sales literature, owner's manuals, & collectibles related to autos, trucks, motorcycles, farm tractors, gas engines, aircraft, boats, & other fine trade catalogs on various subjects. No magazine ads, please.

*Other categories: Mixed Automobilia; Showroom Items; Motorcycle Collectibles*

## L. Robert Hurwitz

4906 Crestwood Ln.
Syracuse, NY 13215-1315 USA
TEL: 315-468-4281

Hupmobile wanted: Literature (sales, factory, showroom, salesmen, dealer),

original artwork, posters, trophies, factory employee badges, banners, signs, pinbacks, showroom photo albums, slides, filmstrips, postcards, business cards, fobs, photos, house magazines entitled "The Hupmobilist" & "Just Between Ourselves," etc., 1909-1941.

*Other categories: Specialized Automobilia; Showroom Items; Marque Specific*

## Bob Johnson's Auto Literature

21 Blandin Ave.
Framingham, MA 01701
TEL: 508-872-9173
FAX: 508-626-0991

Hershey's largest selection of auto and truck literature. 1900 to present. Sales brochures, parts books, owner and shop manuals, etc.

## ICPM Automotive Books

See our main listing under "Books"

## Italian Cars & Related Stuff

See our main listing under "Marque Specific"

## Jimmy Lightning

See our main listing under "Hot Wheels"

## Keith's Hobby Shop

See our main listing under "Models, Kits"

## David M. King Automotive Books

See our main listing under "Books"

## Dan Kirchner

404 N. Franklin
Dearborn, MI 48128 USA
TEL: 313-277-7187

For sale: automotive shop manuals, owner's manuals, sales catalogs, dealer books, & original automotive company artwork. Send SASE with wants.

*Other categories: Art, Original; Books*

## Michael Knittel

105 Roxborough Rd.
Rochester, NY 14619-1417 USA
TEL: 716-328-5131
FAX: 716-328-5131*51
Email: mike@netacc.net

Specialize in collecting all factory/dealer literature & items relating to the Kaiser-Frazer automobiles. I also collect Kaiser-Willys literature & the foreign operations of Kaiser Industries, especially in Argentina. Always looking to purchase or trade for unusual K-F advertising material.

*Other categories: Club/Organization; Marque Specific; Showroom Items*

## Ric Kruse

3199 Caudill Rd.
Batavia, OH 45103 USA
TEL: 513-625-4628

Original auto, truck, gas, tractor advertising, teens to early 1970s. Very extensive inventory. Some aircraft advertising also. Most single-sided ads are mounted on heavy paper stock & laminated for complete protection. Have assorted dealership brochures, pens, freebies, etc. SASE with your interest for list. Try to call after 5pm.

*Other categories: Marque Specific; Photographs; Showroom Items*

## Lilliput Motor Car Co.

See our main listing under "Models, Precision"

## Lincolnia

See our main listing under "Promos"

## Bob Lint Motor Shop

See our main listing under "Mixed Automobilia"

## M&M Automobilia Appraisers

See our main listing under "Appraisal Service"

## Mail Order Service

Neumann Torsten
Reinhurdtstr. 11
Berlin, Germany 12103
TEL: +49-30-757.04394
FAX: +49-30-757.04393
Email: tneumann@mail.blinx.de

Specialize in sales literature, press kits, BBR models, Formula 1 & Indy car prints. We are looking for early buying of new edition deluxe sales literature of US & Japanese cars. We will buy one item or your whole collection of quality automotive materials. Contact us.

*Other categories: Models, Kits; Art, Prints & Posters; Mixed Automobilia*

## Marchbanks Ltd.

See our main listing under "Pedal Cars"

## Charles McCabe

See our main listing under "Toys, Tractor"

## McLellan's Automotive History

Robert C. & Sharon K. McLellan
9111 Longstaff Drive
Houston, TX 77031-2711 USA
TEL: 713-772-3285
FAX: 713-772-3287

Specializing in sales literature, out-of-print books, press kits, magazines, programs & memorabilia. International source of 1,000,000 items - foreign & domestic - from 1900 to present. Racing, classics, antiques, & sports cars. Mail order only. Free 40-page catalog published six times a year.

*Other categories: Books; Showroom Items*

## Mega-Zines

See our main listing under "General Interest"

## Ken Miller Specialties

Ken Miller
Sandbar Road
Mannsville, NY 13661 USA
TEL: 315-387-5644

1923 through 1930 automobile major specifications, plus specific details on engine components; transmissions; clutches; fuel, cooling, braking systems; axles; springs; tires; steering; etc. Also

passenger car wiring diagrams, 1950 through 1956. Misc. magazines, posters, literature, racing programs. SASE with make/model wants.

*Other categories: Art, Prints & Posters; Mixed Automobilia; General Interest*

## Walter Miller

6710 Brooklawn Pkwy
Syracuse, NY 13211 USA
TEL: 315-432-8282
FAX: 315-432-8256

World's largest selection of original literature 1900-present. Automobile, truck, & motorcycle original sales literature, manuals, & showroom items. Over 2,000,000 pieces in stock! I am also a serious buyer.

*Other categories: Books; Retail Store; Showroom Items*

## Edmund F. Molloy, Jr.

PO Box 736
Weimar, CA 95736-0736 USA
TEL: 916-346-8548

Automobile magazines back into the early 1960s. Racing posters & programs into early 1960s. Wooden (1946) & plastic (back to 1952) car kits for sale. Send SASE & which category for list of your interest.

*Other categories: Art, Prints & Posters; Models, Kits; Models, Precision*

## MotoMedia

See our main listing under "Books"

## Motorcycles & Memorabilia

See our main listing under "Motorcycle Collectibles"

## Motordrive

See our main listing under "Motorcycle Collectibles"

## Motorpress

Patrick Daubitz
Hausburgstr. 24
Berlin, Germany 10249
TEL: +49-30-4272942
FAX: +49-30-4278057-1

Have a big collection of car sales brochures worldwide. Only postwar. Buy, sell, trade. Looking for contacts to buy early deluxe items of US cars & imports.

*Other categories: Showroom Items; Specialized Automobilia*

## Mustang Restorations

See our main listing under "Specialized Automobilia"

## Mysteries & Motorcars

See our main listing under "Books"

## Mystic Motorcar Museum

See our main listing under "Museum"

## Jim Newhall Automobilia

See our main listing under "Promos"

## Wayne Noller

See our main listing under "Promos"

## Original Auto Literature

Ron Magnuson
PO Box 448
North Plains, OR 97133 USA
TEL: 503-647-2353

Original auto literature, shop manuals, sales brochures, owner's manuals, data books, etc. All years, US & foreign. Pre-1942 an additional specialty. Reasonable prices & excellent quality.

*Other categories: Books; Showroom Items; Specialized Automobilia*

## Original Ferrari Literature

See our main listing under "Marque Specific"

## Pastimes

See our main listing under "Specialized Automobilia"

## Pat's Parts

See our main listing under "General Interest"

## Pedal Car Guys

See our main listing under "Pedal Cars"

## Paul Politis Automotive Literature

Paul Politis
Box 335, HC 75
McConnellsburg, PA 17233 USA
TEL: 717-987-3702
FAX: 717-984-4284

Over 100,000 shop manuals, owner manuals, showroom sales brochures, postcards, photos, ads, paint chip sets, books, etc. US & import cars & trucks, 1904-present. Reasonable prices, personal service. Serving the hobby & the motoring public since 1974.

*Other categories: Books; Cards, Postal; Photographs*

## Port Jefferson Historical Automobile Research Institute

Henry J. Wertheim
24 Cottonwood Ave.
Port Jefferson Station, NY 11776 USA
TEL: 516-473-8924
FAX: 516-475-1543

A sales literature collector since 1952. We offer for sale or trade surplus brochures from our personal collection. We also have various promotional models. We'd like to purchase your unwanted sales literature. Help us to expand our historical collection. We are dedicated to the service of our fine hobby.

*Other categories: Promos; Showroom Items; Photographs*

## Portrayal Press

Dennis R. Spence
PO Box 1190
Andover, NJ 07821 USA
TEL: 201-579-5781
FAX: 201-579-5781

Military vehicles – manuals & books for all types of historic military vehicles – jeeps, trucks, tanks, etc. – World War II & postwar. Also civilian Jeep. Full-size 48-page catalog mailed first class - $3 (overseas $5). Mail order only. Call in the mornings, EST.

*Other category: Books*

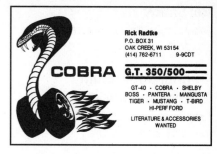

## Rick Radtke

PO Box 31
Oak Creek, WI 53154 USA
TEL: 414-762-6711
FAX: 414-762-6711

Buy, sell, trade. All makes. I deal in original dealer showroom brochures, dealer albums, & other showroom items. I also collect Ford performance Mustang, Shelby, Cobra, T-Bird 1955 to date items as listed above. Call 9-9 CST.

*Other categories: Showroom Items; Mixed Automobilia; Specialized Automobilia*

## Rally Enterprises

See our main listing under "Models, Kits"

## Road Maps Etc.

Peter Sidlow
5895 Duneville St.
Las Vegas, NV 89118 USA
TEL: 702-873-1818
FAX: 702-248-4288

Buying & selling early maps, both oil company & other issues. Colorful graphics preferred. Years 1910-1935 wanted. Have 1000s for sale, write with your specific needs. Buying state-issued maps before 1930 & tour books, travel guides, & brochures, also pre-1935 airline schedules.

*Other categories: Petroliana, Other; Rt. 66 & Roadside; Mixed Automobilia*

## Joseph Russell

See our main listing under "Mixed Automobilia"

## Saab Stories

See our main listing under "Marque Specific"

## SAAB Stuff

See our main listing under "Marque Specific"

## Bill Sandy

See our main listing under "Marque Specific"

## Gunnar Söderblom

Gullbergs Strandgata 34
Göteborg, Sweden 41104
TEL: +46-31-15.70.70
FAX: +46-31-15.10.10
Email: gs@soderblom.se

Dealer in automotive literature, model cars, & automobilia. My shop is open 6 days a week.

*Other categories: Books; Mixed Automobilia; Petroliana, Other*

## SpeedWay MotorBooks

See our main listing under "Books"

## Spyder Enterprises

See our main listing under "Specialized Automobilia"

## Paul E. Szabo

351 Greenwood Ave.
Seekonk, MA 02771 USA
TEL: 508-336-9438

Auto sales literature: 1000 brochures for domestic & foreign cars & trucks. Send SASE with inquiries or $3 for 31-page catalog.

## Taxi Toys & Memorabilia

See our main listing under "Chauffeur/Taxi Items"

## Russell Taylor

See our main listing under "License Plates, Tags, etc."

## TMC Publications

Jeffrey Foland
5817 Park Heights Ave.
Balto, MD 21215-3931 USA
TEL: 410-367-4490
FAX: 410-466-3566
Email: tmcpub@jagunet.com

Automotive literature for Mercedes-Benz, BMW, Jaguar, Porsche, Audi, Lexus, Hyundai, Subaru, Mitsubishi, Suzuki, Toyota, etc. We stock shop manuals, owner's manuals, parts manuals, microfiche, sales brochures 1950-1996. We buy literature collections also.

*Other categories: Books; Publications, Current; Showroom Items*

## Marnix Verkest

See our main listing under "General Interest"

## VIP Ltd.

See our main listing under "Models, Kits"

## Vintage Jag Works

See our main listing under "Marque Specific"

## Douglas Vogel

1100 Shady Oaks
Ann Arbor, MI 48103 USA
TEL: 313-761-2490
FAX: 313-761-3235

Specialize in auto sales literature, shop manuals, owner's manuals, parts books, dealer showroom items, dealer albums, posters, data books, etc. American & foreign cars & trucks, 1900-1996. Mail order only, or spring Carlisle & fall Hershey. Send SASE or fax your wants; over one million items in stock.

*Other category: Showroom Items*

## Ted & Nelda Weems

PO Box 810665
Farmers Branch, TX 75381-0665 USA
TEL: 972-247-8169
FAX: 972-247-8169

Factory shop manuals, owner's manuals, sales brochures, showroom albums, parts catalogs, paint chips, pre-1970 automotive magazines. Best selection in the south central US. Collecting since 1950. Call Monday through Thursday or send your want list with SASE. Also buying, selling, & trading pre-1980 promotional models.

*Other categories: Promos; Models, Kits*

## Paul R. Weiss

11 Ross Rd.
Scarsdale, NY 10583 USA
TEL: 914-723-5880
FAX: 212-861-8376

*Cars & Parts* magazine 1975-1994, mint condition. Best offer.

## Dillon T. Wescoat

14082 Gaswell Rd.
Titusville, PA 16354 USA
TEL: 814-827-3088

I have been collecting automobile literature for over 40 years. I will sell duplicates or trade for literature I don't have.

*Other category: Mixed Automobilia*

## Gerard Wilson

154 Mansion Ave.
Yonkers, NY 10704 USA
TEL: 914-423-7229

Automobile sales literature, 1957-1964, automobile magazines, 1965-1969, for sale or trade. Mostly US, some European. My list upon request, your list sought. I buy literature also.

## The XR-1000 Nut

See our main listing under "Motorcycle Collectibles"

# LUGGAGE/PICNIC SETS

## Auto Epoch

See our main listing under "Publications, Current"

## Elegant Accessories

See our main listing under "Specialized Automobilia"

## Enthusiast's Specialties

See our main listing under "License Plates, Tags, etc."

## Finesse Fine Art

See our main listing under "Mascots/Badges/Emblems"

## Roy Lassen

See our main listing under "Motoring Accessories"

# MANUFACTURER

## Blast from the Past

See our main listing under "Neon"

## Brookfield Collectors Guild

See our main listing under "Models, Precision"

## Brooklin Models, Ltd.

See our main listing under "Models, Precision"

## C & N Reproductions, Inc.

See our main listing under "Pedal Cars"

## Creative Miniature Associates

See our main listing under "Models, Precision"

## Crown Premiums

Mark Hoeger
1029 1st St. SW
Dyersville, IA 52040 USA
TEL: 319-875-2694
FAX: 319-875-2726

Manufacture diecast pedal car replicas & vintage gas pumps in miniature. They are custom imprinted with your company name or logos & utilized in promotional merchandise. Each unit is a replica featuring working lights, coin bank features, sequential numbering, custom carton, & numerous added features. Very realistic – very collectible.

*Other categories: Pedal Cars; Petroliana, Other; Toys, Truck*

## Fairlane Automotive Specialties

See our main listing under "Pedal Cars"

## 4 Tek

See our main listing under "Displays/Fixtures"

## GM Studios, Inc.

See our main listing under "Jewelry"

## David L. Gray

See our main listing under "Mixed Automobilia"

## Robert J. Harrington

See our main listing under "Spark Plugs"

## Harvey Racing Engines

See our main listing under "Specialized Automobilia"

## The Hobby Shop

A.M. Hall
640 Hermitage Lane
San Jose, CA 95134 USA
TEL: 408-433-1694

Desk sets with your favorite car & personalized brass nameplate. Write for complete information stating desired car. The perfect gift for the car enthusiast.

*Other categories: Models, Precision; General Interest*

## Innovative Ideas

See our main listing under "Jewelry"

## Lilliput Motor Car Co.

See our main listing under "Models, Precision"

## Max Neon Design Group

Ed Goralewski
19807 Sussex Drive
St. Clair Shores, MI 48081 USA
TEL: 810-773-5000
FAX: 810-772-6224

Neon clocks & parts: replicas of late 1930/early 40s advertising clocks. Electric movements, 18 in. H x 18 in. W x 6 in. D, 40 stock faces, standard neon colors, custom logos available, one-year guarantee on electrical parts. Non-spinner $279, spinner $299. S.H.I. add $20. Additional information, catalog, photos, remit $5 to cover handling.

*Other categories: Art, Other; Diner Memorabilia; Signs*

## Moviecraft Inc.

Larry Urbanski
Box 438
Orland Park, IL 60462 USA
TEL: 708-460-9082
FAX: 708-460-9099
Email: larryu@moviecraft.com

Producer of TV's Magic Memories Home Video, a historical & nostalgic collection of video releases, including automotive, hot rod, drag racing, stock car, & other films from the 1930s to 1960s. Large illustrated video list $1. We seek 16mm, 35mm films, all types!

*Other categories: Hot Rod Memorabilia; General Interest; Racing Artifacts*

## NASCAR Novelties

See our main listing under "Motoring Accessories"

## Nylint Collector

See our main listing under "Toys, Truck"

## Dan O'Neill Precision Models

Daniel J. O'Neill
1065 Spur Rd.
Souderton, PA 18964 USA
TEL: 215-723-9320
FAX: 215-997-8153

Specialize in developing radio-controlled equipment. Trash, fire, construction machinery, buses are available in static models also. Prototypes developed, machine shop & molding services. For the model or item you want but not available in store or catalog.

*Other categories: Models, Kits; Promos; Toys, Truck*

## Park Drive Garage

See our main listing under "Petroliana, Other"

## Peachstate

See our main listing under "Models, Precision"

## Portell Restorations

See our main listing under "Pedal Cars"

## R & D Unique

See our main listing under "Models, Kits"

## Rare Sportsfilms Inc.

See our main listing under "Racing Artifacts"

## Revell-Monogram, Inc.

See our main listing under "Racing Artifacts"

## Road Race Replicas

See our main listing under "Slot Cars"

## S & H Chrome Plating & Powder Coating, Inc.

See our main listing under "Restoration Service"

## John Snowberger

See our main listing under "Models, Precision"

## Squat Rods

See our main listing under "Pedal Cars"

## SRE Industries

See our main listing under "Mascots/Badges/Emblems"

## Turtle Creek Scale Models

See our main listing under "Models, Precision"

## Vic's Place

See our main listing under "Petroliana, Other"

## Winross Company

Richard Hahn
2060 O'Neill Rd.
Macedon, NY 14502 USA
TEL: 800-227-2060
FAX: 315-986-3849
Email: www.winross.com

America's premier collectible custom truck model manufacturer. New limited edition 1/64-scale truck models offered each month. Oil companies, freight companies, automobile anniversary commemoratives, many other special models. Call to join free mailing list. Join the hobby, join the fun. Collect Winross.

*Other categories: Toys, Truck; Promos*

## Wolo Manufacturing Corp.

See our main listing under "Horns"

# MARQUE SPECIFIC

## AAA Small Car World

Ron Sturgeon
1500 Carlson
Fort Worth, TX 76117 USA
TEL: 817-831-0946
FAX: 817-834-7453

Buying tin cars, specializing in Mercedes, & vehicles with dogs. Over 1,500 pieces of automobilia on display, including German auto training models.

*Other categories: Museum; Specialized Automobilia*

## Auto-Ideas

See our main listing under "Specialized Automobilia"

## Automobile Sportswear Inc.

See our main listing under "Clothing"

## B.A.S.I.C.

See our main listing under "Mixed Automobilia"

## Bob's British Car Parts

Robert W. Paré
513 Deubler Rd.
Camp Hill, PA 17011-2017 USA
TEL: 717-737-1119

British Ford toys, literature, models, accessories, signs, parts, etc. for Anglia, Prefect, Thames, Squire, Consul, Zephyr, Zodiac, Cortina, Pilot, etc. Buy & sell anything English Ford, one piece or a collection. At fall Hershey & several Carlisle shows. Call 5-9pm EST or weekend days.

*Other categories: Toys, General; Literature; Models, Kits*

## Bob's Trucks

See our main listing under "Toys, Truck"

## Alan Bowden

See our main listing under "Models, Kits"

## Cadillac Motorbooks

See our main listing under "Books"

## Checker USA

See our main listing under "Literature"

## Cole Motor Car Club

See our main listing under "Club/Organization"

## Curtis Equipment Co.

See our main listing under "Appraisal Service"

## Eureka Antique & Collectibles

Richard Bitterman
1701 W. Chase Ave.
Chicago, IL 60626 USA
TEL: 773-743-1511
FAX: 773-743-3330

Collecting 356 & other early Porsche toys, manuals, factory promotions, posters, postcards, etc. No kits & no reproductions. Also buy any unrelated objects with the number 356 on them, e.g., hotel keys, coatroom checks, license plates, etc. Send description, price, & SASE. Photos returned if requested.

*Other category: Specialized Automobilia*

## Dick Farnsworth

1034 Henderson
Freeport, IL 61032 USA
TEL: 815-232-3825

Stephens, Henney, Shoemaker, anything for these three makes wanted. I am also looking for miscellaneous mascots, radiator emblems, screw-on hubcaps, body plates, & pre-1930 automotive magazines.

*Other categories: Mascots/Badges/Emblems; Literature; Mixed Automobilia*

## Fast Toys, Inc.

Bruce Hollander
901 S. State Rd. 7, Penthouse C
Hollywood, FL 33023 USA
TEL: 954-964-8000
FAX: 954-964-5969

Porsche collector – literature, models, toys, diecast, tin, books, art, posters, factory pieces, clothing, & plastic. Specializing in Porsche race cars. Interested in vintage sports car racing materials. Purchasing complete collections or single pieces. Buy, sell, trade, consignment. Send large SASE for my list. Send me your list or call.

*Other categories: Racing Artifacts; Books; Models, Precision*

## 4 Tek

See our main listing under "Displays/Fixtures"

## L. Robert Hurwitz

See our main listing under "Literature"

## Italian Cars & Related Stuff

Steve Piantieri
3012 Ardsley Dr.
Orlando, FL 32804 USA
TEL: 407-843-6240
FAX: 407-296-8774
Email:
102752.1362@compuserve.com

Alfa Romeo & Ferrari boutique items. Many odd literature & desktop gifts for enthusiasts of all spaghetti-flavored cars. Send SASE or Email for list. Posters, mugs, sales brochures, temporary tattoos, videos, license plates, promotional items & lapel pins! Many Ferrari 250/330 & Alfa 116/102/106 series parts for sale also.

*Other categories: Specialized Automobilia; Mixed Automobilia; Literature*

## Ed Jacobowitz Cadillac & LaSalle

Ed Jacobowitz
341 Fitch Hill Rd.
Uncasville, CT 06382 USA
TEL: 860-848-8934

Used auto parts, 1905 through 1973, new castings, literature, guidance. I collect vintage cars, most items related: radiator nameplates, mascots, hubcaps, also truck stuff. Insurance appraisals, 35 years' experience. Extensive inventory of parts, parts cars. Primarily Cadillac & LaSalle, but have Packard, Gardner, Graham-Paige Roosevelt, Smith & Briggs motorwheels. Try me.

*Other categories: Mascots/Badges/Emblems; Mixed Automobilia; Specialized Automobilia*

## Jaguar Automobilia Collector

Ian Codling
59 Oxenturn Rd.
Wye, Ashford, Kent TN25 5AY UK
TEL: +44-1233-812416
FAX: +44-1233-813601

Quarterly magazine & sod-lot postal auction for all aspects of Jaguar automobilia: brochures, models, mascots, prints, badges, books, photos, etc. Detailed reports on Jaguar automobilia at other auctions. Interested in Jaguars or automobilia? Then write

now for your free copy of my magazine & auction catalog.

*Other categories: Auction Firm; Publications, Current; License Plates, Tags, etc.*

## Jaguar Drivers Club of South Australia

See our main listing under "Club/Organization"

## Kid Stuff

See our main listing under "Restoration Service"

## Michael Knittel

See our main listing under "Literature"

## Ric Kruse

See our main listing under "Literature"

## Mobil & Morgans

See our main listing under "Petroliana, Other"

## Model A Ford Cabriolet Club

See our main listing under "Club/Organization"

## Original Ferrari Literature

Ken Lewis
Box 23576
Mandarin, FL 32241-3576 USA
TEL: 904-731-5992
FAX: 904-739-3164

Original Ferrari & Lamborghini factory sales literature & related memorabilia. We buy, sell, & exchange. Manuals, brochures & Scuderia Ferrari items & dealer signs. Free 40-page catalog just for asking. 24-hour phone/fax.

*Other category: Literature*

## People Kars

See our main listing under "Toys, General"

## Pirelli Collector

See our main listing under "Specialized Automobilia"

## Ken Poynter

See our main listing under "Specialized Automobilia"

## RJN Automobilia

Richard Niezabitowski
140 Highland Avenue
Rowayton, CT 06853 USA
TEL: 203-852-9527
FAX: 203-852-9527
Email: RNiez@GTE.net

Specialize in posters, books, magazines & related items concerned with American sports car racing from 1948-1970. Also buy, sell & trade collectible spark plugs & related items, mainly pre-WWII. Buying early brass-era plugs, especially French, for my personal collection.

*Other categories: General Interest; Spark Plugs*

## Saab Stories

Bob McNary
672 Sunvale Ave.
Ventura, CA 93003 USA
TEL: 805-654-1646
FAX: 805-988-1129

Private collector wishes to buy, sell, trade Saab automobile paraphernalia with special interest in items from 1950 through 1974, including jewelry, toys, dealer displays, posters, literature, factory manuals, ashtrays, lighters, cans of Saab oil, NOS 2-stoke parts, *Saab Soundings* newsletters. If you have anything odd & Saab let's hobnob.

*Other categories: Specialized Automobilia; Showroom Items; Literature*

## SAAB Stuff

Rob Allen
1318 SE 119 Ave.
Micanopy, FL 32667 USA
TEL: 352-466-4970

SAAB-related items: wanted & for sale. The older & odder the better. Seeking dealer signs, pedal & scale toys, sales literature, promo items, manuals, inventory of old 2-stroke & V4 parts, calendars, etc. to enhance mature collection. Desire correspondence from other collectors to trade.

*Other categories: Literature; Specialized Automobilia; Signs*

## Bill Sandy

115 Route 519
Newton, NJ 07860 USA
TEL: 201-383-9491
FAX: 201-383-9377

Oldsmobile literature, postcards, toys, precision models, & promos from 1897-1997. Our 25th year! World's largest dealer dedicated to America's greatest & longest continuous car maker. Celebrate Oldsmobile's centennial in Lansing, Aug. 1997! Mail order, Oldsmobile clubs' meets, & local shows. Send SASE, state year(s)/interests for current list(s). Chevy, Mopar, & FoMoCo literature closeout sale!

*Other categories: Literature; Toys, General; Cards, Postal*

## Scale Autoworks

See our main listing under "Models, Precision"

## Vintage Jag Works

Walt Osborn
1390 W. Hwy 26
Blackfoot, ID 83221 USA
TEL: 208-684-3554

Jaguar-related. Buy, sell, trade. Literature, toys, models, tools, parts, & cars. Mixed automobilia also: magazines, sales brochures, ads, books, toys, models, signs, & vintage speed equipment. Appraisal & consulting service for cars of the 1930s, 40s, 50s, & all Jaguars.

*Other categories: Literature; Mixed Automobilia; Appraisal Service*

## VW Collector

PO Box 1705
Redondo Beach, CA 90278 USA
TEL: 310-371-3919
Email: AW793@lafn.org

Collector of VW history from 1937 to 1967. Interested in dealership signs, posters, literature, dealer promotional items, inventory, personal photos, factory tour photos, movies. Also EMPI, Meyers Manx, Bug-In: catalogs, jackets, programs, trophies, parts, etc.

*Other categories: Specialized Automobilia; Mixed Automobilia; Photographs*

## Zwart Design Group, Inc.

See our main listing under "Books"

# MASCOTS, BADGES, EMBLEMS

## American Arrow

Don Sommer
105 Kinross
Clawson, MI 48017 USA
TEL: 810-435-6115
FAX: 810-435-4670

Mascots bought, sold, traded. Expert service & knowledgeable advice.

*Other category: Specialized Automobilia*

## American Automobile Sales Literature of Lancaster, PA

See our main listing under "Petroliana, Other"

## BJM

Joe Madonia
12101 Chuck Cir.
Hudson, FL 34669 USA
TEL: 813-863-7033
FAX: 813-863-7033

Specializing in custom-embroidered emblems, American-made patches for your club, organization, or event. Any size or shape, with unlimited colors available. Patches made from your designs or ours. Low minimums & great prices. Custom hat pins & emblematic jewelry also available. Call or write for price quotes & samples.

*Other categories: Jewelry; General Interest; Specialized Automobilia*

## G.R. Beckon

RR 3, Wiley Rd.
Wellandport, Ontario LOR 2JO
Canada
TEL: 905-386-6546
FAX: 905-386-6546

Wanted: mascots, hood ornaments, badges – all kinds & condition. Cash or trade.

*Other category: Mixed Automobilia*

## Casey's Collectibles

See our main listing under "Books"

## Collector Auto Appraisal Co.

See our main listing under "Appraisal Service"

## Dave's Signs & Collectibles

See our main listing under "Petroliana, Other"

## Emblemagic Co.

Raymond Geschke
8367 Shepard Rd.
Macedonia, OH 44056 USA
TEL: 216-467-8755

Prewar car & truck badges in stock & restoration available. Postwar plastic inserts for cars & trucks. This is the clear plastic decorative insert that seems to have its design embedded inside. Your emblem headquarters. Call or write for free catalog.

*Other category: Restoration Service*

## Bob English

See our main listing under "Signs"

## Enthusiast's Specialties

See our main listing under "License Plates, Tags, etc."

## Dick Farnsworth

See our main listing under "Marque Specific"

## Finesse Fine Art

Tony Wraight
91 Coniston Crescent
Weymouth, Dorset DT3 5HA England, UK
TEL: +44-1305-854286
FAX: +44-1305-852888
Email: finesse@fine-art.demon.co.uk

Only the very finest European prewar motoring items. Available here: fine signed mascots, picnic sets, bronzes, René Lalique glass mascots, badges, lamps, silverware, etc. 30 years' experience dealing worldwide. If you want the best, I have it or can find it for you. Free worldwide shipping, photos a pleasure.

*Other categories: Luggage/Picnic Sets; Art, Other; Lamps*

## GM Studios, Inc.

See our main listing under "Jewelry"

## Bob Gerrity

See our main listing under "Restoration Service"

## Philip R. Goldberg

71 Lawton Ave.
Hartsdale, NY 10530 USA
TEL: 914-948-6924

NOS & excellent used, original, fine-quality American & European mascots for sale/trade. Automotive books & literature for sale. 1928-1968 Mopar signs (neon & porcelain) for sale/trade. Free lists, SASE with specific needs.

*Other categories: Literature; Signs*

## Ralph A. Herbst

See our main listing under "License Plates, Tags, etc."

## Hosking Cycle Works

See our main listing under "Motorcycle Collectibles"

## Ed Jacobowitz Cadillac & LaSalle

See our main listing under "Marque Specific"

## Robert Kegler

12937 Broadway Apt. #5
Alden, NY 14004 USA
TEL: 716-937-6889

Collector of cloisonné radiator emblems, looking for any of the following: Adria, Apperson, Climber, Cutting, Davis, Diana 8, Empire, Harding, Havers, Interstate, Jones, Kline Kar, Lambert, Lozier, Lexington, McFarlan, Monroe, Moline Dreadnought, Niagara, Pan American, Pilot, Pathfinder, Revere, Rickenbacker, Pratt, Standard, R & V Knight.

*Other categories: Specialized Automobilia; Mixed Automobilia; General Interest*

## Kneipp's Toy & Collectibles

See our main listing under "Toys, General"

## Sy Margolis

17853 Santiago Blvd, Ste. 107-210
Villa Park, CA 92861 USA
TEL: 714-974-5938
FAX: 714-921-0731

If it went on a radiator cap, I'm interested! Mascots, factory or aftermarket, literature, ads, signs. Buy, sell, trade.

## Motoring Goodies

See our main listing under "Mixed Automobilia"

## SMB Designs

See our main listing under "Signs"

## SRE Industries

Jim Sullivan
3424 W. Magnolia
Burbank, CA 91506 USA
TEL: 818-848-7223
FAX: 818-848-7302
Email: jims@lapelpins.com

Custom hat & lapel pins – for clubs, events, even repro of your collector car. High quality & dependable delivery at modest cost. Check us out on the Internet (www.lapelpins.com) or write or call for catalog.

*Other categories: Manufacturer; Club/Organization; Shows & Events*

## Charles Schalebaum

See our main listing under "Art, Original"

## Seebee Enterprises

See our main listing under "Displays/Fixtures"

## Dan Smith

3410 Wentworth Dr.
Jamul, CA 91935 USA
TEL: 619-442-4314
FAX: 619-442-7480

Mascot collector. Buy, sell, trade. Pre-WW II mascots. Publisher of *Accessory Mascots, the Automotive Accents of Yesteryear, 1910-1940*. Still a few books left. $19.95 + $3 s/h.

*Other categories: Motorcycle Collectibles; Specialized Automobilia; Signs*

## SpeedArt Enterprises

S.R. Reamer
PO Box 298
St. Bonifacius, MN 55375 USA
TEL: 612-446-9527
FAX: 612-446-9527

Longtime collector/trader of pre-1932 US auto radiator emblems, screw-on hubcaps, other early auto memorabilia, racing, 1/43 models, art. Will appraise collections or items at no charge. Interested in starting registry/newsletter for emblem collectors. Write if interested.

*Other categories: Appraisal Service; Mixed Automobilia; General Interest*

## John W. Webster

68 Chesterfield Rd.
E. Lyme, CT 06333 USA
TEL: 860-739-2790

Emblems, nameplates, fobs, pins, badges, photos, & mascots. Restoration of any hard enamel items above. Buy, sell, trade.

*Other categories: Mixed Automobilia; Restoration Service; Specialized Automobilia*

## Workbench

Ray Geweke
1107 Bugbee
Wausau, WI 54401 USA
TEL: 715-675-9983

Specializing in radiator caps/mascots. Buy, sell, trade. I also collect sales literature. Collections or individual pieces purchased/sold. Send SASE for current list. Phone 5-9pm, CST.

*Other categories: Motorcycle Collectibles; Specialized Automobilia; General Interest*

## Zwart Design Group, Inc.

See our main listing under "Books"

# MIXED AUTOMOBILIA

## Ablaze Enterprises Inc.

James & Brenda Anderson
PO Box 129, 4925 Rt 9N
Corinth, NY 12822 USA
TEL: 518-654-9699

Specializing in auto & gas memorabilia, porcelain signs, pump restorations, welding (20 years' experience), & "Cover It" instant garages. Daytime calls, please.

*Other categories: Petroliana, Other; Signs; Restoration Service*

## Adams Flea Market

Don Doyle
Booth 3
Adams, WI 53910 USA
TEL: 608-339-9303

Flea market interest. Buy, sell, trade. Parts, tools, toys, paper. Call after 6pm.

*Other categories: Petroliana, Other; Toys, General; Tools*

## Tom Adams

See our main listing under "Literature"

## Alex & Phil's Filling Station

See our main listing under "Petroliana, Other"

## Allen Oil Sales

See our main listing under "Petroliana, Other"

## Antiques Warehouse of Cape Cod

See our main listing under "Toys, Truck"

## Art's Automobilia

See our main listing under "Toys, General"

## Auto Air & Audio

Todd Kirkpatrick
4869 Old Wire Road
Battlefield, MO 65619 USA
TEL: 417-882-1391
FAX: 417-831-7560

Collect mixed automobilia & gasoline collectibles. Oil cans, globes, old gas station items. Signs: automotive, soft drink, cigarette, general advertising. Signs must be in excellent condition or NOS. I like bright colors. Tin or porcelain.

*Other categories: Signs; Petroliana, Other; Petroliana, Pumps & Globes*

## Auto Literature & Collectibles

See our main listing under "Literature"

## Auto-Cycle Publications

See our main listing under "Literature"

## Autographics

See our main listing under "Books"

## Automobilia Auctions, Inc.

See our main listing under "Auction Firm"

## Automobilia & Collectibles

Kenneth R. Moore
551 W. Main St.
Alpahretta, GA 30201 USA
TEL: 770-664-9426
FAX: 770-664-9426

Automotive, motorcycle, Rt. 66, oil & gas items, both original & reproduction, including advertising signs, clocks, posters, auto & cycle collector cards, lots of decals, metal license plates, & more. Retail store & mail order. Low prices.

*Other categories: Petroliana, Other; Hot Rod Memorabilia; Motorcycle Collectibles*

## Autopia Advertising Auctions

See our main listing under "Auction Firm"

## Autosaurus

See our main listing under "Art, Prints & Posters"

## B.A.S.I.C.

Stephen Ring
182-32 Radnor Rd.
Jamaica Estates, NY 11432-1538 USA
TEL: 718-969-8477
FAX: 718-380-1841
Email: basicnyc@aol.com

We buy & sell toys, models, literature, & other automobilia with a special interest in all things Jaguar or British.

*Other categories: Toys, General; Models, Precision; Marque Specific*

## Barkin' Frog Collectible Co.

See our main listing under "Toys, General"

## G.R. Beckon

See our main listing under "Mascots/Badges/Emblems"

## Bergen Distributors

See our main listing under "Petroliana, Other"

## Andy Bernstein

See our main listing under "License Plates, Tags, etc."

## Big T's Gas Trash

See our main listing under "Petroliana, Other"

## Bowers Collectable Toys

Larry & Dee Dee Bowers
27037 Woodbrook Rd.
Rancho Palos Verdes, CA 90275 USA
TEL: 310-544-0444
FAX: 310-544-7718

Smith Miller trucks. Buy, sell, trade. Ertl & Eastwood banks. Eastwood #1 through #12 mint in boxes. Xonex & Hallmark pedal cars, child-size pedal cars, signs, gas globes. Send SASE with your desires. OK to call until 10pm PST.

*Other categories: Toys, General; Petroliana, Other; Pedal Cars*

## Dennis Brilla

52 Mt. Vernon Rd.
Plantsville, CT 06479 USA
TEL: 860-621-4338

Collector buys, sells, trades auto, motorcycle, gas station items 1900-1960. Pre-1920 items, globes, signs, auto & motorcycle racing wanted. 1 item or a garage full. Indy, Daytona, Sebring, Bonneville items wanted. NASCAR pit badges wanted. Call for free estimate when selling your collectibles 8-11pm EST.

*Other categories: Petroliana, Pumps & Globes; Motorcycle Collectibles; Racing Artifacts*

## The British Garage

See our main listing under "Specialized Automobilia"

## C & C Creations

Carson Acuff
214 Alfred McCammon Rd.
Maryville, TN 37804 USA
TEL: 423-982-6995
FAX: 423-985-4502

Buy, sell, trade, restore pedal cars, Ford Pinto parts, Ford flathead engines, Texaco collectibles, Tonka, Tennessee license plates.

*Other categories: Petroliana, Other; Pedal Cars; Toys, General*

## Joseph Camp

26 Peach Tree Rd.
Oakhurst, NJ 07755 USA
TEL: 908-229-3324

Private collector specializing in Aurora H.O. Model Motoring, Atlas, & Tyco-S slot cars from the 1960s. Buy, sell, trade. Also collect hot rod memorabilia, including "Hot Rod," "Drag," & "Surf" record albums from 1960s. In addition, model kits including annuals, customs, & TV-related. Call after 7pm EST.

*Other categories: Slot Cars; Hot Rod Memorabilia; Models, Kits*

## Canton Classic Car Museum

See our main listing under "Museum"

## Castle Concepts

See our main listing under "Racing Artifacts"

## Clark's Historic Rt. 99 General Store

Bruce W. Clark
82253 Indio Blvd (Historic Rt. 99)
Indio, CA 92201 USA
TEL: 619-342-4776
FAX: 619-347-1415

Specialize in porcelain signs. Buy, sell, trade. Also collect early Union Oil signs, memorabilia; Rt. 99 Washington, Oregon, California signs, memorabilia, & postcards. Porcelain license plates. Complete collections purchased. Call 6am to 2pm PST.

*Other categories: Signs; Cards, Postal; Petroliana, Other*

## Classic Motors

Tony Leopardo
PO Box 1011
San Mateo, CA 94403 USA
TEL: 415-348-8269
FAX: 415-340-9473

Classic Motors is proud to announce the new Coca-Cola collectible Coke bottle '57 car series. '57 pink T-bird, '57 red Corvette, & a '57 yellow Bel-Air

make up the set. Send $20, which includes shipping & handling for each three-bottle set. You can order all of one car too!

## Classic Restoration

See our main listing under "Tools"

## Cotton Candy Classics

See our main listing under "Hot Rod Memorabilia"

## Robert Covarrubias Studios

See our main listing under "Specialized Automobilia"

## Crazy Irishman Collectibles

Pat McCarthy
421 Louisa St.
So. Amboy, NJ 08879 USA
TEL: 908-721-4232

Oil company promos, trucks, signs, advertising items, maps, pens, miscellaneous collectibles. Also auto racing programs, pictures, tickets, etc. Buy, sell, trade. Send want list or call.

*Other categories: Petroliana, Other; Toys, Truck; Racing Artifacts*

## D & K Collectables

See our main listing under "Petroliana, Other"

## Dan's Classic Auto Parts

George, Bob, or Robert
1537 SE Morrison
Portland, OR 97214-2694 USA
TEL: 503-234-6674
FAX: 503-234-2434

Automobilia old & new: a store full of literature, books, photos, posters, maps, decals, signs, toys, gasoline related, cans, old auto accessories, & more. General Motors items a specialty. Send list of wants with SASE, or visit our showroom Mon-Fri 9-5:30, Sat 9-2.

*Other categories: Retail Store; Petroliana, Other; General Interest*

## Dave's Signs & Collectibles

See our main listing under "Petroliana, Other"

## Dave's Tag Barn

See our main listing under "License Plates, Tags, etc."

## Don's Body Shop

See our main listing under "Appraisal Service"

## Doney Enterprises

Kevin Doney
2135 W. Walnut St.
Lebanon, PA 17042 USA
TEL: 717-272-1886

Specialize in restoration & sales of pedal cars, gas pumps, bumper cars, neon clocks. Also original art drawing from photos. Call or mail listing.

*Other categories: Restoration Service; Petroliana, Pumps & Globes; Pedal Cars*

## Electric Dreams

See our main listing under "Slot Cars"

## Elegant Accessories

See our main listing under "Specialized Automobilia"

## David Ellnor

See our main listing under "Books"

## Enterprise Cars

See our main listing under "Signs"

## Enthusiast's Specialties

See our main listing under "License Plates, Tags, etc."

## Fairlane Automotive Specialties

See our main listing under "Pedal Cars"

## Dick Farnsworth

See our main listing under "Marque Specific"

## Formula 1 World

John
Via Vignola 21
Maranello-Modena, Italy 41015
TEL: +39-335-396630
FAX: +39-59-220153
Email: johnf1@mbox.nau.it

I sell, buy, trade only genuine Formula 1 memorabilia items, like: genuine F1 used & signed helmets, genuine F1 used & signed overalls, genuine F1 used & signed visors & gloves, genuine Ferrari F1 body parts, etc.

*Other categories: Signs; Specialized Automobilia*

## Frank's Toys & Adv. Memorabilia

Frank Rothdeutsch
319 Sumner Ave.
Whitehall, PA 18052 USA
TEL: 610-434-0246

Interested in gasoline collectibles, signs, lighters, etc., 1950s memorabilia, soda & gas station adv., diecast toy trucks & cars, 1/64, 1/34, 1/25-scale Danbury & Franklin Mint cars & trucks. Buy, sell, trade. Have Ertl, Winross trucks for sale. Call after 6pm EST.

*Other categories: Signs; Toys, Truck; Petroliana, Other*

## Frontier Group

See our main listing under "Petroliana, Other"

## Frost International Enterprises

See our main listing under "Literature"

## Paul Furlinger

See our main listing under "Petroliana, Other"

## Bob Gajewski

18001 Snow
Dearborn, MI 48124 USA
TEL: 313-336-4762

Specialize in Ford, GM, & Chrysler memorabilia, signs, auto & gas related, Wyandotte trucks, neon, promos, clocks, filling station artifacts, unusual & one-of-a-kind Motor City memorabilia. Call after 6pm EST for latest inventories.

*Other categories: Petroliana, Other; Signs; Neon*

## Gallery Automania

See our main listing under "Art, Prints & Posters"

## Gus Garton Auto

See our main listing under "Literature"

## Gasoline Alley

Roger J. Watt
4407 Solano Ave.
Napa, CA 94558 USA
TEL: 707-226-2359
FAX: 707-226-2981
Email: rjwatt@aol.com

Service, repair antiques, classic autos, vehicles on consignment. Memorabilia for sale & on consignment. Cars & parts locator service.

*Other categories: Restoration Service; Retail Store*

## Gasoline Alley

See our main listing under "Motorcycle Collectibles"

## Get It On Paper

See our main listing under "Retail Store"

## Dwayne L. Gordon

PO Box 381
Rockaway Beach, MO 65740 USA
TEL: 417-561-2482

We specialize in nothing, sell anything we can get, from hubcaps to periodicals to tins to advertising, etc. We are always out searching for automobilia items to resell. Send large SASE for list.

*Other categories: Art, Other; Literature; General Interest*

## David L. Gray

5707 Mills Creek Ln.
North Ridgeville, OH 44039 USA
TEL: 216-327-0401

I collect all automotive-related items, including gasoline memorabilia, promos, Hot Wheels, Matchbox, & racing.

*Other categories: Petroliana, Other; Hot Wheels; Manufacturer*

## Greater Dakota Classics

See our main listing under "Club/Organization"

## Pablo Gudino

See our main listing under "Photographs"

## Robert N. Haldeman

See our main listing under "General Interest"

## Hayes Associates

See our main listing under "Petroliana, Pumps & Globes"

## Hemmings Motor News

See our main listing under "Publications, Current"

## Clyde Hensley

See our main listing under "Motorcycle Collectibles"

## Ralph A. Herbst

See our main listing under "License Plates, Tags, etc."

## Joseph Herr

See our main listing under "Toys, General"

## Hiway 79 Classic Collectibles

David & Sally Edwards
PO Box 890994
Temecula, CA 92589 USA
TEL: 909-699-4586
Email: hiway79@aol.com

Do you like cars, planes, personalities, & images from a simpler age? Hiway 79 offers diecast & plastic models, hand-signed prints, signs, & more for your nostalgic collecting. Send $2 for a fully illustrated catalog.

*Other categories: Toys, General; Art, Prints & Posters; General Interest*

## Horseless Carriage Club of America

See our main listing under "Club/Organization"

## Hot Stuff By Tri-C

See our main listing under "Hot Wheels"

## Hudson Motor Car Company Memorabilia

See our main listing under "Specialized Automobilia"

## Stan Hurd Auto Literature

See our main listing under "Literature"

## Richard Hurlburt

See our main listing under "License Plates, Tags, etc."

## Iowa Gas Swap Meet & Auctions

See our main listing under "Petroliana, Other"

## Alan J. Isselhard

See our main listing under "Racing Artifacts"

## Italian Cars & Related Stuff

See our main listing under "Marque Specific"

## Jim & Connie's Collectibles

See our main listing under "Specialized Automobilia"

## Ed Jacobowitz Cadillac & LaSalle

See our main listing under "Marque Specific"

## S.L. Jaffe, Inc.

See our main listing under "Appraisal Service"

## Ron Johnson

See our main listing under "General Interest"

## Robert Kegler

See our main listing under "Mascots/Badges/Emblems"

## Kirk's Ghetto Garage

Kirk Bible
301 S. Paulsen Ave.
Compton, CA 90220 USA
TEL: 310-608-5492
FAX: 310-608-0537

Dress up your collectibles with hand-built miniature garages. Each one comes with dustcover. Also gas islands, 1/15 & 1/24 scale, complete with air & water lines. Most brands available. Pumps in 1940s & 50s styles. Send $3 for brochure.

*Other categories: Petroliana, Pumps & Globes; Art, Other; Toys, General*

## Kneipp's Toy & Collectibles

See our main listing under "Toys, General"

## Dan Kruse Classic Car Productions

See our main listing under "Auction Firm"

## L'art et l'automobile

See our main listing under "Art, Prints & Posters"

## Dave Leopard

See our main listing under "Toys, General"

## License Plates, Etc.

See our main listing under "License Plates, Tags, etc."

## LMG Enterprises/Gallery L'Automobile

See our main listing under "Books"

## Bob Lichty Enterprises

See our main listing under "Shows & Events"

## Bob Lint Motor Shop

Bob Lint
101 Main, Box 87
Danville, KS 67036 USA
TEL: 316-962-5247

Old car brochures, sales pamphlets, parts books, car tags, magazines, wire wheels, radiators. Thousands of hub-caps. Old car magazines, pictures out of old magazines, thousands of parts. Write or call.

*Other categories: License Plates, Tags, etc.; Literature; Spark Plugs*

## M&M Automobilia Appraisers

See our main listing under "Appraisal Service"

## Larry Machacek

See our main listing under "License Plates, Tags, etc."

## Magazine Man

See our main listing under "Books"

## Mail Order Service

See our main listing under "Literature"

## John Mancino's Garage

See our main listing under "Petroliana, Other"

## Mike Martin

See our main listing under "Racing Artifacts"

## Ron & Carol Martinelli

See our main listing under "Petroliana, Other"

## McLong Tags & Ads

See our main listing under "License Plates, Tags, etc."

## Memory Lane Collectibles

See our main listing under "Toys, General"

## Metropolitan & British Triumph

See our main listing under "Toys, General"

## Ken Meyer

5408 CTH "TT"
Sturgeon Bay, WI 54235 USA
TEL: 414-743-4440

Old "drive-in" speakers $25, mounting "head & basket" $50: both for $70 PPD lower 48. Miscellaneous old oil cans, Chev "409" parts, WWII US Army "half-track" & parts for sale. Call noon to 7pm CST only.

## Ken Miller Specialties

See our main listing under "Literature"

## Mobilia

See our main listing under "Publications, Current"

## Mobilia South Africa

See our main listing under "Petroliana, Other"

## Moonlight Peddler

See our main listing under "Pedal Cars"

## Morris Manor Collectables

See our main listing under "Toys, General"

## Motordrive

See our main listing under "Motorcycle Collectibles"

## Motorhead

4311 45th Ave. NE
Tacoma, WA 98422
TEL: 206-924-0776
FAX: 206-924-0788

The source for collectors of automotive fine art. L:arge illustrated catalog, $5.

## Motoring Goodies

Bob Figenskau
4551 Tonkawood Rd.
Minnetonka, MN 55345 USA
TEL: 612-935-7909

Automobilia, specializing in MG & British memorabilia & model toys. Gasoline/oil company/service station memorabilia – banks, toys, thermometers, S&P, tire ashtrays, or anything you can classify as motoring goodies. Call or write to buy, sell, or trade.

*Other categories: Petroliana, Other; Mascots/Badges/Emblems; Toys, General*

## Motoring Memories

See our main listing under "General Interest"

## The Museum of Automobile History

See our main listing under "Museum"

## Mystic Motorcar Museum

See our main listing under "Museum"

## Park Drive Garage

See our main listing under "Petroliana, Other"

## Past Gas

See our main listing under "Restoration Service"

## Pirelli Collector

See our main listing under "Specialized Automobilia"

## Pro Drop

Mark Blackman
PO Box 1421
Denison, TX 75021-1421 USA
TEL: 903-464-0226

Mixed automobilia, Hot Wheels series sets, event steins & Budweiser steins, movie posters of Corvette Summer,

Chevy P/U body parts 1972-87, antique irons, 1947 MacClatchie tri-bike mint condition.

*Other categories: Hot Wheels; Promos; Art, Prints & Posters*

## Purveyor of Petroleum Paraphernalia

See our main listing under "Petroliana, Pumps & Globes"

## R & G Automobiles & Collectables

Greg & Ru Howard
4159 Electric Way
Pt. Charlotte, FL 33980 USA
TEL: 941-766-7007
FAX: 941-766-7009

Buy, sell, trade pre-1972 automobiles & 'Vettes, automobilia, Coke, Pepsi, beer collectibles, coin-op machines, gas pumps, neons, antiques & collectibles. Open 9-5 Mon-Fri, Sat & Sun appointments only.

*Other categories: General Interest; Petroliana, Other; Neon*

**Race Place Collectables**

See our main listing under "Retail Store"

**Rader's Relics**

See our main listing under "Retail Store"

**Rick Radtke**

See our main listing under "Literature"

**Remember Woodward, Inc.**

Bill Stinson
1555 Chapin
Birmingham, MI 48009 USA
TEL: 810-646-0584
Email: remwood@earthlink.net

Woodward Avenue: The Midwest's cruising & street racing capital since the 1930s. We specialize in T-shirts, pins, caps, jackets, & trading cards by mail, in conjunction with our huge annual cruise each August. Write or phone for prices & availability. Some '96 shirts left: (L, XL, XXL) $10 + $3 s&h.

*Other categories: Art, Other; Art, Original; Specialized Automobilia*

**Road Maps Etc.**

See our main listing under "Literature"

**Route 66 Accessories Co.**

See our main listing under "Rt. 66 & Roadside"

**Route 66 Decanters**

See our main listing under "Specialized Automobilia"

**Joseph Russell**

455 Ollie St.
Cottage Grove, WI 53527 USA
TEL: 608-839-4736

Automotive & petroleum memorabilia in Madison, Wisconsin, at the Antiques Mall of Madison, 4748 Cottage Grove Rd. Oil cans, ornate radiator caps, spark plugs, handy oilers, gas globes, tire ashtrays, literature, chauffeur's badges, DAV tags, employee badges, signs, toys, much more. Booth 77, Joseph Russell's Automobilia, open every day.

*Other categories: Petroliana, Other; License Plates, Tags, etc.; Literature*

**SMB Designs**

See our main listing under "Signs"

**Ed Schwartz**

See our main listing under "Petroliana, Other"

**Shelley's Foreign Auto**

See our main listing under "Specialized Automobilia"

**Sign of the Times**

See our main listing under "Signs"

**Al Simonenko**

See our main listing under "Signs"

**Snyder's Oil & Gas Collectibles**

Marvin J. Snyder
105 Gray Place
Marshall, MN 56258 USA
TEL: 507-532-6273

For sale: tire/tube repair kits, model kits, toys, DAV key chain tags, games. Send SASE with your want list, or call in the afternoons.

*Other categories: Toys, General; Models, Kits; Games*

**Gunnar Söderblom**

See our main listing under "Literature"

**South Shore Auto Sports**

See our main listing under "Shows & Events"

**Southern Cross Automobilia**

Barry Wilkins
P.O. Box 5565
Stafford Heights, Queensland 4053 Australia
TEL: +61-7-33534999
FAX: +61-7-33534996
Email: sca@elf.brisnet.org.au

We specialize in hat pins, key rings, patches, license plates, decals, T-shirts, buckles, etc. We have a 250-page catalog available @ 7.50AUD plus postage. We do mail order & accept Visa.

**SpeedArt Enterprises**

See our main listing under "Mascots/Badges/Emblems"

**SpeedWay MotorBooks**

See our main listing under "Books"

**David C. Start**

See our main listing under "Signs"

**Dennis C. Stauffer**

See our main listing under "Petroliana, Other"

**Philip Stellmacher**

See our main listing under "Toys, General"

**Steve's Antiques**

See our main listing under "Signs"

**The Strong Collection**

David K. Strong
2013 Nelson Dr.
Thief River Falls, MN 56701-3811 USA
TEL: 218-681-5749
FAX: 218-681-5749

Antique women's shoes. Miscellaneous pre-1930 literature. Miscellaneous brass-era auto accessories.

*Other category: General Interest*

**7 Russell Taylor**

See our main listing under "License Plates, Tags, etc."

**Te Amo J**

See our main listing under "Lamps"

**Tee-Pee Model Toy Collectibles**

See our main listing under "Toys, General"

**Ron Throckmorton**

See our main listing under "Petroliana, Other"

**Edward Tilley Automotive Collectibles**

See our main listing under "Promos"

**Toys & Cars**

See our main listing under "Petroliana, Other"

**Mike Tyler**

See our main listing under "Petroliana, Other"

## Vintage Autos & Automobilia

Peter R. Zobian
Fern Oaks, 2698 Ernest Place
Cambria, CA 93428 USA
TEL: 805-927-5802
FAX: 805-927-5802

Collecting, selling, & trading since 1954. I specialize in rare & unusual autos & automobilia with a strong interest in European sports & racing cars, CCCA Classic cars, & brass era too. Original art, prints, posters, books, magazines, toys, models, badges, emblems, antique parts, & period accessories bought & sold.

*Other categories: Toys, General; Books; Art, Prints & Posters*

## Vintage Jag Works

See our main listing under "Marque Specific"

## VW Collector

See our main listing under "Marque Specific"

## David Wasserman

See our main listing under "Motorcycle Collectibles"

## Weber's Nostalgia Supermarket

See our main listing under "Petroliana, Pumps & Globes"

## John W. Webster

See our main listing under "Mascots/Badges/Emblems"

## Dillon T. Wescoat

See our main listing under "Literature"

## Wheels of Fun, Inc.

See our main listing under "Slot Cars"

## Willys/Jeep Collectibles

See our main listing under "Specialized Automobilia"

## Wizard's

See our main listing under "Racing Artifacts"

## Wizzy's Collector Car Parts

Lee Wisniewski
1801 S. 2nd St.
Milwuakee, WI 53204 USA
TEL: 800-328-6554
FAX: 414-645-5457

Retail auto parts store since 1914 with emphasis on collector car parts. Screw-on hubcaps from the 1920s, litho fuse tins from the 30s, striking packages from many years, & much more. We buy cast-iron & pressed-steel toys. SASE or fax for free list.

*Other categories: Art, Prints & Posters; General Interest; Retail Store*

## Wyckoff Auto

Ed Natale, Sr.
410 Russell Ave.
Wyckoff, NJ 07481 USA
TEL: 201-891-4252
FAX: 201-891-4252

Interested in oil cans, grease cans, auto/petro signs, Buick items, New Jersey porcelain plates, BMW, NSU motorcycle stuff, etc. Send list of your items for sale.

*Other categories: Petroliana, Other; Specialized Automobilia; General Interest*

## Yosemite Sam's Auto Art

See our main listing under "Art, Original"

# MODELS, KITS

## Abbott & Hast Ltd. Auto Promos & Kits

Paul J. Nix
9416 Gullo Ave
Arleta, CA 91331 USA
TEL: 818-893-3412
FAX: 818-830-0612

We specialize in dealer promo & friction cars, both plastic & metal, all makes & models, 1930s to 1990s. We buy, sell, & trade, & can appraise your collection. We also deal in unbuilt model kits, 1950s to 1980s. Call or fax with wants. No list has too much stuff!

*Other categories: Appraisal Service; Toys, General*

## David T. Alexander

See our main listing under "Literature"

## Auto Racing

See our main listing under "Racing Artifacts"

## Back In Time Toys

See our main listing under "Models, Precision"

## Bart Cars

See our main listing under "Promos"

## Bill Behlman

See our main listing under "Racing Artifacts"

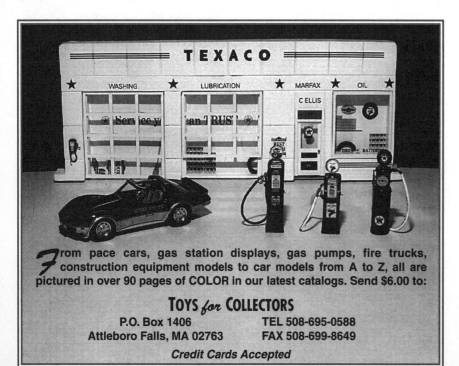

## Bill's Garage

William H. Smith
443 Orleans Ave.
Battle Creek, MI 49015 USA
TEL: 616-968-2762
FAX: 616-963-9355

Reproduction antique toys in cast aluminum. Pre-1950 open wheel racing items, KK patches, Mobil stickers, midget & sprint photos, T-shirts, & hats. Original models & toys (of open wheel racing) found, bought, & sold.

*Other categories: Racing Artifacts; Hot Rod Memorabilia; Toys, General*

## Bob's British Car Parts

See our main listing under "Marque Specific"

## Alan Bowden

9913 E. Pinewood Ave
Englewood, CO 80111 USA
TEL: 303-771-1418
Email: abow@gwl.com

Duesenberg memorabilia – buy models, sales literature, ads, misc. related to Duesies!

*Other categories: Art, Prints & Posters; Literature; Marque Specific*

## Brooklin Models, Ltd.

See our main listing under "Models, Precision"

## C & N Reproductions, Inc.

See our main listing under "Pedal Cars"

## Joseph Camp

See our main listing under "Mixed Automobilia"

## Car Crazy

See our main listing under "Hot Rod Memorabilia"

## Carney Plastics Inc.

See our main listing under "Displays/Fixtures"

## City Classics

Jim Sacco
PO Box 16502
Pittsburgh, PA 15242 USA
TEL: 412-276-1312
FAX: 412-276-1312

Manufacturer of HO scale 1/87 building kits. Our line includes a model of a classic 1940s porcelain-paneled gas station, a 1950s stainless steel diner, as well as stores, factories, etc. City Classics kits are available at most hobby shops that carry model trains. Send SASE or $1.00 for brochure.

*Other categories: Rt. 66 & Roadside; Diner Memorabilia; General Interest*

## Creative Miniature Associates

See our main listing under "Models, Precision"

## Doc & Jesse's Auto Parts

A.J. Grimaldi
6 Holly Blvd.
Scotia, NY 12302 USA
TEL: 518-346-8553
Email: antski@aol.com

Specialists in American Motors memorabilia, scale models, promos, toys, slot cars, literature, dealer signs, key fobs, car parts, etc. Send a stamp for each of the following lists (please specify request): 1) car parts, 2) literature, 3) Johnny Lightning, 4) models & toys. We buy, sell, & swap anything AMC!

*Other categories: Literature; Toys, General; Slot Cars*

## Cliff Douglas

See our main listing under "License Plates, Tags, etc."

## Dragster Australia

See our main listing under "Art, Prints & Posters"

## Early Racing Classics

See our main listing under "Models, Precision"

## Electric Dreams

See our main listing under "Slot Cars"

## Fast Art

See our main listing under "Art, Prints & Posters"

## Get It On Paper

See our main listing under "Retail Store"

## Great Planes Model Distributors

See our main listing under "General Interest"

## HC Designs

PO Box 1132
Arlington, TX 76004-1132
TEL: 817-457-1311

Authentic wood building kits, in 1:24
and 1:34-scale. Send for free brochure.

## HO Motoring & Racing

See our main listing under "Slot Cars"

## Peter E. Hoyt

PO Box 15808
Pittsburgh, PA 15244 USA
TEL: 412-269-7807

Specialize in 1950s to 90s promotional
model cars & trucks. Also have very
large selection of showroom literature
(domestic & foreign) from 1946 to present. Will buy or trade for collections of
either promos or literature. Vendor at
most Carlisle & toy shows. Send SASE
for listing of models or literature.

*Other categories: Promos; Literature; Toys, Truck*

## Jamar Company

See our main listing under
"Displays/Fixtures"

## John's Scale Autos

See our main listing under "Promos"

## Keith's Hobby Shop

Graham Lloyd
5205 Yonge St.
Willowdale/Toronto, Ontario
M2N 5A7 Canada
TEL: 416-222-4721
FAX: 416-222-4895

Supplying modelers & collectors
worldwide since 1958. Kits, diecast,
paints, decals, reference books, detailing supplies, tools from worldwide
sources. Free mail order product list.
Easy access via freeway & public tran-
sit. Help, advice always available from
our staff & customers. When visiting
Toronto, stop in, have some coffee, &
browse!

*Other categories: Retail Store; Literature; Books*

## Ted Knorr

See our main listing under "Racing
Artifacts"

## Let's Get Small

George Zurowski
20 Bradish Lane
Bayshore, NY 11706 USA
TEL: 516-665-2770
FAX: 516-665-2770

Specialize in large scale model kits.
Offer resin replicas in 1/8, 1/12 scale,
1/8 flathead engines, 426 Hemi Replica. I buy collections of model kits. Will
trade rare 1/24, 1/25- scale kits for rare
1/8 scale. Also sell original masters in
1/8 & 1/12 scale.

*Other category: Models, Precision*

## Lincolnia

See our main listing under "Promos"

## Mail Order Service

See our main listing under "Literature"

## Merchandising Incentives Corp.

See our main listing under "Promos"

## Milwaukee Miniature Motors

Mike Dunn
N3W31535 Twin Oaks Dr.
Delafield, WI 53018-2807 USA
TEL: 414-646-4115

Model car swap meets. Buy, sell, trade
model cars, diecast, promos, racing
memorabilia.

*Other categories: Cards, Trading; Hot Wheels;
Promos*

## Model Car Journal

See our main listing under "Publications,
Current"

## Model Kit Hobbies

Matthew D. Rodkey
PO Box 1012
Clearfield, PA 16830 USA
TEL: 814-768-7899
FAX: 814-234-9626

We are your full-service model company. Competitive prices on new & discontinued plastic kits, paints, decals, &
building supplies. Also, full line racing
diecast dealer for NASCAR, Indy, F1, &
drag racing collectibles. Professional
model building service available for
precision replicas. Model or racing
diecast lists are $2 each.

*Other categories: Models, Precision; Racing
Artifacts; Promos*

## The Model Shop

Dean Kulas
PO Box 68 Dept. SB
Onalaska, WI 54650 USA
TEL: 608-281-1864
FAX: 608-281-7143
Email: dkulas@centuryinter.net

Check out The Model Shop! We specialize in NASCAR model kits & decals.
We also offer current, limited edition, &
discontinued model cars & trucks. Plus
a full line of tools, paints, bare metal
foil, glues, photo-etched parts, & more.
Send $3 for our 104-pg. catalog. Satis-
faction guaranteed.

*Other categories: Models, Precision; Specialized
Automobilia; Tools*

## Edmund F. Molloy, Jr.

See our main listing under "Literature"

## Moto-Mini

See our main listing under "Motorcycle Collectibles"

## Motor Cycle Days

See our main listing under "Motorcycle Collectibles"

## NAV, Inc.

See our main listing under "Models, Precision"

## Bob Neubauer

1491 Billington Rd.
East Aurora, NY 14052 USA
TEL: 716-655-3124

Specialize in model kits, cars, trucks, & promos. Diecast including Hot Wheels, NASCAR cars, haulers, banks, cards, Matchbox. Also Hallmark ornaments, examples: '57 Chevy, '69 Camaro. I collect, buy, sell, trade, with interest in Riviera, Buick items. Send LSASE with request for current model kit or diecast list.

*Other categories: Promos; Hot Wheels; Toys, General*

## Jim Newhall Automobilia

See our main listing under "Promos"

## Wayne Noller

See our main listing under "Promos"

## Nostalgia Productions, Inc.

See our main listing under "Art, Other"

## Dan O'Neill Precision Models

See our main listing under "Manufacturer"

## Pacific Restoration

See our main listing under "Slot Cars"

## Paul Garnand Sales

Paul Garnand
203 Campus Drive - Box 68
Garden City, KS 67846 USA
TEL: 316-275-9552
FAX: 316-275-1770

Specializing in discontinued car model kits & limited edition diecast pieces from 1/18 Ertls, Hot Wheels, Johnny Lightnings, Action Drag Racing to full-size 1962-72 Chevrolet/GM restoration parts & detailing items. We are active

buyers of model car collections & drag race memorabilia. Our catalog is large & available for $2 to cover mailing.

*Other categories: Retail Store; Hot Wheels; Promos*

## Frank A. Poll

2601 E. Oakland Pk. Blvd #505
Fort Lauderdale, FL 33306 USA
TEL: 954-568-1334
FAX: 954-568-1335

Specialize in early model kits (Corvette, NASCAR, drag racing). Buy, sell, trade. Also collect & sell original drag strip decals & Japanese motorcycle literature.

*Other categories: Hot Rod Memorabilia; Motorcycle Collectibles*

## R & D Unique

D.J. VanderWal
17113 SE 149th St.
Renton, WA 98059-8057 USA
TEL: 206-772-2507
FAX: 206-277-5296
Email: curbsided@aol.com

Multimedia model kit manufacturer. Product line is "Curbside Dioramics." Over 100 1/24-scale kits with more coming. Precision model assembly kits with street rod focus. The only truly 1/24-scale gas pump assembly kits available. $1 for catalog. Visa/MC. Custom resin & white metal casting services available.

*Other categories: Petroliana, Pumps & Globes; Models, Precision; Manufacturer*

## Rally Enterprises

Ray G. Olson
2 Sinclair Cir.
Indialantic, FL 32903 USA
TEL: 407-727-0275
FAX: 407-853-7780
Email: larkris@aol.com

Specialize in various automobilia & aviation collections. Interests are literature, models, books, & magazines. Sports cars & aircraft from postwar era are prime. Have lists of literature, kits, books for sale or trade. No stock cars. Large SASE for listings. Call after 5pm EST.

*Other categories: Literature; Specialized Automobilia; Art, Prints & Posters*

## Rare Sportsfilms Inc.

See our main listing under "Racing Artifacts"

## Revell-Monogram, Inc.

See our main listing under "Racing Artifacts"

## Road Race Replicas

See our main listing under "Slot Cars"

## San Remo Hobby and Toy

See our main listing under "Promos"

## Scale Autoworks

See our main listing under "Models, Precision"

## Smith Automotive Group

See our main listing under "Hot Rod Memorabilia"

## Snyder's Oil & Gas Collectibles

See our main listing under "Mixed Automobilia"

## Philip Stellmacher

See our main listing under "Toys, General"

## Supercar Collectibles

See our main listing under "Toys, General"

## T and D Toy & Hobby

See our main listing under "Retail Store"

## Thunder Road

See our main listing under "Retail Store"

## Vintage American Classics

Marcus V. Allen
1247 W. Marquette Rd.
Chicago, IL 60636 USA
TEL: 312-783-7783

Specialize in classic models, cars, built/unbuilt from 1930s, 40s, 50s. Buy, sell. 1/24, 1/25, 1/12, 1/18, 1/8 metal or plastic; looking for Packards, Duesenberg, Cadillac, Lincoln. Also collect Rolls, Mercedes, Bugatti, Mercedes-Benz 540, kits unbuilt for sale. Please inquire. Please call after 7pm CST.

*Other categories: Models, Precision; Promos*

## VIP Ltd.

W.L. (Bill) Walters
3983 So. McCarran #255
Reno, NV 89502 USA
TEL: 702-857-2662

Specialize in Porsche, Volkswagen model cars, Matchbox cars (all kinds), 1950s, 1960s, 1970s car magazines, owner's manuals, sales brochures, workshop manuals, trading cards, some tin cars & toys, Hot August Nights Coca-Cola commemorative gift sets, bottles, glasses, event pins, Avon automobile decanters, some Hot Wheels models also.

*Other categories: Hot Rod Memorabilia; Literature; Toys, General*

## Ted & Nelda Weems

See our main listing under "Literature"

## Wheels of Fun, Inc.

See our main listing under "Slot Cars"

# MODELS, PRECISION

## The Auto Collectibles Co.

See our main listing under "Retail Store"

## B.A.S.I.C.

See our main listing under "Mixed Automobilia"

## Back In Time Toys

Raymond D. Stewart
111A Marblehead St.
North Andover, MA 01845 USA
TEL: 508-686-0158

Specialize in diecast. First Gear® authorized producer. Designers of the "Boston Hooker" 1957 IHC wrecker & "Beantown Bandit" 1951 Ford flatbed, 1956 Ford stock car. We sell a variety of plastic car & truck kits, Hot Wheels, old & new Johnny Lightnings. Complete collections purchased. Send us your sell or want list.

*Other categories: Models, Kits; Toys, Truck; Specialized Automobilia*

## Barnett Design Inc.

John A. Barnett
PO Box 160
Twin Lakes, WI 53181 USA
TEL: 800-997-0200
FAX: 414-877-9320

Large 1/10-scale stylized models crafted in an artistic form to capture the essence of the original. The 34 coupe, first in the series, was inspired by the high-tech rods of the 80s. The 14.5-inch-long car is cast in resin. Built in a limited edition of 950.

*Other categories: Hot Rod Memorabilia; Art, Other; Racing Artifacts*

## Bob's Promotional Cars

See our main listing under "Promos"

## Bill Brisbane

See our main listing under "Toys, General"

## Brookfield Collectors Guild

Ken Dahlke, President
16312 W. Glendale Dr.
New Berlin, WI 53151 USA
TEL: 800-657-0765
FAX: 414-796-0472

Manufacturer of diecast precision models, including automobiles, sport-utility vehicles, & trucks. Known for quality & attention to detail. Wide variety of vehicles from Chevrolet, GMC, Oldsmobile, Dodge, Chrysler, & Plymouth. Winston Cup Racing collectibles include Dale Earnhardt, Jeff Gordon, Terry LaBonte, etc. Call for our free newsletter on the latest releases.

*Other categories: Promos; Toys, Truck; Manufacturer*

## Brooklin Models, Ltd.

John A. Hall
Unit A3 Pinesway Ind. Est.,
Ivo Peters Rd.
Bath, Somerset BA2 3QS England
TEL: +44-1225-332400
FAX: +44-1225-447438

Manufacturers of 1/43-scale model automobiles from the United States, Britain, & Sweden. Historic, classic, & special-interest cars from the 1930s to the 1960s, hand produced in metal. Our U.S. agent is Brasilia Press, PO Box 2023, Elkhart, IN 46515, fax 219-262-8799.

*Other categories: Models, Kits; Manufacturer; Specialized Automobilia*

## Caribbean Sun Gold

J. Yasuk
PO Box 92-4533
Homestead, FL 33092 USA
TEL: 305-256-7201

NASCAR & race-related diecast collectibles. Founding Fathers series by Ertl. Legends of Racing Buck Baker 1956 Chrysler & Tim Flock 1952 Hudson. Racing Champions & others. Also pre-1928 US paper money.

*Other categories: Toys, General; Toys, Truck*

## Collector's Studio Motorsport Gallery

See our main listing under "Racing Artifacts"

## Craco Showcase Sales Gallery

See our main listing under "Displays/Fixtures"

## Creative Miniature Associates

Marshall Buck
105 Columbus Place, No. 5
Stamford, CT 06907 USA
TEL: 203-329-7823
FAX: 203-329-2416

Manufacturing & sales of 1/12 & 1/24-scale very limited edition, extremely high quality hand-built & scratch-built automotive models for serious collectors. Also offer limited edition kits. Vintage motorcycles as well. Brokerage, consulting, pattern making, & production services. International mail order. Catalog: USA $9, overseas $11.

*Other categories: Models, Kits; Motorcycle Collectibles; Manufacturer*

## DKC & Company

Dean Clark
15 Militia Lane
Scarborough, ME 04074-9333 USA
TEL: 207-883-8472
FAX: 207-883-8472
Email: dkc44@aol.com

Private eclectic collection of factory-built high-quality models. Mostly 1/43 scale. Specialize in Jaguars & road racing models. Also, a 20+ year collection of showroom brochures. Plus, extensive library of hardcover books. Large collection of magazines. Framed & unframed posters & auto art prints. Sell or trade for Jaguar-related automobilia. Fax needs.

*Other categories: Art, Prints & Posters; Books; Showroom Items*

## Durham Classics Automotive Miniatures

595 Wentworth Street, Unit #63
Oshawa, Ontario, Canada L1H 3V8
TEL: 905-436-9140
FAX: 905-436-9140

"In house" producer of 1:43-scale whitemetal hand-built models of American classic automobiles. Produce limited quantities of each model.

## Early Racing Classics

Karl J. Stark
103 George Rogers Rd.
Charlottesville, VA 22911 USA
TEL: 804-979-7534

Specialize in limited edition scale models of early stock cars from the 1940s & 50s as well as many resin-cast bodies, frames, & tire/rim sets. An autographed card included with built-ups. Cars include Ford, Chevy, Mopar coupes & coaches from the 1930s plus Pintos, Vegas, etc.

*Other categories: Models, Kits; Racing Artifacts; Personalities*

## EWA & Miniature Cars USA, Inc.

205 US Highway 22
Green Brook, NJ 08812
TEL: 908-424-7811
FAX: 908-424-7814
Email: ewa@ewacars.com

North America's largest source for scale model automobiles. Over 6,000 models from 200 manufacturers. Catalog $4

($6 overseas), includes $5 gift certificate. Visit our large retail showroom!

See our display ad on p. 4

## Fast Toys, Inc.

See our main listing under "Marque Specific"

## Finger Lakes Diecast

Lowell Korb
26 Hickory Trail
Ithaca, NY 14850 USA
TEL: 607-539-7019

Collectible 1/43-scale model cars & trucks. Models by Brooklin, Durham Classics, Motor City USA, Robeddie, & US Model Mint. Available by mail order or model shows in the Northeast. Call or write for competitive prices & show attendance.

*Other categories: Toys, General; Toys, Truck; Shows & Events*

## Wm. P. Fornwalt, Jr.

103 Dartmouth Ave.
Johnstown, PA 15905 USA
TEL: 814-536-8081

Scale models. Precision-built large-scale renderings in mixed media. Hand-built for advanced collectors in brass, copper, aluminum, & various other materials. Accurate miniatures in 1/8 or 1/12 scale. Commissions cheerfully discussed. Phone calls before 4:30pm EST, please. Mail welcome.

*Other categories: Art, Other; Toys, General; Pedal Cars*

## Frost International Enterprises

See our main listing under "Literature"

## Joseph R. Golabiewski

See our main listing under "Toys, Truck"

## Great Planes Model Distributors

See our main listing under "General Interest"

## Junkyard Dog

See our main listing under "Petroliana, Other"

## The Hobby Shop

See our main listing under "Manufacturer"

## Kato USA, Inc.

Brent Runzel
100 Remington Rd.
Schaumburg, IL 60173 USA
TEL: 847-781-9500
FAX: 847-951-9570

Manufacturer of highly detailed 1/43-scale precision automobile models. Nissan 300ZX & Toyota Supra. For details or to order, call 1-800-548-5286. Dealer inquiries accepted.

## Legendary Collectibles

Ken & Eileen Mausolf
PO Box 371223
Denver, CO 80237 USA
TEL: 303-761-4680
FAX: 303-741-1013

Appraisals – autos 1900 to new. Models all sizes. Old, new. 50 years' experience worldwide. Highest reputation in 62 car clubs everywhere. Specializing in Rolls-Royce models & memorabilia. Worldwide appraisals on anything on wheels – one or 18.

*Other categories: License Plates, Tags, etc.; Jewelry; Appraisal Service*

## Let's Get Small

See our main listing under "Models, Kits"

## Lilliput Motor Car Co.

Ray Paszkiewicz Jr.
PO Box 156
Clarksburg, NJ 08510 USA
TEL: 908-446-9381
FAX: 908-446-9297

Specialize 1/43 hand-built precision models; autos, trucks, buses. Manufacturer "Victory Models" plus exclusive offerings "DeHanes" truck models, Shrock toy Studebakers. Unusual

Lowell Korb
Owner

FINGERLAKES DIECAST
Specializing in 1/43 diecast models

26 Hickory Trail
Ithaca, NY 14850

(607) 539-7019
Phone - Fax

British, European, Russian models. Diecast: Corgi, Minichamps, Vitesse. Buy, sell auto sales brochures, postcards. 8x10 in. photos, advertising, books, mixed automobilia. Mail order, 30 East Cost shows.

*Other categories: Literature; Manufacturer; Toys, Truck*

## Marvelous Auto Miniatures

Gregory L. Gunn
PO Box 266
Swanton, OH 43558 USA
TEL: 419-825-1238
FAX: 419-825-1238

Store specializing in 1/43 to 1/12-scale diecast & hand-built models, display cases, videos. 1/43-scale detail & restoration service. Largest selection in Ohio of auto miniatures. We also buy collections. Locating service, catalog available. Get updates, specials, etc. Send $3. 24-hour fax.

*Other categories: Toys, General; Retail Store; General Interest*

## Milestone Motorcars

Mark Tyra
12910 Sunnybrook Dr.
Prospect, KY 40059 USA
TEL: 502-228-5945
FAX: 502-228-1856

Stocks over 700 different diecast cars & dealer promos. 1/18 scale is our specialty. If you are looking for a limited edition piece or a discontinued item please check with us. We have a free 16-page catalog available.

*Other categories: Promos; Toys, General; Specialized Automobilia*

## Miniatures by Jack

Jack Harris
8720 E. Edward Ave.
Scottsdale, AZ 85250 USA
TEL: 602-998-1735

Scale model gas stations & stores, 1920s, 30s, 40s. 1/12 & 1/24 scale, all wood, handcrafted, highly detailed. Six basic plans to work from, or will build to your specs, pictures, etc. Scaled pumps, accessories, signs, logos, etc. Reasonable prices. Brochure w/ pics available. Call or write. Custom models also!

*Other categories: Rt. 66 & Roadside; Specialized Automobilia*

## Minichamps
14261 SW 136th Street, Bay 7
Dept. Edi
Miami, FL 33186

Over 1,000 superior models in diecast metal with full detail accuracy. Find us at your local hobby shop or your favorite mail order catalog.

## Model Car Journal
See our main listing under "Publications, Current"

## Model Kit Hobbies
See our main listing under "Models, Kits"

## The Model Shop
See our main listing under "Models, Kits"

## Edmund F. Molloy, Jr.
See our main listing under "Literature"

## Moto-Mini
See our main listing under "Motorcycle Collectibles"

## Motor Cycle Days
See our main listing under "Motorcycle Collectibles"

## NAV, Inc.
John Schwickert Jr.
PO Box 263
Mt. Sterling, KY 40353 USA
TEL: 606-498-4446
FAX: 606-498-4446

Fine scale models, hand-built & kits of sports, racing, LSR, & others in 1/43 scale. Also books & magazines. Catalog $3.

*Other categories: Models, Kits; Toys, General*

## Palmer Motor Racing
Mark Palmer
8350 Melrose Ave
Los Angeles, CA 90069 USA
TEL: 213-651-0400
FAX: 213-651-5612

Specializing in 1/43-scale out-of-production Minichamp 1990-1993 DTM

race cars – BMW E30 M3s, Mercedes EVO I & EVO IIs, Opel Omega 3000 EVOs, Audis, & Alfas. Buy, sell, trade. Also 1/43-scale out-of-production Indy & Formula 1 Onyx 1988-1993 race cars & current DTM/ITC race cars.

*Other categories: Toys, General; Racing Artifacts; Specialized Automobilia*

## Peachstate
Tom Long
PO Box 1537
Winder, GA 30680 USA
TEL: 770-307-1042
FAX: 770-867-0786
Email: peachgmp@mindspring.com

The Peachstate Musclecar Collectibles Club is well into their second year of exclusive, short-run, diecast muscle car offerings. These 2,500-piece serialized 1/18 replicas are produced just for Peachstate by The Ertl Co., the best in the business. Call, fax, Email, or write.

*Other categories: Manufacturer; Racing Artifacts; Toys, General*

## People Kars
See our main listing under "Toys, General"

## ProScale Models
3861 Gala Loop
Bellingham, WA 98226
TEL: 360-676-4166

We manufacture the '69 Camaro Pace Car, Z-28, RS, SS, & Yenko. The '67 Camaro is offered as a pace car or convertible, all in correct colors. Each model is hand-built in very limited quantities. Full color brochure available for $2.00, refundable.

## R & D Unique
See our main listing under "Models, Kits"

## Replicarz
99 State Street
Rutland, VT 05701
TEL: 802-747-7151
FAX: 802-775-1981
Email: replicarz@aol.com

Ayrton Senna series of quality diecast replicas. Call, write, fax, or Email for a free catalog of high-quality diecast.

## Jeffrey Rosen
133 Maple Ave.
Red Bank, NJ 07701 USA
TEL: 800-891-5238
FAX: 908-219-7119

I buy & sell white metal factory built 1/43 scale auto models. I am interested in the following manufacturers: Brooklin, Durham, Conquest, Motor City, Mini Marque, & Design Studio. I have models by SMTS, Kenna, Landsdowne, Western, GPM, Somerville, SAMS, & Small Wheels to sell or trade. Call or fax.

## Route 66 Accessories Co.
See our main listing under "Rt. 66 & Roadside"

## Royal Coach
See our main listing under "Specialized Automobilia"

## San Francisco Bay Brooklin Club
PO Box 61018
Palo Alto, CA 94306 USA
TEL: 415-591-9580
FAX: 415-591-9580

The San Francisco Bay Brooklin Club is an information exchange for collectors of Brooklin 1/43 white metal models. Membership includes six issues of the newsletter "Limited Editions" & an

updated listing of Brooklin models. Membership is $25 for one year ($30 in Canada & overseas).

*Other categories: Club/Organization; Toys, General; General Interest*

## Scale Autoworks

Brady Ward
313 Bridge St #4
Manchester, NH 03104-5045 USA
TEL: 603-623-5925
FAX: 603-623-5925

A professional model-building shop focusing on large-scale classic European cars, especially the Pocher 1/8 "Classics" models. All models are given concours-quality paint jobs, leather interiors, & many extra details. Custom mahogany coachwork & hardwood cases are available. Shop open by appointment only. AMEX, MC/Visa accepted. Fax available mornings only.

*Other categories: Art, Other; Marque Specific; Models, Kits*

## Seebee Enterprises

See our main listing under "Displays/Fixtures"

## Sharaku

6-1-10 Shinohara Minamimachi Nada
Kobe, Japan 657
FAX: +81-78-881-5622

We are retailers of model cars in Japan. We started mail order business of Japanese 1/43-scale models for foreign collectors last year. Now we can supply you with Epoch, Hasegawa, Kato, Tamiya, & Tomica. Please fax or write for free catalog.

## Sinclair's Mini-Auto

Box 8403 (M)
Erie, PA 16505
TEL: 814-838-2274
FAX: 814-838-2274

Wide variety of models from around the world. Catalog $2 refundable.

## Smith Automotive Group

See our main listing under "Hot Rod Memorabilia"

## John Snowberger

PO Box 4395
Centerline, MI 48015 USA
TEL: 810-978-1143

Specializing in handcrafted Indy 500 race car models, 1/8-scale, 1911 through 1960s by the son of famed Indy great Russell Snowberger. Each car is crafted using the same materials as the real ones were. As seen on display at the Indianapolis Motor Speedway Hall of Fame & Museum.

*Other categories: Museum; Manufacturer; Racing Artifacts*

## Clifford D. Stubbs

See our main listing under "Hot Wheels"

## Thunder Grass Ltd.

Young S. James
516 Butler Ave.
Columbus, OH 43223-1699 USA

For sale: information 1949 Danbury Mint Mercury also Franklin Mint 1949 Buick Roadmaster. Both $160 cash, money order. Send SASE for photo information. Models have papers. Mint

condition. Request payment before shipping to the first inquirer.

## Tiger Automotive
See our main listing under "Promos"

## Tompkins Collectible Toys
See our main listing under "Toys, General"

## Toys for Collectors
PO Box 1406
Attleboro Falls, MA 02763
TEL: 508-695-0588
FAX: 508-699-8649

Wide variety of models. Full-color 90-page catalog $6.

## Turtle Creek Scale Models
Gene Arner
2420 E. Ridge Rd.
Beloit, WI 53511 USA
TEL: 608-365-0579

Specializing in 1/16-scale model trucks. First release: Topkick/Kodiak stakerack – each numbered, limited edition of 400. Approx. 12 in this series, milk truck second in series. American-

made, cast metal, highly detailed. Future projects: licensed Freightliner semi & line of vintage race cars. All 1/16 scale & hand-built.

*Other categories: Toys, Truck; Manufacturer; Specialized Automobilia*

## Victory Models
Ray Paszkiewicz, Jr.
PO Box 156 Clarksburg, NJ 08510
TEL: 908-446-9381
FAX: 908-446-9297

Great selection of American, British and European handbuilt models.

## Vintage American Classics
See our main listing under "Models, Kits"

## Kirk F. White
See our main listing under "Gas-Powered Racers"

# MOTORCYCLE COLLECTIBLES

## Antique Toys
Scott Johnson
RR 1 Box 74
Leroy, MN 55951 USA
TEL: 507-324-5772

Collector buys motorcycle toys. Highest prices paid for rubber, plastic, tin, or cast-iron motorcycle toys made from the 1920s through the 1960s. Call or write with description. Also have other toys, cars, trucks, for trade or sale.

*Other category: Toys, General*

## Antique & Vintage Motorcycle
Mick Stamm
3401 S. 1st St.
Abilene, TX 79605-1708 USA
TEL: 915-676-8788

Antique & Vintage Motorcycle Restoration & Museum. Buy, sell, trade. Bikes, parts, & quality motorcycle memorabilia. Always interested in original-paint motorcycles, parts, oil cans, literature, license plates, clocks, mirrors, chalkboards & misc. memorabilia. Needing restoration OK. Purchasing complete collections or by the piece. V-Twin

restoration catalog $15.95+$3.95p/h. Memorabilia list $3 w/SASE.

*Other categories: Petroliana, Other; License Plates, Tags, etc.; Literature*

## Auto-Cycle Publications
See our main listing under "Literature"

## Automobilia & Collectibles
See our main listing under "Mixed Automobilia"

## Automotive Fine Art
See our main listing under "Art, Prints & Posters"

## Barkin' Frog Collectible Co.
See our main listing under "Toys, General"

## Andy Bernstein
See our main listing under "License Plates, Tags, etc."

## Greg Bowden
22225 Ten Mile Rd.
St. Clair Shores, MI 48080 USA
TEL: 810-773-6439

Specializing in antique motorcycles – 1900 through 1960s, any memorabilia, pins, buttons, fobs, photos, literature, signs, m/c license plates, Gypsy Tour awards, clothing, anything motorcycle-related! Top cash paid for one piece or entire collection. Buy, sell, trade.

*Other categories: Literature; License Plates, Tags, etc.; Signs*

## Dennis Brilla
See our main listing under "Mixed Automobilia"

## British Only Motorcycles & Parts, Inc.
Ken Grzesiak
32451 Park Lane
Garden City, MI 48239 USA
TEL: 313-421-0303
FAX: 313-422-9253
Email: info@british-only.com

Motorcycle collectibles of all kinds, toys, trophies, art, clothing, dealer displays, pins, patches, dealer giveaways, oil cans, paint tins, signs, anything paper. World's largest supplier of British

motorcycle parts. Free catalog. Find us on the World Wide Web at http://www.british-only.com

*Other categories: Racing Artifacts; Literature; Art, Original*

## Bullivant Gallery

See our main listing under "Art, Prints & Posters"

## Classic Performance

See our main listing under "Hot Rod Memorabilia"

## Creative Miniature Associates

See our main listing under "Models, Precision"

## Dave's Tag Barn

See our main listing under "License Plates, Tags, etc."

## Demarest Motorbooks

See our main listing under "Books"

## Dunbar's Gallery

Leila & Howard Dunbar
76 Haven St.
Milford, MA 01757 USA
TEL: 508-634-8697
FAX: 508-634-8698
Email: dunbar2bid@aol.com

1900-1970s American motoring & motorcycle collectibles bought, sold,

appraised, & auctioned by Howard & Leila Dunbar. Call us for information about our upcoming auctions, consignments, sales, etc.

*Other categories: Signs; Petroliana, Other; Auction Firm*

## Gasoline Alley

Ed Natale, Jr.
Box 222
Wyckoff, NJ 07481 USA
TEL: 201-848-8485

Buying motorcycle-related items – tins, oil cans, club/gang memorabilia, patches, photos, pins, etc.; handy oil, lighter fluid cans, mini oil can banks, small tin/porcelain signs, etc. Selling all types of petroliana – cans, signs, giveaways, patches, etc. Send SASE with specific wants.

*Other categories: Petroliana, Other; Mixed Automobilia; Signs*

## Herb Glass

RD 1 Box 506A
Pine Bush, NY 12566 USA
TEL: 914-361-3657

Private collector wants pre-1915 American motorcycling literature & advertising items: factory sales catalogs, manuals, magazines, pins, fobs, trophies, medals, & related items.

## William Goetzmann

3385 Harlem Rd.
Buffalo, NY 14225 USA
TEL: 716-636-8904
FAX: 716-833-2265

Specialize in British & European motorcycles. All motorcycles, literature, license plates, dealer display items, AMA, racing artifacts, toys. Buy, trade. Messages returned.

*Other categories: Showroom Items; License Plates, Tags, etc.; Literature*

## Robert N. Haldeman

See our main listing under "General Interest"

## Clyde Hensley

6251 N. Lotz Rd.
Canton, MI 48187 USA
TEL: 313-981-1385

Harley factory letters, posters, *Enthusiast* mags, literature, oil cans, ink pens, matches, cycle toys, transportation toys, auto sales brochures, mechanical pencils, spark plugs. Ford Motor Co. collectibles, hot rod toys, promos, live steam toys, Lionel, Flyer trains. Street rods, pro street cars, bought, sold, traded. Some old tools also.

*Other categories: Mixed Automobilia; Toys, General; Spark Plugs*

## Hosking Cycle Works

Jim Hosking
136 Hosking Lane
Accord, NY 12404 USA
TEL: 914-626-4231
FAX: 914-626-3245

Specialize in shop manuals, parts books, back-issue motorcycle maga-

zines. World's largest collection motorcycle lapel pins. Also ROKON 340cc motorcycles & parts. Catalog $1 (first class).

*Other categories: Books; Mascots/Badges/Emblems*

## J. Hubbard Classic Cycles & Collectibles

Jeff J. Hubbard
2900 91st St.
Sturtevant, WI 53177 USA
TEL: 414-886-0477

Buy, sell, trade, collect, restore 1969-1978 Kawasaki motorcycles, models H1, H2, KH, Z1900/KZ1000 (main interest is early 2 stroke, 3 cyl.). Also Harley-Davidson items (any/all), Hot Wheels, Matchbox & Hubley diecast cars/toys. Also Harley *Enthusiast* mags (early) quarterly publication.

*Other categories: Restoration Service; Toys, General; General Interest*

## Stan Hurd Auto Literature

See our main listing under "Literature."

## Inside Only

See our main listing under "Toys, General."

## Meow

See our main listing under "Clothing."

## Moto-Mini

Steve Hooper
Rt 4, Box 516A-M
McKinney, TX 75070-9642 USA
TEL: 972-837-2686
FAX: 972-837-2356
Email: motomini@waymark.net

Motorcycle collectibles exclusively. Diecast models & kits. Plastic model kits. White metal scale models, finished & in kit. Hand-carved custom-built wood models of your personal motorcycle. Model kit-building service. Hard-to-find items as well as name-brand toys & models. Motorcycles only. Catalog $1.

*Other categories: Models, Precision; Models, Kits*

## Motor Cycle Days

David Gaylin
PO Box 9686
Baltimore, MD 21237 USA
TEL: 410-665-6295
FAX: 410-687-6867

America's largest source for original & reprinted motorcycle literature. Motorcycle advertising & movie posters also a specialty, including glossy photographs of celebrities on bikes. Send SASE for list or see us at most major antique motorcycle events.

*Other categories: Models, Precision; Models, Kits*

## Motorcycles & Memorabilia

Bill Pelissier
Box 1952
Englewood, CO 80150 USA
TEL: 303-797-8354
FAX: 303-904-4538

Buying: motorcycle memorabilia: ANY MAKE, signs, clocks, banners, literature, posters, etc. Have many items to trade or sell. Not interested in any reproductions!

*Other categories: Signs; Literature; Specialized Automobilia*

## Motordrive

Jim Demetropoulos
RR 1 Box 273
Yarmouth, ME 04096 USA
TEL: 207-846-5827

Items related to motorcycles bought & sold. Wanted items: brochures, magazines, manuals, programs, pins, awards, toys, posters, tools, postcards, photos, license plates, models, clothing, trophies, showroom items, racing memorabilia, & anything else. Motorcycles & parts wanted also. Evenings best time to call.

*Other categories: Literature; Mixed Automobilia; General Interest*

## Nighthorse Inc.

Ben Nighthorse Campbell
PO Box 639
Ignacio, CO 81137 USA
TEL: 970-563-0067
FAX: 970-563-0067

Specialize in motorcycle-related memorabilia. Buy, sell, trade. Display motor-

cycle movie posters. Also interested in petroliana collectibles.

*Other categories: Art, Prints & Posters; Rt. 66 & Roadside; Petroliana, Other*

## PL8MAN

See our main listing under "License Plates, Tags, etc."

## Frank A. Poll

See our main listing under "Models, Kits."

## Pumping Iron

See our main listing under "Petroliana, Other."

## Dan Smith

See our main listing under "Mascots/Badges/Emblems."

## Marnix Verkest

See our main listing under "General Interest."

## David Wasserman

16 Ashwood Lane
Morgantown, WV 26505 USA
TEL: 304-291-2058
FAX: 304-291-2058

Buying/selling American motorcycles & related memorabilia, 1965 & earlier. Always have vintage bikes & signs, toys, medals, badges, clothing, clocks, oil/paint cans. 10 years' collecting & dealing. Top quality. No reproductions or fantasies.

*Other categories: Toys, General; License Plates, Tags, etc.; Mixed Automobilia*

## Workbench

See our main listing under "Mascots/Badges/Emblems."

## The XR-1000 Nut

William Armstrong
9 Oak St.
Pittsfield, MA 01201 USA
TEL: 413-447-9797

Specializing in Harley-Davidson XR-1000 related items, as well as H-D competition motorcycle literature, posters, photos, etc. Anything related to flat-track motorcycle racing 1955 to present. Buy, sell, trade. Write or call after 5pm EST.

*Other categories: Literature; Racing Artifacts*

## Yankee Trader

See our main listing under "Toys, General"

# MOTORING ACCESSORIES

## Auto Epoch

See our main listing under "Publications, Current"

## Auto-Ideas

See our main listing under "Specialized Automobilia"

## The British Garage

See our main listing under "Specialized Automobilia"

## Christie's

See our main listing under "Auction Firm"

## Classic Restoration

See our main listing under "Tools"

## Elegant Accessories

See our main listing under "Specialized Automobilia"

## Innovative Ideas

See our main listing under "Jewelry"

## Roy Lassen

29 Betty Dr.
Santa Barbara, CA 93105 USA
TEL: 805-569-7160
Specialize in 1920s-1950s dealer aftermarket accessories. Examples: Superay road lights, fog lights, Lorrain-Appleton spotlights, backup, fender cow lights. Sidemount rear spare tire covers, mirrors, trunk racks, trunks, radios, heaters, glass, Bakelite, shift, brake, steering, knobs, compass, cat's eye cigar lighter. Buy, sell, trade. Appraisal: write car year, send SASE.

*Other categories: Luggage/Picnic Sets; Horns; Lamps*

## NASCAR Novelties

DeeDee Hubbard
P.O. Box 422
Bloomfield Hills, MI 48303 USA
TEL: 810-332-7646
FAX: 810-334-5927
Email: webmaster@middleburgonline.com
NASCAR novelties, lugnut keychains. The actual lugnuts from NASCAR & super truck racing are used in our keychains.

*Other categories: Manufacturer; Promos; General Interest*

## SABAR International

Barry Hautman
481 Grand Avenue
West Trenton, NJ 08628 USA
TEL: 609-883-1827
I sell & collect antique & new diecast tin cars/trucks & antique & new auto race posters of European auto races of the 1920s-1950s.

*Other categories: Toys, General; Art, Prints & Posters*

## Mark Suozzi

PO Box 102
Ashfield, MA 01330 USA
TEL: 413-628-3241
FAX: 413-628-3241
Motoring accessories. Antique motoring artifacts bought & sold. Paying your prices for celluloid pinbacks, fobs, medals, china display pieces, advertising art, signs, photographs of pre-1920 races, pennants, tin toy windup autos with glass windows over 10 ins. long. Send photos & condition of any sport racing artifacts for immediate offer.

*Other categories: Specialized Automobilia; Racing Artifacts; Toys, General*

## Wolo Manufacturing Corp.

See our main listing under "Horns"

## Yesterday's Highways Newsletter

See our main listing under "Publications, Current"

# MUSEUM

## AAA Small Car World

See our main listing under "Marque Specific"

## Allen Oil Sales

See our main listing under "Petroliana, Other"

## Canada's All Canadian Service Station Museum

Don Loughren
RR 2 Site 200 Box 47
Regina, Saskatchewan 54P 2Z2
Canada
TEL: 306-757-8976
Museum offers: over 300 signs, advertising clocks, oil bottles, thermometers, & display racks. Tin, porcelain, neon, cardboard, & light-ups. Early pumps, globes, & some 3,500 cans. Coca-Cola, soda pop, ice cream, & country store. Learn the history of early Canadian oil companies. Items for sale.

*Other categories: Neon; Petroliana, Other; Retail Store*

## Canton Classic Car Museum

Bob Lichty, Director
555 Market Ave. S.
Canton, OH 44703 USA
TEL: 330-455-3603
FAX: 330-456-4256
Museum consisting of over 40 cars & 20 years of automobilia collecting. Toys, highway, tourism, clothing, Lincoln Highway, travel, & Canton, Ohio, emphasis. Open seven days 10-5. Adults $4, seniors/students $2.50. Great gift shop too.

*Other categories: Mixed Automobilia; Rt. 66 & Roadside*

## Himes Museum of Motor Racing

Marty Himes
15 O'Neil Ave.
Bayshore, NY 11706 USA
TEL: 516-666-4912
Old stock cars, midgets, sprints, & more. Uniforms, helmets, 1000s of rare photos, posters, pieces of famous racetracks, buildings. You name it, "nobody

has more stuff." Open year-round. Please call ahead. Donations gratefully accepted. Featured in *Car & Driver*, *Stock Car Racing Magazine*, & more.

*Other categories: Racing Artifacts; Specialized Automobilia; Photographs*

## Imperial Palace Auto Collection

Hagan L. Stewart
3535 Las Vegas Blvd. S.
Las Vegas, NV 89109 USA
TEL: 702-794-3174
FAX: 702-369-7430

Over 200 antique, classic, & special-interest automobiles are on display in a plush, gallery-like setting. Located on the fifth floor of the hotel's parking facility, the Auto Collection is open seven days a week. It also features a unique gift shop with a wide selection of automotive memorabilia & books.

*Other categories: Toys, General; General Interest; Books*

## Innovative Ideas

See our main listing under "Jewelry"

## Edward E. Moberg, Jr.

See our main listing under "Art, Original"

## The Museum of Automobile History

Walter Miller
321 N. Clinton St.
Syracuse, NY 13202 USA
TEL: 315-478-2277
FAX: 315-432-8256

World's largest museum of its kind! Over 10,000 objects on display. Devoted to the history of automobiles, trucks, & motorcycles from the 19th century to the present. Open Wed-Sun 10-5.

*Other categories: Mixed Automobilia; Retail Store; General Interest*

## Mystic Motorcar Museum

David J. Bishop, Director
PO Box 282
Mystic, CT 06355-0282 USA
TEL: 860-572-9190
Email: david.bishop@snet.net

Recently formed nonprofit auto museum. Membership $25, expires one year after we open. Many vehicles & automobilia ready to display. Fund-raising begun to acquire a building with possible locations in Connecticut or Rhode Island. Donations of all automobilia welcomed & tax deductible. Newsletter available. Thanks for your interest & support.

*Other categories: Mixed Automobilia; Literature; General Interest*

## National Automotive & Truck Model & Toy Museum of the United States

NATMATMUS is in Auburn, Indiana. A museum within a museum, it is housed at NATMUS & contains 1000s of model & toy automobiles & trucks from cast iron to diecast. The Roadside Market (219-925-9100) sells a wide selection of automobilia.

*Other categories: Toys, General; Retail Store; Petroliana, Pumps & Globes*

## National Automotive & Truck Museum of the United States (NATMUS)

John Martin Smith, President
PO Box 686
Auburn, IN 46706 USA
TEL: 219-925-4560
FAX: 219-925-4563

NATMUS is located in the former factory buildings of the Auburn Automobile Company at Auburn, Indiana. It houses over one hundred collector cars & trucks & thousands of toy & model cars & trucks. The Roadside Market (219-925-9100) sells a wide selectio nof automobilia.

*Other categories: Toys, General; Retail Store; Petroliana, Pumps & Globes*

## Pacific Communications

See our main listing under "Rt. 66 & Roadside"

## Rineyville Sandblasting Model A Ford Museum

Ernest J. Pyzocha
179 Arvelwise Ln.
Elizabethtown, KY 42701 USA
TEL: 502-862-4671

Packed with a constantly rotating stock of nearly 40 unrestored 1928 through 1931 Model A Ford cars & trucks. Also porcelain signs, license plates, antique gasoline pumps, old tools, many NOS & used parts & accessories. Located off Hwy 1538 (between Fort Knox & Elizabethtown, Kentucky) open year-round by phone or chance. Admission $2.

## James T. Sandoro

See our main listing under "Appraisal Service"

## John Snowberger

See our main listing under "Models, Precision"

## John J. Zolomij, Inc.

See our main listing under "Appraisal Service"

# NEON

## Blast from the Past

Ron Van Oeveren
1824 M St. Suite 1
Lincoln, NE 68508 USA
TEL: 402-438-7283
FAX: 402-438-7283
Email: blast2past@aol.com

Manufacturer & distributor of nostalgic neon signs & clocks. Wholesale/retail. Designs include garage, gas, diner, Rt. 66, auto, service, many more; plus custom neon of all types including clock & neon sign restoration service. We buy, sell, trade, restore porcelain neon signs & auto/soda/gas/oil advertising signs.

See our web site at http://pmadt.com/blastpast

*Other categories: Signs; Manufacturer; Restoration Service*

## Canada's All Canadian Service Station Museum

See our main listing under "Museum"

## Bob Gajewski

See our main listing under "Mixed Automobilia"

## R & G Automobiles & Collectables

See our main listing under "Mixed Automobilia"

## Rick's Gallery

See our main listing under "Art, Prints & Posters"

# ONLINE SERVICE

## Autosaurus

See our main listing under "Art, Prints & Posters"

## Bullivant Gallery

See our main listing under "Art, Prints & Posters"

## Car Crazy, Inc.

See our main listing under "Retail Store"

## GameRoomAntiques

See our main listing under "Games"

## LMG Enterprises/Gallery L'Automobile

See our main listing under "Books"

## Victory Lane

See our main listing under "Toys, General"

# PEDAL CARS

## S. Adams Inc.

See our main listing under "Specialized Automobilia"

## Antiques Warehouse of Cape Cod

See our main listing under "Toys, Truck"

## Astro Automotive, Inc.

10 Kenwood Circle
Franklin, MA 02038
TEL: 800-527-8762

Mustang Pedal Car replica in all-metal design. Passed Ford Motor Company quality test.

## Bowers Collectable Toys

See our main listing under "Mixed Automobilia"

## C & C Creations

See our main listing under "Mixed Automobilia"

## C & N Reproductions, Inc.

Carl Kriewall
1340 Ashover Ct.
Bloomfield Hills, MI 48304 USA
TEL: 810-852-1998
FAX: 810-852-1999
Email: ckcn@ix.netcom.com

Pedal car parts, pedal plane parts, kits for pedal cars & pedal planes. Visit our website at www.pedalcar.com.

*Other categories: Manufacturer; Models, Kits; Books*

## Chuck's Collectibles

See our main listing under "Restoration Service"

## Clapper Restorations

See our main listing under "Petroliana, Pumps & Globes"

## Classic Transportation

Jerry Dixey
3667 Mahoning Ave.
Youngstown, OH 44515 USA
TEL: 330-793-3026
FAX: 330-793-9729
Email: gadmak@aol.com

Since 1989 Classic has carried a complete line of pedal cars & parts, auto art, neon clocks, vintage signs, gas pumps & parts, price guides, hot rod videos, & other related automobilia. A 32-page full-color catalog is available for $2. Complete in-house restoration facilities available.

*Other categories: Hot Rod Memorabilia; Petroliana, Other; Restoration Service*

## Crown Premiums

See our main listing under "Manufacturer"

## D&S Pedal Car Restorations

Dave or Sno Kleespies
15257 S. 24th St.
Phoenix, AZ 85048 USA
TEL: 602-759-5131

Professional restoration of all types of pedal cars, wagons, & tractors. Free estimates. Restorations range from riding condition to museum quality. Upholstery, chrome plating, custom graphics, airbrush, & pin-striping all available. Changing stock of restored & unrestored pedal cars. Locating service available.

## Doney Enterprises

See our main listing under "Mixed Automobilia"

## Dooley & Sons

See our main listing under "Signs"

## East Coast Classics

See our main listing under "Petroliana, Pumps & Globes"

## Fairlane Automotive Specialties

Keith Ashley
107 W. Railroad St.
St. Johns, MI 48879 USA
TEL: 517-224-6460
FAX: 517-224-9488

Manufacturer of fiberglass-bodied pedal cars, fiberglass gas pumps, fiberglass shapes for neon signs, fiberglass signs. Custom fiberglass molding. Handcrafted full-size 1936 Ford roadster bodies, fenders, etc.

*Other categories: Specialized Automobilia; Mixed Automobilia; Manufacturer*

## Fineline Car Co.

See our main listing under "General Interest"

## Wm. P. Fornwalt, Jr.

See our main listing under "Models, Precision"

## G & L Collectibles

See our main listing under "Toys, Truck"

## Half-Pint Motors

David J. Jundt
2903 Valleyview Ave.
Bismarck, ND 58501 USA
TEL: 701-258-6345

Specialize in pedal cars of all types. Restore pedal cars. Collect all items regarding pedal cars, including paper items & parts. Buy, sell, trade. Also collect NASCAR diecast & model kits. Interested in all types of hot rod memorabilia, especially hot rod comic books. Call after 6pm CST.

*Other categories: Hot Rod Memorabilia; Racing Artifacts*

## Hi-Tec Customs

See our main listing under "Restoration Service"

## Inside Only

See our main listing under "Toys, General"

## Juvenile Automobiles

Matt Vaznaian
101 Main St.
Woonsocket, RI 02895 USA
TEL: 401-762-9661

Specializing in pedal cars, parts, Art Deco tricycles, & wagons. Buy, sell, trade. Send $5 for our parts catalog. Looking to buy toy trucks: 1920s American National, Toledo, Genron Bulldog Macks, pressed-steel trucks. Give us a call if you have any questions on toys.

*Other categories: Toys, Truck; Toys, General*

## Brad Kellogg

PO Box 398
Wakefield, NE 68784 USA
TEL: 402-287-2729

Mainly collector. Buy, sell, trade pedal cars, gas pumps, signs. Restoration of gas pumps & pedal cars.

*Other categories: Petroliana, Pumps & Globes; Petroliana, Other; Signs*

## Kneipp's Toy & Collectibles

See our main listing under "Toys, General"

## Marchbanks Ltd.

C. R. Marchbanks
314 Candelaria Rd.
Albuquerque, NM 87107 USA
TEL: 505-344-3359

Pedal cars, small toys, license plates, pictures, photos, literature, titles.

*Other categories: License Plates, Tags, etc.; Literature; Toys, General*

## Memory Lane Collectibles

See our main listing under "Toys, General"

## Moonlight Peddler

Veronica A. Doster
PO Box 287
Athens, GA 30603 USA
TEL: 706-548-2739
Email: pedalangel@aol.com

Collects pedal cars. Buy, sell, trade, show. Also collects signs, vending machines, diner displays. Also cars of all types 1950s-70s. Toys (Barbie-wagons). Email or call.

*Other categories: Diner Memorabilia; Mixed Automobilia; Toys, General*

## New Era Toys

See our main listing under "Restoration Service"

## Nostalgia Productions, Inc.

See our main listing under "Art, Other"

## Pedal Car Guys

Chris Swingley
4457 - 45 Ave. So.
Minneapolis, MN 55406 USA
TEL: 612-724-4598
Email: pedalguys@aol.com

Specialize in the collection & sale of pedal car materials. Original manufacturer catalogs, sales literature, art illustrations, photographs, full-page magazine advertising, posters, postcards, greeting cards, books. Also diecast pedal cars, retired Hallmark kiddie car classics. Always interested in unrestored pedal cars. Seeking European, Eureka, Triang, Austin Junior.

*Other categories: Literature; Cards, Postal; Art, Prints & Posters*

## Pedal Car News

Craig Fleetwood
26861 Trabuco Road, E-303
Mission Viejo, CA 92691 USA
TEL: 714-768-0665
FAX: 714-768-0665

*Pedal Car News* is a monthly publication dedicated to pedal car collecting. The publication features collector profiles, show coverage & information, new products, cars for sale, a complete line of pedal car parts for sale, restoration tips, & more. For a sample issue send $2 for s & h.

*Other categories: Publications, Current; Toys, General; Toys, Truck*

## Perma Coatings

See our main listing under "Restoration Service"

## Portell Restorations

Dan & Lindia Portell
Box 91
Hematite, MO 63047 USA
TEL: 314-937-8192
FAX: 314-931-2806

Manufacturer of pedal car parts before 1940. Have complete suspensions, hood ornaments, wheels, tires, hubcaps. Buy, sell, trade pedal cars before 1940. Also collect pressed-steel trucks & tin & porcelain advertising signs. Parts catalog $4.

*Other categories: Manufacturer; Toys, Truck; Signs*

## Rader's Relics

See our main listing under "Retail Store"

## Rick's Restorations/Custom Toys

See our main listing under "Restoration Service"

## Ron's Relics

Ron Hirtreiter
8601 Clarence Center Rd.
Clarence Center, NY 14032 USA
TEL: 716-741-2818

Buy, sell, restore, & collect pedal cars. Also restore & sell gas pumps & automobilia. Classic auto restoration. Auto appraisals for insurance & estate settlements.

*Other categories: Petroliana, Pumps & Globes; Appraisal Service; Restoration Service*

## Squat Rods

Edward O'Brien
7475 Woodbine Rd.
Macungie, PA 18062 USA
TEL: 610-366-0606

Design & production of new & original pedal cars. Available as kits or as completely painted & lettered vehicle. DIVCO snub-nosed milk truck currently in production. Send SASE for brochure.

*Other categories: Toys, Truck; Manufacturer; Hot Rod Memorabilia*

## Thomas Toys, Inc.

See our main listing under "Toys, General"

Continued on p. 81

# THE AUTOMOBILIA TOP TEN

## Your Best Buys for 1997

**W**elcome to this special bonus section to the *MOBILIA Sourcebook* featuring our Top 10 Automobilia Collectibles. This is *MOBILIA* magazine's second annual look at great automobilia to collect for the future. The picks come from our regular magazine columnists and other acknowledged experts in the hobby.

Here you'll find 10 great automobilia collectibles that are flying below the radar screens of most collectors. But they're poised—in the opinion of those in the know—for powerful gains in public attention and in value.

As before, we're guided by the criteria "Accessible, Affordable, and Available." That is: 1) The item selected has broad popular appeal; 2) It is emerging into prominence, therefore not yet prohibitively expensive; and 3) Though uncommon, it is obtainable for a reasonable amount of time and determination.

To make our Top 10 list as useful as possible, each entry also provides essential stats: Prices (values based on condition); Sources (contact info for key dealers or suppliers, or other tips on finding the item); and Recommended Reading—books, periodicals, club newsletters, etc. covering the item.

We hope that you enjoy this bonus section of your *MOBILIA Sourcebook,* and that it adds a little spice to your collecting fun. We're also grateful for the help of one and all in naming this year's Top 10—and wish all of our readers luck in latching on to some of these rising stars!

# A HONEY OF A COLLECTIBLE

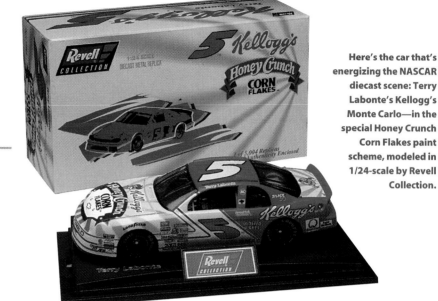

Here's the car that's energizing the NASCAR diecast scene: Terry Labonte's Kellogg's Monte Carlo—in the special Honey Crunch Corn Flakes paint scheme, modeled in 1/24-scale by Revell Collection.

## The Year's Sweetest NASCAR Diecast

TOM FUNK

NASCAR fans just don't march in lockstep. Ask who's *really* the top driver, or whether Ford, Chevy, or Pontiac is the *real* chariot of fire—and you'll elicit something between a healthy diversity of opinion and a mud-wrestling bout. Which is why it came as a surprise that when we asked dealers in the field to name their hottest NASCAR collectible for 1997, their choices were nearly unanimous.

"Revell Collection." We heard those two words time and again—from dealers stocking collectibles, both new and old, by the whole gamut of manufacturers. Frankly, we were hoping for something with a few years of history, and relative scarcity on its side. Can we really expect something big out of a mass manufacturer's brand-new line of diecasts? What makes Revell Collection—and one car in particular—so desirable?

According to our friends in the retail trenches, it's simple: high quality, attention to detail, low production runs, and affordable prices. Betty Arnold, of R&K Cards & Collectibles in Norfolk, Virginia, named the Revell Collection line, in both 1/24 and 1/64 scales, as her top pick for 1997, praising them as "very popular and moderately priced." Frank Carpenter, of Inside Track in Warwick, Rhode Island, had the same nomination: "The Revell Collection stuff is outstanding. The 1/24-scale diecasts are absolutely incredible, the quality and attention to detail—it's some of the best stuff we've ever seen in the hobby. And it sells so well, since it's reasonably priced."

Robert Bataglia, of Buck Fever Racing, called the collection "probably one of the better lines out there. It's top-of-the-line stuff, with lots of detail and lots of weight to the cars. Everything is tampo-printed, so it's very bright, very detailed. And the price is in range with most people's spending money. The

Honey Crunch is a significant car," concluded Bataglia. "It made a tremendous impact on the market. It came out at just the right time—and they didn't make enough of them."

Revell has exercised admirable restraint by holding production levels down and limiting the number of authorized dealers. Though superstar Jeff Gordon merited about 8,000, said Carpenter, for many of the cars, production has been limited to 5,000 copies—and in some cases as little as 2,500-3,000. That exclusivity has collectors so fired up about the Revell Collection race cars—and one car in particular.

That car is our Top 10 NASCAR collectible for 1997—a car so coveted that its $29 initial retail price has rocketed to $100 in a mere three weeks. That car is the 1/24-scale Kellogg's Monte Carlo driven by NASCAR iron man and points champion Terry Labonte, in its special "Honey Crunch Corn Flakes" paint scheme.

A mere 5,004 were made, and allocated to dealers in the strictest fashion. Rumor has it some 1,000 of them were shipped to QVC shopping network, which sold out of them in *three minutes.* The special, sunshiny paint job, the driver's champion status, and the sheer scarcity of the product fueled a frenzy that shows no sign of abating.

Where can you get one? The dealers listed below are great sources for any NASCAR collector. But they'll all be working the phones, struggling to restock the product. "It's gone!" said Carpenter. Buck Fever

Racing is a master distributor of the Revell Collection line—but even they may not be able to help you with the car. "Sold out!" Robert Bataglia exclaimed. "You just can't keep them in stock," said Betty Arnold of the entire Revell Collection line. "And it's like pulling teeth to get the new ones."

*MOBILIA* readers don't need a lesson in supply and demand to recognize that the 1/24-scale Honey Crunch car is a smart NASCAR buy for 1997. That is, if you can find one.

## VALUES

- Terry Labonte's Honey Crunch Corn Flakes Monte Carlo (mint). . . . . . . $100
- Most other Revell Collection diecasts (mint) . . . . . . . . . . . . . . . . . . . . . . . . . $30

## TIPS & SOURCES

- **R&K Cards & Collectibles,**1846 E. Little Creek, Norfolk, VA 23518; TEL 757-583-0155; FAX 757-583-1120
- **Inside Track,** 2443 West Shore Rd., Warwick, RI 02886; TEL 401-738-2299; FAX 401-738-1323
- **Buck Fever Racing,** P.O. Box 230, Marion, VA 24354; TEL 800-888-BUCK

# ALL OVER THE MAP

## Vintage Shell Road Maps Are a Road to Riches

**Colorful vintage Shell road maps are at the very top of the genre—and likely to take off in value from their currently affordable levels. The 1932 and 1933 maps struck a note of boundless possibility with their collages of far-flung license plates and portraits of lady motorists at the wheel.**

### CARL BOMSTEAD

As the full-service gas stations of yore evolved into the convenience stores of today, one of the many traditions that fell by the wayside was the offering of courtesy road maps. Today's stations will, of course, sell you a generic Rand McNally map, dispensed from a machine for a handful of quarters—a far cry from the free-for-the-asking, distinctive offerings of the past. These early maps, often with highly stylized graphics, served as a positive reminder of your visit. Once a prominent form of advertising, they long ago gave way to the gas companies' increasing reliance on television ads.

The main suppliers of service station maps were Rand McNally and Company and the N.M. Gousha Company, both of Chicago. They both used a code to date their maps; Rand McNally started in alphabetical order in 1919 and changed to a numerical code in 1945. Gousha also utilized the alphabet starting in 1927 and

switched to double letters in 1953. The Gallup Map and Supply Co. of Kansas City, Missouri, was a lesser-known supplier in the Midwest, and the W.C. Eubank Company provided maps for Richfield and others on the West Coast.

The most desirable—and the most expensive—maps are the colorful ones depicting detailed scenes, often of the stations themselves. Conoco maps from the Twenties featured the Continental soldier in yellow, red, and blue, and a view of a period station. Sinclair road maps from the Thirties usually featured a view of a station but were more Art Deco in design. Standard Oil featured a distinctive Art Deco design with geese prominently displayed in flight.

Shell offered two series of wide appeal. The 1929 offering featured a wooden runabout boat at speed, a biplane in flight, and five automobiles, one parked at a period Shell station and others in motion. The strong yellow, red, and blue color scheme conveys boldness and power. For their 1932 and 1933 maps Shell offered a collage of license plates against period artwork by Robert E. Lee. The 1932 example featured a lovely lady, with scarf flowing, driving a convertible, with a male passenger glancing out the window. For 1933 an equally attractive lady motorist traded in her disinterested male passenger for a white terrier.

Gas and oil collectors are beginning to appreciate the more graphically appealing and colorful maps, and values are beginning to creep up. However, maps can still be uncovered at flea markets and antique and garage sales—and some real treasures are often found within a stack of maps priced at three for $10. The more desirable maps were available for $5-20 a few years ago, but the

range is now more like $40-60, with some, such as the 1929 Shell series of maps, going for $100 in excellent condition. The popularity of these vintage items should continue to increase over the next few years as other gas and oil enthusiasts are exposed to their graphic appeal. For the time being, though, these collectibles are still very affordable.

As with any other collectible, condition is key. The only reason to purchase anything but a pristine example is if it is so rare that you can't be assured of another coming your way in the near future. The Shell maps, while not common, can be found in excellent condition with a little patience and persistent hunting.

**The 1929 offering featured a host of vehicles—from cars to a boat to a biplane—benefiting from Shell gas.**

---

## VALUES

### 1932-33 Shell License Plate Maps

| | |
|---|---|
| Mint | $45 |
| Good | $28 |
| Lesser Condition | PASS |

## TIPS & SOURCES

- **Vendor: Peter Sidlow, 5895 Duneville, Las Vegas, NV 89118; TEL 702-873-1818**
- **Other sources include antique shows, flea markets, garage sales, and gas bashes.**

# DIECAST DYNAMITE

Collectors have fond memories of Johnny Lightnings—the diecasts that appeared in 1969, blew the doors off Matchbox, and ate into Hot Wheels' market share. Here's the Johnny Lightning Leapin' Limo from Topper, 1970. Value: $40-45.

## Johnny Lightnings— Diecasts to Die For

**DANA JOHNSON**

Johnny Lightnings actually cover both eras of diecast toys. The original Johnny Lightnings issued by Topper Toys from 1969 to 1971 are currently gaining in popularity, in part because of the resurrection of the brand name three years ago by the Indiana firm Playing Mantis. The Johnny Lightning commemorative series from Playing Mantis has sparked renewed interest in the original Topper models. And the popularity of the originals continues to drive the surging success of new issues.

Tom Lowe remembers when Matchbox's sedate models were the only game in town. Then Hot Wheels diecasts came along in 1968 and burned up orange tracks all over the country. But they didn't have the diecast toy market all to themselves—Johnny Lightnings were introduced in 1969, and by the time they were two years old in 1971, they were stealing one third of the market from Hot Wheels...and had left Matchbox behind in the dust.

Johnny Lightnings may have gone on to wipe out Mattel's Hot Wheels if it weren't for the fact that Henry Orenstein, Topper's top guy, got greedy. Allegations of business fraud were followed by bankruptcy. No new Johnny Lightnings were issued after 1971, although many were planned. By 1973,

Topper Toys was out of business.

Only 47 of the 81 planned Johnny Lightning models were put into production. The first year's models were custom versions of American production cars, while the second year featured bizarre designer models. By the third year only five new models were marketed, and Orenstein's company started its irreversible nosedive. Johnny Lightning production models from Topper's first year are now worth up to $200. Second year models are worth up to $75.

Fast forward to 1993. Tom Lowe is now in his thirties and pining for the Johnny Lightnings he remembered from childhood. A successful businessman looking for a new direction, Tom discovers that the brand name is up for grabs, and grabs it. Beginning with commemorative reissues of eight popular Johnny Lightning models, Lowe's company, Playing Mantis, produced about 17,000 of each model—replicas of the Movin' Van, Wasp, Custom XKE, Custom El Camino, Vicious Vette, Custom GTO, Bug Bomb, and Custom '32 Roadster. That was Series A. Playing Mantis followed with another 17,000 or so of each model in another color scheme and called it Series B. Ten color variations later, they had successfully sold over 1.3 million models. Playing Mantis is a blazing success!

The future of Playing Mantis's line of Johnny Lightning diecasts is secure, while Topper's original models are still out there

waiting for the lucky collector to find them, often for far less than they are worth. The reason? Most people who currently own them don't recognize them as anything more than a cheap Hot Wheels knockoff—testimony to Orenstein's original concept of "copying a good thing."

**Playing Mantis's Johnny Lightning Custom Continental, 1996. Value: $4-5.**

### VALUES

Johnny Lightnings from Topper's first year (1969) are worth up to $200 in mint condition, and second-year models up to $75. Contemporary Johnny Lightnings are worth about $3-5, and promotionals $12-15.

### TIPS & SOURCES

- *Johnny Lightning News Flash*, Playing Mantis, P.O. Box 3688, South Bend, IN 46619-3688; TEL 800-MANTIS-8; FAX 219-233-3788
- New Johnny Lightnings: major retailers, or from Playing Mantis; TEL 800-MANTIS-8
- Original Johnny Lightnings: toy shows, and vendors such as J.B. Collectables TEL 888-JBC-TOYS; A&M Collectibles TEL 800-787-5559; and Tailfin Productions TEL 813-684-3785
- Promotionals: Bob's Toy Show TEL 510-889-6676; Toy Time TEL 508-827-5261; and Greater Seattle Toy Show TEL 360-668-7144.

The Johnny Lightning FAO Schwarz Custom XKE from Playing Mantis, 1995. Current value: $12-15

# COURTLAND'S CAPTIVATING COLLECTIBLES

This manufacturer's "case" assortment of Courtland toys was recently discovered in the New England area by a house painter. Twelve tin-plate mechanical toy trucks from 1950, with their original boxes, in a factory carton represents a fantastic find.

## Their 225% Surge in Value Outperforms all Postwar Motor Toys

**JOE AND SHARON FREED**

A nearly impossible challenge presented by *MOBILIA:* Identify an antique toy or tightly focused class of antique toys that are still inexpensive, available, and yet poised for toy stardom. Perhaps this would not be that difficult when selecting a contemporary toy, but to choose an antique toy or group of toys that have been ignored by collectors for 40 to 90 years, and are just now poised for rediscovery, would seem to be an impossible task. With a little luck and perseverance, however, we believe we have done it. We have identified a family of toys that meets the *MOBILIA* criteria, and then some!

Courtland Toys, with manufacturing facilities in Camden, New Jersey, produced miniature mechanical automotive toys in tinplate from the late Forties to about 1954. Research shows that Courtland Manufacturing was one of the few toy manufacturing concerns to continue using tin-plate as the material of choice after World War II, when most toy companies were exploiting the wonders of the "new-age" plastic. During this period, Courtland tin toys were second in production volume only to the offerings of Louis Marx.

During the past five years, we have monitored the performance of Courtland Toys in the collecting arena. Our research reveals that toy collectors are quickly discerning the potential of these mechanical beauties. The in-depth study of auction sales figures, along with many private transactions, indicate that Courtland Toys, as a group, have outperformed all other postwar automotive toy collectibles with an amazing 225% increase in collector dollar value during the past three years. The potential for investment growth in this category is substantial.

"Why the sudden surge in Courtland collectibility?" you may be asking. Courtland products are handsomely lithographed, highly animated, and are—comparatively speaking—less expensive than similar postwar tin toys such as Marx. Interested collectors also can still obtain Courtland Toys in their original factory boxes (along with the "Motor-Guaranteed-For-Life" certificate). There are many styles to choose from: sedans; taxis; moving vans; farm tractors; tractor-trailer rigs; dump, milk, gasoline, and tanker trucks; a mechanical train—and this is just the beginning. Several boxed sets were offered, each containing from two to five toys, packaged in an attractive "set" box, the tops of which are fully illustrated with beautiful art.

Our guidance for collecting Courtland Toys, or any toy for that matter, is: Always buy the best toy affordable. It is always bet-ter to purchase one toy in pristine condition than several near-excellent or lower-quality examples. Toy values will always be determined by condition, so buy only the best. Forties and Fifties Courtland stock toys in their original boxes are still available in mint or near-mint condition. The photographs accompanying this article are of Courtland Toys recently acquired by a well-known Pennsylvania toy collector during the past year and a half. Have patience and you will be rewarded. So, my collecting colleagues, have fun. There is no caveat emptor here! You can take this advice to the bank.

## VALUES

**$50-$250 in mint condition for all but the rare, unique examples.**

## TIPS & SOURCES

**Most major auction houses including:**
- Bill Bertoia Auctions, 1881 T-Spring Rd., Vineland, NJ 08360
- Richard Opfer Auctioneering, Inc., 1919 Greenspring Dr., Timonium, MD 21093
- New England Auction Gallery, P.O. Box 2273, West Peabody, MA 01960

**Most major toy shows including:**
Chicago, Dallas, Los Angeles, and Allentown (PA).

**For the armchair shopper:**
- Toy Trader, 100 Bryant St., Dubuque, IA 52003
- Toy Shop, 700 East State St., Iola, WI 54990
- Bob Smith, The Village Smith, 62 West Ave., Fairport, NY 14450 (mail order and toy shows)
- Charles Gilbert, 1103 Camelot Ct., Johnstown, PA 15904 (mail order and toy shows)

The beautiful lithography on this Courtland "American Dairies" truck should appeal to even the most critical of toy vehicle collectors.

## Remember Those Souvenir Window Decals? Now's the Time to Buy!

**MICHAEL KARL WITZEL**

**Intense color, bold graphics, and nostalgic themes make these window decals from the Forties, Fifties, and Sixties appealing to today's collectors. They speak of simpler times when driving was an adventure, and the trip was more important than the destination.**

Remember those cross-country trips in the family automobile, and all those station wagons you passed on the highway with their windows plastered with tacky tourist decals? Well, those colorful icons of American travel are back and they are showing up at flea markets, collectibles shows, ephemera events, and other well-known automobilia gatherings.

Once upon a time during the Forties, Fifties, and Sixties, long before the children of America realized what endless fun can be had by playing with "stickers," window decals were all the rage. During their travels, Mom and Dad liked to pick them up at tourist traps, motels, gasoline stations, and every other imaginable roadside attraction.

Most boasted of favorite destinations, such as "Jesse James's Hideout" at Meremec Caverns along old Route 66, or the Grand Canyon in Arizona. Others promoted particular brands of gasoline, tourist accommodations, and service businesses of similar ilk. Many were die-cut in the shape of a particular state and featured important points of interest within the borders. Of course, Indian trading posts were a favorite subject, as were the hackneyed expressions and comical themes now found imprinted on today's standard-issue bumper stickers.

With their intense color, highly stylized graphic motifs, and nostalgic themes, these whimsical window decals are excellent examples of the art techniques that were once used by commercial advertisers in America. They speak volumes of a much simpler time, when traveling across the country was really an adventure, and the ride was more important than the destination.

Some might ask, "But how do I collect decals that were stuck on the windows of cars that are probably turned into scrap metal by now?" The answer is simple: Over the past decade, unused decals of this genre have surfaced at all the usual swap meets and collector gatherings (Hershey, etc.). Somehow, a good number of these gems survived—buried in the bottom of a drawer or hidden away in a shoebox. Because their owners never quite got around to affixing them to the back window of the family flivver, they remain in pristine condition.

For those that like to collect the artifacts categorized as automobilia, this forgetfulness is a boon. Today, collectors may pick up fine examples of these water-application decals in excellent shape for well under $10. Often, the decals are in brand new condition and come in their original glassine envelope, complete with the detailed instructions on how to apply them!

Whether arranged in a plastic album, mounted in a framed and matted series, or blown up with a color copier for individual display, these fine bits of retro art are a great addition to any collector's exhibit.

For those with classic cars, it's extremely tempting to actually use some of these decals—and some do. Along with those decals of the hot rod and speed equipment variety, tourist appliqués can provide just the right touch to make things look "original."

Considering their appealing nature and general rarity, one would think that tourist-themed window decals are in big demand. Not yet so. A few ardent fans are just beginning to appreciate their beauty, while the bulk of decal collectors still clamor over the racing-themed decals.

These always colorful travel-type window decals of yesteryear are a great way for the automobilia collector to imagine what it was like during those crazy days of two-lane travel and tourist traps. The only drawback to collecting them is having to resist the temptation to slap them on the family station wagon and hit the road.

## VALUES

| Condition | Expect to Pay |
|---|---|
| Mint | $15-25 |
| Good | $10-15 |
| Fair | $5-10 |
| Poor | nil to $5 |

## TIPS & SOURCES

**Source Listing:**
- **Lost Highway Art, P.O. Box 164, Bedford Hills, NY 10507-0164. Specializes in mint original decals**
- **Past Lane Auto, P.O. Box 69, Athol Springs, NY 10410. Catalog ($3) features some decals.**

# CLASSICS IN MINIATURE

**Durham's own promo was made to celebrate their selection as best stand at the 1994 Modelex show. Only 100 of these gold-trimmed models were made.**

## Durham Classics Models Are "Created, Not Manufactured"

**WAYNE E. MOYER**

The excellent 1/43-scale white-metal models "created, not manufactured" by Durham Classics may be among the biggest "sleepers" in the model collecting hobby. Many collectors are either unfamiliar with Durham Classics models (even though they've been made since 1981) or are unaware that many unique promotional versions offered by other companies are actually produced by Durham. Adding to the mystique, there's no easy way, at present, to accurately date a Durham Classics model, or to determine just how many examples of a particular version were made. The formation of a new club, The Durham Collector, should change all that for fans of these Canadian-made models.

Today Durham Classics makes 21 different "standard" models, with many limited-run variations and promotionals, and is ready to introduce an exciting new series, Cruisin' Classics, featuring American hot rods.

Several factors have kept Durham Classics' models from reaching the popularity of Brooklin or Western models. One is the simple lack of information, as the majority of collectors worldwide usually aren't aware that they exist.

A second factor has been the choice of subject. Except for the Airflow, the 1938 Lincoln-Zephyr, 1941 Ford, and 1941 Chevy, and a single run of 1951 Canadian Monarch models, all D.C. models have been light commercial van or pickup truck models. And several variations of the '41 Chevy have been police cars. Commercial vehicles are a minuscule part of the market compared to the demand for sports and racing cars, or even the classics.

Price has been a third factor. From the beginning, Durham's models have cost 60%

to 80% more than a comparable Brooklin. Part of this cost reflects the cost of research and production of the master model. Durham's masters are crafted by some of the best artisans in the business. Durham's colors and graphics have always been carefully researched and 100% accurate, and the finish itself is always superb—noticeably better in most cases than that of their competitors.

Another influence on Durham model prices is the production quantity; where Western makes a couple thousand of each model, and Brooklin some 3,000 to 4,000, Durham typically makes only a few hundred of each standard version. Limited numbers and high quality simply mean higher costs.

Determining the collector value of a Durham model is difficult at this point. Each of those 21 standard models is still in production, though Durham, like some continental companies, makes only a small batch at a time. When those are sold out, another batch will be made.

Besides normal small variations between batches, the models have improved with time and technology. While one of the very first batch of 25 Airflows should be worth $500 or more, the Indy Stewards model currently sells for less than $100.

The Durham models to look for right now are those club and show promotional models. By my count there are at least 88 different versions of those basic 21 models. A collector could establish several Durham themes, such as models made for the Toronto Toy Show ('39 Ford panel van, 1987; '53 Ford pickup, '88; '38 Lincoln Zephyr, '89; '53 Ford utility truck, '90; '41 Chevy "Fire Chief" coupe, '91; '41 Chevy convertible, '92; '41 Chevy panel delivery, '93; '54 Ford courier, '94; '41 Chevy ambulance, '95; '41 Chevy Suburban railcar, '96). I'd expect to

pay upwards of $200 each for these models. Probably the most desirable promotional is the unique '39 Ford "Toronto Telegram" model with signboards announcing Durham's first-place stand at the 1994 Modelex exhibition in England.

If The Durham Collector is successful, we can expect the club to develop an accurate database on Durham's models and their values. As more and more people become aware of these beautifully finished little gems, those values can only go up.

The two known types of Vermont Automobile Register, the top one a dealer plate.

# THE ROAD LESS TRAVELED

## Non-Passenger Issues Are Heating Up

### DAVE LINCOLN

Although to most folks an expired license plate has value comparable to yesterday's newspaper, some thrifty individuals have always recognized in these bits of colored metal scrap, at very least, material to patch the roof or seal a rodent hole—and at best a memento or a decoration for an outbuilding. Thus enough plates survived over decades of negligence and willful destruction to make the field quite interesting to today's collectors of automotive and cultural artifacts.

Thus for reasons of economy (of space, of finances) perhaps more than any other, there became established in the patterns and activities of these first collectors a heavy focus on passenger-plate issues to the exclusion of other types. Most folks of the era did not ride motorcycles, drive pickups or other commercial vehicles, or work at a dealership—so they found passenger issues more appealing. Odd types, especially the smaller-size ones, were collected sporadically, but more often rejected, traded, or given away for a pittance.

Today that attitude is changing rapidly, and it's not hard to understand why: It's much too crowded and expensive to travel the well-established highways of collecting. But don't wait too long, because a paradigm shift is taking place within the hobby. Newer collectors have no incentive to abide by the old prejudices.

So, you can always abandon the "auto" trip and adopt a motorcycle, or 4-wheel-drive truck. That, figuratively, is what many active collectors now are doing, turning their attention to these and other non-passenger series such as dealer, bus, farm, and so forth. These once obscure types, as well as city and local issues, now attract as much as or more interest than the more familiar passenger issues.

This trend shows no sign of abating; rather it seems that a few of the more popular non-passenger types, dealers and cycles in particular, will soon easily eclipse their passenger counterparts—if indeed they have not already. These are the plates to watch out for when hiking your favorite flea market or bidding on that peach basket of sheetmetal at the local country auction.

A perfect example comes from MOBILIA's home state of Vermont. The first plate issued in this state, the 1905/06 "Vermont Automobile Register" porcelain, or "VAR," is quite scarce. Somewhere around a thousand were produced, in passenger format, numbered sequentially, and dealer, with an "0" prefix. Approximately 50 are known today, only two of these in the dealer format. This plate is the "stopper" for collectors endeavoring to complete "runs" from first year to present of all the New England states. For a long time the dealer plate No. 010 pictured here waited patiently in one of these collections, available to anyone who would offer an equal-condition passenger example in exchange, so the owner could consider his set properly complete. Finally, someone was able to make the swap, becoming the new, proud owner of one of the very, very few surviving porcelain plates from these six northernmost states. It's rated scarcity-level "E" (for Elusive, six or fewer known). Go figure. Better yet, go find the ones still missing!

# TOP TRUCKS

Lesney Toys of England produced this "heavy breakdown/wreck" truck as part of their Matchbox King Size collection, a line of trucks which serious collectors are now giving a closer look.

## Matchbox Rigs Shift into High Gear

**MARK H. MACREADING**

As we enter 1997, toy truck collectors are drowning in a sea of diecast trucks of all sizes, shapes, and colors. Some of the new models are now as costly as the early pieces, which is causing a lot of concern and confusion within collector circles.

You can break toy trucks down into three categories: real toys (designed for children); adult replicas (by First Gear, etc.); and promotional trucks (produced to advertise a company or product). To make it more complicated, promotional trucks may be designed either as children's playthings or as adult collectibles.

My pick of an emerging truck for collectors in 1997 fits the real toy truck category. For many of us, collecting the real toy trucks has become cost prohibitive. At a recent show I was looking at trucks I know many collectors would love to own but just can't afford: Arcade AC Macks in the $4,500 neighborhood; Fifties Tonkas around $500; and early Dinkys, Hubleys, etc. at similar prices. So what's left in nice old trucks that are still affordable and still not completely impossible to find? How about the Sixties Matchbox King Size series?

The Matchbox King Size series, produced by Lesney Toys of England, were introduced in 1960. The name King Size echoed the marketing of the then-popular king-size cigarettes. Lesney introduced the line as a high-end complement to their miniature 1/75-scale line. The move was probably an attempt to break into what was referred to as the "standard scale" used by Dinky and Corgi Toys.

At the time, the King Size line was not particularly successful. People who collected that scale were very loyal to the other brands. During the Eighties, most of these models could be found at toy shows for very reasonable prices and still did not sell very well. Now serious collectors are taking a closer took at the old King Size line, and realizing that this was actually a desirable line of trucks, with some unique and detailed castings.

Although the line was produced from 1960-88, the pre-1970 models make the most desirable collectibles. After 1969 Lesney renamed the line Super Kings, the wheels were changed to the Super Fast style, and the trucks became less realistic. The Seventies saw a dramatic change in the market, with companies producing unrealistic cars and trucks in bright colors in an attempt to create more "kid appeal" in their toys.

The series consists mainly of commercial vehicles, although a few cars were introduced into the line in 1968—a Mercury Cougar, a Dodge Charger, a Mercury police car, and a Lamborghini Miura. The Dodge Charger seems to be the hardest to find of the cars.

With the increasing popularity of these models at toy shows, it is just a matter of time before the whole line comes into its own. The good thing is that with a little work and searching, you can still find all the models in this line. Many of them are now passing the $50 mark, although you can still find many mint models at various shows for under $50. This is a bargain if you consider what Dinky Toys of the same era are selling for. Prices will increase on many of these pieces, so it is not a bad time to get into them. The most expensive piece you will find in the line is the K8 Prime Mover, consisting of a truck, trailer, and a Caterpillar tractor. You will probably pay from $150-200 for a mint, boxed model.

Depending on how deeply you get into model variations, you can put together a fairly complete Matchbox King Size collection with some 40 or 50 models. And they make up many a beautiful commercial vehicle display. If I hear any interest in this line of trucks from MOBILIA readers, I will explore them more for my monthly column.

By the way, for folks interested in the "adult collectibles" category, I recommend the Hartoy PEM line. These are beautiful 1/64-scale replicas, and you can still find most of the trucks Hartoy has produced—and at a decent price. Since it's a relatively new line, not all that many different trucks have been produced. Price range: $35-48 for the standard models. The two gold Coca-Cola models can be found for $85-100. Some early models may sell for as much as $65.

---

## VALUES

- Mint, boxed models cost around $50, but can be found cheaper at some shows.
- Early construction models may bring up to $100, and the Prime Mover will bring $150-200.
- Make sure the treads on the Caterpillar models are not dry-rotted.

## TIPS & SOURCES

**Matchbox King Size Reading**
- *Collecting Matchbox Diecast Toys—The First Forty Years* by Kevin McGimpsey and Stewart Orr. A beautiful book that is a must for any serious Matchbox collector.
- *Matchbox USA*, c/o Charles Mack, 62 Saw Mill Rd., Durham, CT 06422. Offers a monthly newsletter on the Matchbox hobby, with classified ads.

# FANTASTIC PLASTIC

## Model Kit Lovers— Go Small in '97

**TOM FUNK**

If you want to catch the next wave in plastic model kit collecting, buy these neglected classics—1962 Aurora hot rod kits, in 1/32 scale.

Collector enthusiasm for plastic model kits—particularly for popular models made in the late Fifties, the Sixties, and Seventies—has risen dramatically. As those who grew up in the era seek to relive their fond memories of buying and assembling their favorite street rods, fantasy rods, funny cars, and muscle cars, prices of those old kits have ballooned to serious money—in some cases hundreds of dollars apiece. Not bad for items that, when new, typically retailed for about $1.49 or so!

The days of finding them at a bargain-basement price are over—and mint-in-box examples in top-notch condition are harder and harder to come by. But the kits that most baby boomers have bid up so strongly are—almost exclusively—modeled in 1/24 scale, the perennial scale of choice for model builders.

In short, if you're seeking to find model kits that the rest of the world hasn't already discovered, you'll have to think small. No less an authority than Mike Goyda, of Car Crazy, advises us that the fervor for 1/24-scale kits leaves collectors with a super opportunity to inexpensively acquire the 1/32-scale kits that nostalgic model builders have overlooked. These kits were never as popular with hobbyists, because their smaller size meant fewer and less intricate details.

But when it comes to the current-day collector market, nobody cares about building the models—the idea is obtaining a great and memorable kit, in a colorful original box, for purposes of display.

"People are buying kits for the graphics—the box art," says Goyda. "Absolutely." And that's where Mike's Top 10 pick comes in. His favorite early-Sixties 1/32-scale hot rod kits by Aurora have everything a collector could ask for: wild cars, gorgeous box art (guaranteed to whisk you back to the days of poodle skirts and letter sweaters), and affordable price tags.

For specific Aurora models, Goyda names three 1962 gems: the T for Two (a rodded 1921 Ford high coupe), the Sad Sack (a 1927 Model T Ford), and the Wolf Wagon (a 1928 Ford pickup). The box art is simply great: a pair of lovers sharing their romantic "Blueberry Hill" lookout with the T for Two; young rodders packing their belongings for college; coeds flocking to the proud male occupants of the Wolf Wagon. It's hard to believe such eminently displayable blasts from the past are still undiscovered by the automobilia rank and file.

Goyda says, "1/32-scale kits have always cost collectors less money." But don't expect the disparity to last forever. "Prices are now just starting to go up, due to increased demand. There's no question that there's more and more interest in these kits," he says—particularly among hot rod enthusiasts who grew up anytime between the mid-Fifties and the late Sixties. "And that kind of interest always drive the prices up."

For now, though, collectors can find these Aurora kits all over the place. You might pay $20 for a nice, complete kit in a less-than-mint box. Some $50 buys you a pristine mint-in-box example. Traditionally in the vintage model kit hobby, built-up models without the box are worth little or nothing.

Where to find such kits? Goyda says the burgeoning interest in old kits of all kinds has resulted in their appearance almost anywhere collectibles are sold—including general flea markets and, of course, special-interest swap meets. Knowledgeable dealers like Goyda himself are excellent sources, as are classified ads in *MOBILIA* or modeling publications.

---

### VALUES

| Condition | Expect to Pay |
|---|---|
| • Mint in box | $50 |
| • Complete kit, with a less-than-mint box | $20 |
| • Built-up model, no box | Nil |

### TIPS & SOURCES

- **Car Crazy**, P.O. Box 192, East Petersburg, PA 17520; TEL 717-569-7149
- **The Model Shop**, P.O. Box 68, Onalaska, WI 54650; TEL 608-781-1864
- **Ghoulie Motors**, 288 Portland St., Rochester, NH 03867; TEL 603-335-0555; FAX 603-335-8683

- *Model Car Journal*, P.O. Box 154135, Irving, TX 75015-4135
- *Scale Auto Enthusiast*, Highland Productions, P.O. Box 10167, Milwaukee, WI 53210; TEL 414-783-7723; FAX 414-783-7710

# AWESOME OFFY!

**OFFENHAUSER**

THE LEGENDARY RACING ENGINE AND THE MEN WHO BUILT IT
GORDON ELIOT WHITE

*In light of the past and present popularity of Indy cars, their drivers, and the Indy 500 race itself, this book is a surefire winner.*

## The Best Addition to Your Motorsport Library

**NORM MORT**

What's the best automotive book to get your hands on? Selecting the top automotive book, hot off the press or recently published, is no easy task. We've been fortunate to see many new important titles published in the past year—most of them appearing in the Reviews pages of *MOBILIA.* Some were limited editions and priced accordingly, such as *The French Sports Car Revolution* by Anthony Blight, or *Vauxhall 30-98* by Portway. Others such as *Cord 810/812—A Timeless Classic* by Josh Malks were destined for a niche market. The latest award-winning edition of *Mercedes-Benz Quicksilver Century* by Karl Ludvigsen, or *Sebring* by Ken Breslauer, are must buys for the racing enthusiast.

But for my money, the best addition to the enthusiast's library is the new title *Offenhauser,* by Gordon Eliot White (Motorbooks International, 10 x 10 in. hardcover, 192 pp., 200 illus.). When you consider the past and present popularity of Indy cars, their drivers, and the Indy 500 race itself, you begin to appreciate the widespread appeal of this book. The writing and production is of top quality, and I feel the book is an incredible value at its $39.95 price. All these factors will ensure an enthusiastic response. And let us not forget the fact that the Offenhauser story has been long awaited by both Miller and Midget racing fans.

For these reasons this edition should be a bookshelf winner, and 20 years from now, long out of print, it should stand as an important work much in demand by the next generation of automobile enthusiasts.

Before the move to rear engines, Ford power, and the British invasion, the all-American Offenhauser engines were the power plants of champions in oval-track,

sprint-car, and Pikes Peak racing. Every Memorial Day, the American twin-cam, four-cylinder engine with the German-sounding name—and odd "Offy" nickname—was as familiar as cornflakes around the breakfast table.

Author Gordon Eliot White—a racing enthusiast all his life—was twice nominated for a Pulitzer Prize for his political reporting. He is now retired from newspaper journalism and acts as auto racing adviser to the Smithsonian Institution no less. His understanding of racing is much more profound than might first be imagined; he is also the owner-driver of the international record-holding Tassi Vatis Offy.

As noted in the preface, "Any Offy-powered car was like the New York Yankees of the time: unbeatable." White picks up the story of the Miller-Offenhauser metamorphosis touched on by Borgeson and Dees in their excellent Miller volumes. He covers the engine's evolution and development, and its entire racing history through to the "Final Defeat" in 1989.

The final pages include comprehensive specifications: a full engine production listing (including number, date sold, purchaser, cubic inch capacity, and remarks); an Offy racing record on AAA & USAC Championship cars 1935-78; engine specs from 1926-79; a list of employees from 1913-75. Also provided is an extensive bibliography and index for research and reference. Liberally sprinkled throughout the text are crisp,

action-packed black-and-white photographs. Many have never been published before, or haven't been seen since the Thirties.

Wherever possible, White researched firsthand accounts, and cross-referenced them with published accounts and record books. Unfortunately, he found most of the principal personalities are no longer with us.

With Offenhauser's glorious and extensive racing record, it would have been very easy to produce a superficial photo history, but this is a written account, and an important work. White has carefully blended history, technical details, enlightening sidebars, and personality profiles to document America's most popular and dominant racing engine. A thoroughly enjoyable read!

## VALUE

**$39.95 at retail**

## TIPS & SOURCES

**Available in general bookstores, from vendors of used and new automotive books, and direct from the publisher, Motorbooks International (P.O. Box 1, 729 Prospect Ave., Osceola, WI 54020; TEL 800-826-6600).**

# VINTAGE MINIATURE GAS-POWERED RACE CARS

## FREE APPRAISALS –
## PURCHASE OR TRADE

We provide free appraisals of cars, total collections, or prospective purchases – avoid the fakes, repros, or assembled bits and pieces.

The J&E Spindizzie Collection will also acquire important collections, unrestored prewar models, rare cars, and memorabilia such as literature, trophies, or photos.

Since we are not dealers and do not buy for resale, we can offer the highest prices for the highest quality, or offer rare models in trade.

### J&E Spindizzie Collection
17337 Aspenglowe Lane
Yorba Linda, CA 92686
TEL. (714) 993-5482; FAX (714) 572-8696

Continued from p. 64

## US Toy Collector Magazine

See our main listing under "Toys, Truck"

## Vintage America

See our main listing under "Restoration Service"

## Bill Walls

682 Ridgeview Lane
Columbus, IN 47201 USA
TEL: 812-342-2504

Special interest in buying pedal cars built before 1950. Also collect early police toys & vehicles. Available for appraisal, general information, & a limited number of high-quality restorations of pedal cars. Also interested in unique tricycles, wagons, & early automotive toys. I like almost anything with wheels. Call evenings.

*Other categories: Toys, Truck; Toys, General; Restoration Service*

## Wee Wheels Restoration

Richard Klein
1426 E. Commercial
Algona, IA 50511 USA
TEL: 515-295-2159
FAX: 515-295-2159

Restoration of pedal cars, gas cars, & metal toys.

*Other categories: Gas-Powered Racers; Slot Cars*

## Keith Wendt

See our main listing under "Toys, General"

## Western Industrial

See our main listing under "Toys, Tractor"

## Wheel Goods Trader Magazine

John Rastall
PO Box 435
Fraser, MI 48026 USA
TEL: 810-949-6282
FAX: 810-949-6282

Great pedal car information in *The Wheel Goods Trader*. Articles, auction & show reports, buy, sell, trade, classifieds. Subscribe today. $20 USA, $40 foreign (US funds). Send check or money order.

*Other categories: Publications, Current; Club/Organization; Toys, General*

## Wheels Art & Memorabilia

See our main listing under "Art, Original"

# PERSONALITIES

## Back Issue Car Magazines

See our main listing under "Literature"

## Early Racing Classics

See our main listing under "Models, Precision"

## Ron Johnson

See our main listing under "General Interest"

## Richard's

Richard Gerow
Box 895
Liberty, NY 12754 USA
TEL: 914-292-3967

Formula 1 autographed posters, photos, & display presentations. Jim Clark, Jochen Rindt, Schumacher, Damon & Graham, etc. Fully autographed "Legends of Motorsport" only $400. Send for current list. No calls, please.

*Other categories: Art, Prints & Posters; Racing Artifacts*

# PETROLIANA, PUMPS & GLOBES

## Alex & Phil's Filling Station

See our main listing under "Petroliana, Other"

## Auto Air & Audio

See our main listing under "Mixed Automobilia"

## Benkin Pump Co.

Ben Staub
14 E Main St.
Tipp City, OH 45414 USA
TEL: 513-667-5975

New visible style gas pumps from 1920s. Available in 8 ft or 10 ft tall. All aluminum construction. Available in kit form or completely finished.

## Dennis Brilla

See our main listing under "Mixed Automobilia"

## The Can Man

See our main listing under "Petroliana, Other"

## Peter Capell

See our main listing under "Petroliana, Other"

## Check the Oil! Magazine

See our main listing under "Petroliana, Other"

## Chuck's Collectibles

See our main listing under "Restoration Service"

## Clapper Restorations

Chad Clapper
22219 Indigo Ave
Clear Lake, IA 50428 USA
TEL: 515-423-3108

Collector of all types of gas pumps, globes, signs, pedal cars, pop machines, oil containers, & maps. Also offering high-quality restorations & a full line of gas pump restoration parts, all of which are reasonably priced. I am a low-budget connection, for the low-budget collector.

*Other categories: Restoration Service; Signs; Pedal Cars*

## Collectors Auction Services

See our main listing under "Auction Firm"

## Doney Enterprises

See our main listing under "Mixed Automobilia"

## Dooley & Sons

See our main listing under "Signs"

## East Coast Classics

Laurin Cooper
1905 Gillespie St.
Fayetteville, NC 28306 USA
TEL: 910-483-3854

Gas pump sales - parts - restaurant-quality restorations. Display cabinet & TV/radio pump conversions. Oil racks, cans, signs, stop lights, parking meters, advertising items, general store items. Pedal cars, tractors, drink boxes, toys, games. We will custom-build to your specs. Buy - sell - trade - restorations.

*Other categories: Restoration Service; Pedal Cars; Petroliana, Other*

## Frontier Group

See our main listing under "Petroliana, Other"

## Full Serve

Bradley A. Grabow
5128 Spring Rd.
Verona, NY 13478 USA
TEL: 315-363-0932

Gas pumps from 1930s to 60s for sale. Restored & original condition. Also have porcelain signs, air meters, & misc. items for older service stations. Write or call for list. Call after 6pm; Exit 33 on NYS Thruway.

*Other categories: Petroliana, Other; Signs; Restoration Service*

## Gulf Oil Collector

See our main listing under "Petroliana, Other"

## Hayes Associates

Patrick M. Hayes
97 Main Street
Monson, MA 01057-1320 USA
TEL: 413-267-9651
FAX: 413-267-4380

Restoration parts & supplies for gas pumps & air pumps. Globes, new pump faces, decals, signs, hoses, gasket, fry parts. Distributor for genuine ECO parts. Sconces (wall brackets), books on gas station memorabilia, clocks, table lamps, mini & 38-inch gas pumps, magnets. Catalog available for $3 (refundable with first order).

*Other categories: Petroliana, Other; Specialized Automobilia; Mixed Automobilia*

## Iowa Gas Swap Meet & Auctions

See our main listing under "Petroliana, Other"

## Jim Jalosky

14783 Shirley
Warren, MI 48089 USA
TEL: 810-774-7236

Specialize in display gas pumps, Islander cabinets, oil cabinets, & display racks. Buying, unrestored preferred. Also collect general petroliana.

*Other categories: Petroliana, Other; Signs*

## Junkyard Dog

See our main listing under "Petroliana, Other"

## Brad Kellogg

See our main listing under "Pedal Cars"

## Key Telephone Co.

See our main listing under "Signs"

## Kirk's Ghetto Garage

See our main listing under "Mixed Automobilia"

## John Mancino's Garage

See our main listing under "Petroliana, Other"

## Bob McClernan

See our main listing under "Petroliana, Other"

## Mid-State Collectibles

See our main listing under "Petroliana, Other"

## Mobil Maniacs

See our main listing under "Petroliana, Other"

## Mobilia South Africa

See our main listing under "Petroliana, Other"

## Paul Mote

See our main listing under "Petroliana, Other"

## Motoring Memories

See our main listing under "License Plates, Tags, etc."

## National Automotive & Truck Model & Toy Museum of the United States

See our main listing under "Museum"

## National Automotive & Truck Museum of the United States (NATMUS)

See our main listing under "Museum"

## The Oil Barron

See our main listing under "Art, Prints & Posters"

## Oil Company Collectibles

Scott Benjamin
411 Forest St.
LaGrange, OH 44050 USA
TEL: 216-355-6608
FAX: 216-355-4955

Gasoline globes – buy, sell, trade. Originals only. Collector buying any brands, singles or collections. Call us about *Petroleum Collectibles Monthly* – the magazine for the petroleum collectibles hobby. Visa, MC, AmEx welcome.

## Oniell's Collectibles

See our main listing under "Petroliana, Other"

## Park Drive Garage

See our main listing under "Petroliana, Other"

## Past Gas

See our main listing under "Restoration Service"

## Rick Pease

See our main listing under "Petroliana, Other" [1]

## Perma Coatings

See our main listing under "Restoration Service"

## Petrolitis

See our main listing under "Petroliana, Other"

## Prime Pumps

Leonard Mort
11 Juniper Drive
Millbury, MA 01527 USA
TEL: 508-865-3507

Vintage gasoline pump museum-quality restorations, for the most discriminating of customers, gas pumps, lubesters, Coke machines, barber chairs, porcelain signs. Gasoline collectibles. Buy, sell, trade. See us at Fall Hershey Green Field 215-217 & Mass Gas.

*Other categories: Restoration Service; Petroliana, Other; Specialized Automobilia*

## Pumping Iron

See our main listing under "Petroliana, Other"

## Purveyor of Petroleum Paraphernalia

Tom King
432 45th St.
West Palm Beach, FL 33407 USA
TEL: 561-842-8983

Specialize in gas pumps – buy, sell, trade.

*Other categories: Petroliana, Other; Restoration Service; Mixed Automobilia*

## R & D Unique

See our main listing under "Models, Kits"

## Ron's Relics

See our main listing under "Pedal Cars"

## Thomas Rootlieb

815 S. Soderquist Rd.
Turlock, CA 95380 USA
TEL: 209-632-2203
FAX: 209-632-2201

Collector seeking West Coast globes, 15 in. only. Will pay for quality & rarity. Will buy collections. All transactions kept in strict confidence. Also buying cigarette lighters with raised logos. Interested in quality signs. Trading & selling duplicates of above. Always at Turlock, Portland, Chickasha, Pate, NSRA Nats, & fall Hershey.

*Other category: Signs*

## Ed Schwartz

See our main listing under "Petroliana, Other"

## Al Simonenko

See our main listing under "Signs"

## Dennis C. Stauffer

See our main listing under "Petroliana, Other"

## Steve's Antiques

See our main listing under "Signs"

## Steve's Service Station Stuff

See our main listing under "Petroliana, Other"

## Time Passages, Ltd.

Scott & Debbie Anderson
PO Box 65596
West Des Moines, IA 50265 USA
TEL: 800-383-8888
FAX: 515-223-5149

Mail order suppliers of restored & unrestored vintage gasoline pumps, replacement parts, restoration supplies, including oil company globes, decals, signs, literature, hoses, nozzles, ID tags, novelty gifts, & more! Design/decor consultants for trade shows, showrooms, restaurants, movie sets, etc. We ship overseas. Wholesale dealers welcome. Mail order catalog $4.

*Other categories: Petroliana, Other; Signs; Showroom Items*

## Toys & Cars

See our main listing under "Petroliana, Other"

## Mike Tyler

See our main listing under "Petroliana, Other"

## Unocal 76 Products

See our main listing under "Petroliana, Other"

## Valenti Classics, Inc.

See our main listing under "Restoration Service"

## Robert Van Gilder

See our main listing under "Petroliana, Other"

## Vic's Place

See our main listing under "Petroliana, Other"

## Vintage America

See our main listing under "Restoration Service"

## Weber's Nostalgia Supermarket

Tim & Marsha
6611 Anglin Dr.
Fort Worth, TX 76119 USA
TEL: 817-534-6611
FAX: 817-534-3316
Email: webers@flash.net

Leader of gas pump restoration supplies. Items in stock, ready to ship worldwide. Globes, decals, hoses, nozzles, signs, rubber, glass, cylinders, parts, parts, more parts. Nostalgia photos, gift items, Coke items. Charge card orders: 800-433-PUMP. Satisfaction guaranteed! Full-color catalog – FREE with order, or $4, refundable.

*Other categories: Mixed Automobilia; Signs; Retail Store*

## Clifford Weese

See our main listing under "License Plates, Tags, etc."

## Greg Wheeler

See our main listing under "Petroliana, Other"

## Walt Wimer, Jr.

See our main listing under "Petroliana, Other"

## Wright's Custom Repair, Inc.

Barry L. Wright
504 N. 20th St.
Billings, MT 59101 USA
TEL: 406-252-4220

Vintage gas pump restoration & sales. I install TVs, VCRs, mailboxes, book cases, etc. in electric pumps. Also original restorations. We also offer a sandblasting service & painting. Buying & selling of restored & unrestored vintage pumps. Also collect Mobil & maps.

*Other categories: Petroliana, Other; Restoration Service; Showroom Items*

## Wyoming Vintage Tin

See our main listing under "Appraisal Service"

# PETROLIANA, OTHER

## Ablaze Enterprises Inc.
See our main listing under "Mixed Automobilia"

## Adams Flea Market
See our main listing under "Mixed Automobilia"

## S. Adams Inc.
See our main listing under "Specialized Automobilia"

## Alex & Phil's Filling Station
Richard S. Bio
6 Stella Drive
North Providence, RI 02911 USA
TEL: 401-231-8918

All kinds of gas station collectibles: Texaco, Shell, Mobil, Cities Service, oil cans, bottles, maps, pens, key chains, toy tankers, literature. Inventory always changing, call ahead for wants. Send SASE for complete listing of items for sale.

*Other categories: Petroliana, Pumps & Globes; Mixed Automobilia; Specialized Automobilia*

## Allen Oil Sales
Michael Allen
1100 W. Locust St.
York, PA 17404 USA
TEL: 717-843-9957
FAX: 717-843-9959

Specialize in Kendall Motor Oil collectibles. Visit my Kendall Museum when you're in the area. By appointment only. Also buy, sell, & trade all brands of gas & oil collectibles, advertising signs, globes, & other related items. Mail order, or spring & fall Carlisle. Call 9-5 M-F.

*Other categories: Museum; Signs; Mixed Automobilia*

## American Automobile Sales Literature of Lancaster, PA
Douglas R. Eyman
2707 Kimberly Rd.
Lancaster, PA 17603 USA
TEL: 717-397-2597
FAX: 717-397-2597
Email: dbnmops@aol.com

Specialize in 4-oz. cans & bottles: Handy Oil, lighter fluid, etc. Trade, buy. Send your list/photos. Also collect American Automobile sales literature. Buy, trade prewar. Also collect factory-issued automobile postcards in complete sets. Need mid-70s & earlier. Also collect hood ornaments, mid-60s & newer. Want unusual.

*Other categories: Literature; Mascots/Badges/Emblems; Cards, Postal*

## Antique & Vintage Motorcycle
See our main listing under "Motorcycle Collectibles"

## Art's Automobilia
See our main listing under "Toys, General"

## Auto Air & Audio
See our main listing under "Mixed Automobilia"

## Automobilia
See our main listing under "Retail Store"

## Automobilia & Collectibles
See our main listing under "Mixed Automobilia"

## Automotive Magazines
See our main listing under "Literature"

## Autopia Advertising Auctions
See our main listing under "Auction Firm"

## Bob Baker
See our main listing under "Toys, Truck"

## Bare Necessities
See our main listing under "General Interest"

## Barkin' Frog Collectible Co.
See our main listing under "Toys, General"

## Bart Cars
See our main listing under "Promos"

## Bergen Distributors
Steve Butler
PO Box 222
Franklin Lakes, NJ 07417 USA

Have NOS gas & oil items, 1000s of uniform patches, tin & comp. oil cans, station premiums, ephemera, & more. Send brand(s) desired with LSASE. No repros. Looking for license plate bolt-ons, one-lb. grease cans, pump signs, etc.

*Other categories: Specialized Automobilia; Mixed Automobilia; General Interest*

## Big T's Gas Trash
Terry Thacker
Box 81
Gladstone, IL 61437 USA
TEL: 309-627-2434

Buy, sell, trade gas & oil-related cans, signs, additive cans, bottles, anything gas station or auto-related. Also toy race cars & gas trucks. A true collector. Please no repro stuff, only originals. Will purchase entire collections if possible or extras.

*Other categories: Mixed Automobilia; Signs; Toys, General*

## Blast from the Past, Inc.
See our main listing under "Retail Store"

## Bowers Collectable Toys
See our main listing under "Mixed Automobilia"

## C & C Creations
See our main listing under "Mixed Automobilia"

## The Can Man
Barry Baker
1942 N. Lincoln Ave., 3-R
Chicago, IL 60614 USA
TEL: 312-280-7905
FAX: 312-337-3185

Collector & dealer specializing in rare or unusual motor oil cans. Quart, gallon, & half-gallon sizes with good graphics or picture. Also want all small gas/oil items: banks, blotters, pinbacks, fobs, badges, maps, postcards, signs, globes, handy oilers. Appraisals – show me your can!

*Other categories: Petroliana, Pumps & Globes; Specialized Automobilia*

## Canada's All Canadian Service Station Museum

See our main listing under "Museum"

## Peter Capell

1838 W. Grace St.
Chicago, IL 60613-2724 USA
TEL: 773-871-8735

Independent branded gasoline/service station items wanted: gas pumps, salt & pepper sets, plastic pole sign thermometers, gas pump & mini oil can banks & other memorabilia. Collector of gas pump globes, early (1920s-50s) maps from independent oil companies. Trade or sell duplicates only. Help wanted! Call evenings.

*Other category: Petroliana, Pumps & Globes*

## Check the Oil! Magazine

Jerry Keyser
PO Box 937m
Powell, OH 43065-0937 USA
TEL: 614-848-5038
FAX: 614-436-4760

Not just another newsletter, *Check the Oil!* is a high-quality color magazine dedicated exclusively to petroliana. Now in our 15th year, we pioneered free ads for subscribers. Find out what 4,000 collectors already know. A subscription is $20/year in USA or $4 for sample. Bankcard orders toll-free 1-800-2CTOMAG.

*Other categories: Petroliana, Pumps & Globes; Specialized Automobilia; General Interest*

## Clark's Historic Rt. 99 General Store

See our main listing under "Mixed Automobilia"

## Classic Transportation

See our main listing under "Pedal Cars"

## Collector Auto Appraisal Co.

See our main listing under "Appraisal Service"

## Collectors Auction Services

See our main listing under "Auction Firm"

## Crazy Irishman Collectibles

See our main listing under "Mixed Automobilia"

## Crown Premiums

See our main listing under "Manufacturer"

## D & K Collectables

Don/Kathie Irvin
11270 Markab Dr.
San Diego, CA 92126 USA
TEL: 619-280-0527
FAX: 619-566-1178

Buy, sell, trade gasoline, automobilia, hot rod memorabilia. Let's trade lists.

*Other categories: Hot Rod Memorabilia; Mixed Automobilia*

## Dan's Classic Auto Parts

See our main listing under "Mixed Automobilia"

## Dave's Signs & Collectibles

Dave Nicoll
17 McLean Blvd. Box 29
Maitland, Ontario KOE 1PO Canada
TEL: 613-348-3252
FAX: 613-345-7192

Buy, sell, trade gas pumps, air meters, or anything petro-related. Signs, cans, bottles. Also collect & have for sale antique radios, advertising signs for sale or trade.

*Other categories: Signs; Mixed Automobilia; Mascots/Badges/Emblems*

## Davison Street Garage

See our main listing under "General Interest"

## Don's Body Shop

See our main listing under "Appraisal Service"

## Dunbar's Gallery

See our main listing under "Motorcycle Collectibles"

## East Coast Classics

See our main listing under "Petroliana, Pumps & Globes"

## Enterprise Cars

See our main listing under "Signs"

## Frank's Toys & Adv. Memorabilia

See our main listing under "Mixed Automobilia"

## Frontier Group

James Hollabaugh
PO Box 460, 3800 Congress Pky
Richfield, OH 44286 USA
TEL: 216-659-3888
FAX: 216-659-9410

Wanted to buy Shell & Frontier petroliana, toys, globes, cans, promotion items, Shell pocket watches. I will buy all or part of your gas station collectibles of any brand. I specialize in Frontier & Shell.

*Other categories: Petroliana, Pumps & Globes; Toys, Truck; Mixed Automobilia*

## Full Serve

See our main listing under "Petroliana, Pumps & Globes"

## Paul Furlinger

PO Box 12971
Mill Creek, WA 98082 USA
TEL: 206-486-8724

Auto, gas, oil, & soda pop advertising wanted. Signs, clocks, thermometers, hats, clothing, badges, & other smalls wanted.

*Other categories: Signs; Mixed Automobilia; Diner Memorabilia*

## Bob Gajewski

See our main listing under "Mixed Automobilia"

## Gasoline Alley

See our main listing under "Motorcycle Collectibles"

## Genuine Collectibles

See our main listing under "Toys, Truck"

## Bob Gerrity

See our main listing under "Restoration Service"

## David L. Gray

See our main listing under "Mixed Automobilia"

## Gulf Oil Collector

Buzz Houston
Box 848
Oxford, KS 67119 USA
TEL: 316-455-2579

Specialize in Gulf Oil. Buy, sell, trade. Also deal in other related gas & oil items. Attend most Midwest events. Would appreciate hearing from all collectors.

*Other categories: Petroliana, Pumps & Globes; Signs; Shows & Events*

## Robert N. Haldeman

See our main listing under "General Interest"

## Hayes Associates

See our main listing under "Petroliana, Pumps & Globes"

## Todd P. Helms

1023 E. 5th Ave.
Lancaster, PA 43130 USA
TEL: 614-681-6151
FAX: 614-681-6076
Email: thelms@greenapple.com

Author of *The Conoco Collector's Bible & Roadside Memories: A Collection of Vintage Gas Station Photos*. Also collector of Conoco & Marland-related memorabilia. Usually have some duplicates for sale. Email or send SASE for updated list.

*Other category: Books*

## Ralph A. Herbst

See our main listing under "License Plates, Tags, etc."

## Hi-Tec Customs

See our main listing under "Restoration Service"

## Hot Rod Art

See our main listing under "Art, Prints & Posters"

## Iowa Gas Swap Meet & Auctions

John Logsdon
2417 Linda Dr.
Urbandale, IA 50322 USA
TEL: 515-251-8811
FAX: 515-242-7358

Held every August, Iowa Gas is the nation's largest oil, gas, & auto-related advertising swap meet & auction. Expect to find signs, globes, cans, pins, paper, etc. The 11th annual event occurs on Aug. 7, 8, 9, 1997. Swap meet on Thursday & Friday. Auctions Friday evening & Saturday. Call after 5pm.

*Other categories: Petroliana, Pumps & Globes; Signs; Mixed Automobilia*

## S.L. Jaffe, Inc.

See our main listing under "Appraisal Service"

## Jim Jalosky

See our main listing under "Petroliana, Pumps & Globes"

## Junkyard Dog

Daniel Sell
1030 N 20th St.
Lafayette, IN 47904 USA
TEL: 317-447-3088

Restored gas pumps 1940s, 50s, & 60s. Other miscellaneous oil & gas items. Also Hot Wheels, Ertl trucks, & other diecast toys. Sinclair items wanted.

*Other categories: Petroliana, Pumps & Globes; Models, Precision; Hot Wheels*

## K & K Old Time Toy Store

See our main listing under "Toys, General"

## Brad Kellogg

See our main listing under "Pedal Cars"

## Key Telephone Co.

See our main listing under "Signs"

## Lights Up

See our main listing under "Specialized Automobilia"

## John Mancino's Garage

John Mancino
135-141 Edison St.
Syracuse, NY 13204 USA
TEL: 315-425-0299
FAX: 315-425-0951
Email: jmancino@aol.com

Always buying, selling, trading cans, pumps, globes, signs. What do you have? What do you need? M-F 7:30-5:30 EST.

*Other categories: Petroliana, Pumps & Globes; Mixed Automobilia; Signs*

## Ron & Carol Martinelli

229 Budlong Dr.
Cranston, RI 02920 USA
TEL: 401-946-4223

Buying & selling quality gas & oil company related advertising items: smalls, signs, cans, pins, badges, pocket mirrors, handy oilers, lube tags, paper advertising, etc. Photos available upon request. Please call M-F after 6pm or anytime weekends.

*Other categories: Mixed Automobilia; Signs; Specialized Automobilia*

## Leo Mathieu

49 Treetop Park
Westboro, MA 01581
TEL: 508-366-6309

Investment quality advertising; high-grade porcelain, gas globes, posters, motorcycle, automobilia for sale. Buy, sell, trade.

## Bob McClernan

34 Shetland Dr.
Clementon, NJ 08021-4220 USA
TEL: 609-346-2776
FAX: 609-346-2776

Mfg. of replica gas pumps. Visibles, electrics, clockfaces, Wayne 60. Call or write for details! Buyer of petro handy oilers, pedal cars, Texaco & Hess premiums, toys, signs, handouts. Also steel, plastic, & diecast toys from the 1950s to current. We buy, sell, or trade. Mention *MOBILIA Sourcebook*!

*Other categories: Petroliana, Pumps & Globes; Specialized Automobilia; Toys, Truck*

## Mid-State Collectibles

Thomas Stratford
42 Burbank St.
Millbury, MA 01527 USA
TEL: 508-865-2044
FAX: 508-865-6668

Specialize in Oilzum products, signs, cans, clocks, etc. I have many other cans for sale or trade. Also, I have a tool for resealing one-quart oil cans. I can be found at the September Mass Gas Bash!

*Other categories: Petroliana, Pumps & Globes; Signs; Shows & Events*

## Mobil Maniacs

Randy & Cyndi Heldenbrand
TEL: 913-782-0752
FAX: 913-782-0752

Advanced collectors of Mobil. Always looking for excellent to mint items only. Pre-1950s signs, cans, globes, smalls. Emphasis on older gargoyle &

pegasus pieces. Also collect White Eagle, Socony, Magnolia, Wadhams, Gilmore items. We are the Maniacs; call us first!

*Other categories: Signs; Petroliana, Pumps & Globes; Specialized Automobilia*

## Mobil & Morgans

Charley Lloyd
213 Maple Dr.
New Holland, PA 17557 USA
TEL: 717-354-7767

Discriminating buyer & seller of Mobil petroliana (1946-1956) & Morgan automobilia. Always upgrading quality of both collections & making room for the rare & unusual. Prompt response to all inquiries.

*Other categories: Marque Specific; Art, Original; Specialized Automobilia*

## Mobilia South Africa

Victor Knowles
39 Hamilton Avenue
Hurlingham, Sandton 2196
South Africa
TEL: +27-82-6536782
FAX: +27-11-4457101
Email: mobilia@iafrica.com

Collect & restore visible, hand-operated, gas pumps – in particular French-made Satam & Carbox (now owned by Tokheim). Some eclectics, Wayne, Tokheim. Will search South Africa for any models as requested. Also old G/Motors brochures, vehicle workshop manuals & spares catalogs. Cape Dutch furniture, African curios, & porcelain dolls.

*Other categories: Mixed Automobilia; Petroliana, Pumps & Globes; General Interest*

## Monday's

See our main listing under "General Interest"

## Kirk Monson

See our main listing under "Spark Plugs"

## Paul Mote

Modesto, CA
TEL: 209-544-6683

Collector of gas pumps, globes, & signs. Buy, sell, trade. Actively seeking globes, signs for my personal collection. Especially want West Coast items. Always looking for Mohawk or Golden Eagle stuff. Gas pump restoration service available.

*Other categories: Petroliana, Pumps & Globes; Signs; Restoration Service*

## Motoring Goodies

See our main listing under "Mixed Automobilia"

## Motoring Memories

See our main listing under "License Plates, Tags, etc."

SMALL ELECTRIC PUMP (top); PRICE BOXES (left)

WAYNE 60 PARTS

REPRODUCTION AIR METER (right); WAYNE 615 PARTS (left)

CROWN GLASS GLOBE (left); GLASS BODY GLOBE (right)

**Park Drive Garage**
(402) 592-1710
5734 So. 86th Circle • Omaha, NE 68127-4147

*CALL OR WRITE FOR CATALOG*

"SCHOOL ZONE" SIGN AND OIL RACK STANDS (above); REPRODUCTION GAS PUMPS (left)

GLOBES & SIGNS; TALL DISPLAY RACKS

### Nighthorse Inc.

See our main listing under "Motorcycle Collectibles"

### Thomas Novinsky

189 Spring Rd.
North Haven, CT 06473 USA
TEL: 203-239-8060

Collecting service station signs, including specific items as restroom key tags, restroom signs & expired gasoline credit cards. Willing to trade actual roadside billboard posters for any service station signs, key tags, expired credit cards. Current automotive & motorcycle billboard posters available. Call after 7pm for current availabilities.

*Other categories: Signs; Art, Prints & Posters; Cards, Trading*

### The Oil Barron

See our main listing under "Art, Prints & Posters"

### The Old Road

See our main listing under "Signs"

### Oniell's Collectibles

Pat Oniell
3440 Grant Ave.
Groves, TX 77619 USA
TEL: 409-962-3332

Dealer in oil company memorabilia & other collectibles such as signs, filling station giveaways, service pins, china, toys, & other smalls from any oil company. My specialty is Texaco.

*Other categories: Signs; Petroliana, Pumps & Globes; Jewelry*

### Park Drive Garage

Andy Anderson
5734 So. 86th Circle
Omaha, NE 68127 USA
TEL: 402-592-1710
FAX: 402-592-1882

Park Drive Garage manufactures reproduction pumps, parts, & miscellaneous items. We carry globes, signs, & gasoline items. Call for free catalog.

*Other categories: Petroliana, Pumps & Globes; Mixed Automobilia; Manufacturer*

### Past Gas

See our main listing under "Restoration Service"

### Rick Pease

3705 Pecan Park Dr.
Weatherford, TX 76087 USA
TEL: 817-596-9328
FAX: 817-596-9328

Specialize in gasoline collectibles. Buy, sell, trade. Restore gasoline pumps, air pumps, pedal cars. Collect one-lb. grease (picture) cans. Collect small signs, particularly pump plates. Display at several automobilia-related events. Author of books related to gasoline collectibles.

*Other categories: Petroliana, Pumps & Globes; Signs; Books*

### Petrolitis

Pete D. Clarke
PO Box 638
Sabattus, ME 04280 USA
TEL: 207-375-4206

Pumps, globes, signs, visible & hand-crank pump restoration. Cast-iron pump parts reproduced. Porcelain signs repaired. 1950s rear-clip sofas also available while supply lasts. Authentic creations only.

*Other categories: Petroliana, Pumps & Globes; Signs; Restoration Service*

### Prime Pumps

See our main listing under "Petroliana, Pumps & Globes"

### Pumping Iron

Fred Hunt, Jr.
49 Streeter Pond Drive
Sugar Hill, NH 03585 USA
TEL: 603-823-7012

We specialize in gas pump restoration & buying & selling of gas pumps & gas pump parts. Restoration parts & supplies available, new, used, & N.O.S. We also buy & sell all other gas-related collectibles. We attend many East Coast shows & mail order. Call or write with inquiries.

*Other categories: Petroliana, Pumps & Globes; Signs; Motorcycle Collectibles*

### Purveyor of Petroleum Paraphernalia

See our main listing under "Petroliana, Pumps & Globes"

### R & B Collectibles & Marketing

PO Box 406
Frenchtown, NJ 08825
TEL: 908-996-2141
FAX: 908-996-7856

Texaco collectibles. Buy, sell, trade.

### R & G Automobiles & Collectables

See our main listing under "Mixed Automobilia"

### Road Maps Etc.

See our main listing under "Literature"

### Roadkill Decorators Supply Company

See our main listing under "Signs"

### Robert Covarrubias Studios

See our main listing under "Specialized Automobilia"

### Route 66 Accessories Co.

See our main listing under "Rt. 66 & Roadside"

### Joseph Russell

See our main listing under "Mixed Automobilia"

### Ed Schwartz

PO Box 173
Deerfield, IL 60015-0173 USA
TEL: 847-945-6361

Gas station/oil company memorabilia. Over 500 duplicate items from my collection: globes, signs, cans, banks, toys, s & p shakers, thermometers, tire/tube repair kits, ashtrays, lighters, radios, pen/pencil, etc. Free list. Send large SASE.

*Other categories: Petroliana, Pumps & Globes; Mixed Automobilia; General Interest*

### Shelley's Foreign Auto

See our main listing under "Specialized Automobilia"

## Sign of the Times

See our main listing under "Signs"

## Silver Creek Antiques

See our main listing under "Retail Store"

## Al Simonenko

See our main listing under "Signs"

## Ed Smith

2720 SE Cushman Court
Milwaukie, OR 97267-3833 USA
TEL: 503-659-4791
Email: edandsal@teleport.com
Texaco & Shell collectibles. Specializing in smalls.

*Other category: Toys, Truck*

## Gunnar Söderblom

See our main listing under "Literature"

## Dennis C. Stauffer

455 Lockport St.
Youngstown, NY 14174 USA
Serious collector of quality gasoline/oil automobilia items: globes, porcelain signs, neon signs, hat badges, corpo-rate desk toppers, display items, toys, smalls, "anything gas/oil or Chevrolet." Buy, sell, trade. 10th year. Open by appointment. Finder/locator service. Appraisals. Please send large SASE with all inquiries, lists. Thanks! Happy hunting.

*Other categories: Petroliana, Pumps & Globes; Signs; Mixed Automobilia*

## Philip Stellmacher

See our main listing under "Toys, General"

## Steve's Antiques & Restoration

See our main listing under "Restoration Service"

## Steve's Service Station Stuff

Steve Lospennato
PO Box 113
Windham, NH 03087 USA
TEL: 603-893-9347
Buy, sell, or trade gas & oil porcelain signs, globes, pumps, cans, s & p shakers, & other small collectibles. Also like soda, barber shop, telephone & diner stuff. Will buy one item or whole collection.

*Other categories: Signs; Petroliana, Pumps & Globes; Diner Memorabilia*

## Ron Throckmorton

2650 Ossenfort Rd.
Wildwood, MO 63038 USA
TEL: 314-458-3577
FAX: 314-458-3585
Email: http://www.aol.throcksals.com
Oil bottles: I currently have 134 for sale or trade. Ranging from $22 to $135. Mobil Diamond Gargoyle, Standard ISO-vis, Esso, Imperial, Sunoco, Kalamazoo, U-Neek, Tiolene, Shell X-100 pints, Jay B. Rhodes, some extra racks available. Send SASE for free list. Trades accepted, large lots purchased.

*Other categories: Rt. 66 & Roadside; Specialized Automobilia; Mixed Automobilia*

## Time Passages, Ltd.

See our main listing under "Petroliana, Pumps & Globes"

## Toys & Cars

John Cruickshank
2424 Main St.
Keokuk, IA 52632 USA
TEL: 319-524-9740
Always buying & selling gas station, automotive signs, oil cans, porcelain advertising signs, car parts, soda pop & tobacco signs.

*Other categories: Petroliana, Pumps & Globes; Signs; Mixed Automobilia*

## Mike Tyler

PO Box 175
Moore, MT 59464 USA
TEL: 406-374-2458
Collect, buy, trade, sell gas pumps, globes, signs, cans, maps, & other gas/oil items wanted. Montana oil & gas company globes, signs, cans, maps, license plate attachments, neons, any advertising from Grizzly, Glacier, Laureleaf, Litening, Hi-Line, Montana Chief, Powerized, Mule, Hart, Silver Gas, Husky Aronows, Weiloffs, Heccolene, Big West.

*Other categories: Petroliana, Pumps & Globes; Signs; Mixed Automobilia*

## Unocal 76 Products

Daniel Stiel
PO Box 25376
Santa Ana, CA 92799 USA
TEL: 714-428-6129
FAX: 714-428-8094

Union Oil Company of California, dba UNOCAL, is one of America's largest & oldest oil companies. We vigorously protect our registered trademarks, which include the orange "76" ball, & the Pure Oil Company trademarks. Companies looking to obtain rights to produce likenesses of any of Unocal's trademarks should contact us.

*Other categories: Petroliana, Pumps & Globes; Legal Service; General Interest*

## Valenti Classics, Inc.

See our main listing under "Restoration Service"

## Robert Van Gilder

1526 Cherrywood Dr.
Modesto, CA 95350 USA
TEL: 209-521-6009

Collector of Signal oil & gas memorabilia, dealer in other fine petroleum collectibles, such as globes, signs, oil cans, gas pumps, coin banks. Looking for salt & pepper shakers, hat badges, lighters, & coin banks I don't have. Buy, sell, trade, collect. Send SASE for current sales list or call.

*Other categories: Petroliana, Pumps & Globes; Signs; Specialized Automobilia*

## Vanished Roadside America Art

See our main listing under "Art, Prints & Posters"

## Vic's Place

Vic Raupe
124 N. 2nd St.
Guthrie, OK 73044 USA
TEL: 405-282-5586
FAX: 405-282-6850
Email: www.vicsplace.com

Mail order manufacturer & supplier of gas pump restoration parts & supplies. New, used, & reproduction pumps, parts, globes, signs, decals, clocks, neon, oil cans, racks, books, etc. Showroom, warehouse phones open Mon-Sat 8-6.

Catalog $3, credit cards accepted, UPS daily, restoration service available. We buy, sell, & trade.

*Other categories: Petroliana, Pumps & Globes; Manufacturer; Restoration Service*

## Clifford Weese

See our main listing under "License Plates, Tags, etc."

## West Coast Replicas

See our main listing under "Toys, Truck"

## Greg Wheeler

5878 Hill Ave.
Toledo, OH 43615 USA
TEL: 419-865-0323

Buy, sell, & trade Sunoco & Sohio items but will deal with all gas & oil co. & buy, sell, & trade country store items, with Coca-Cola being a favorite. Gas pump restoration service available. Call after 6pm.

*Other categories: Petroliana, Pumps & Globes; Signs; Restoration Service*

## Walt Wimer, Jr.

456 Vista Dr.
Butler, PA 16001-3237 USA
TEL: 412-285-3577

Private collector of gasoline items, especially road maps. In addition collect oil cans, globes, station photos, matchbooks, & other paper items. Also collect beer cans, brewery advertising items & auto racing items such as programs & yearbooks. Buy, sell, trade.

*Other categories: Petroliana, Pumps & Globes; Racing Artifacts; Rt. 66 & Roadside*

## Wright's Custom Repair, Inc.

See our main listing under "Petroliana, Pumps & Globes"

## Wyckoff Auto

See our main listing under "Mixed Automobilia"

# PHOTOGRAPHS

## AiLE bv

See our main listing under "Art, Prints & Posters"

## Frank Ashley

See our main listing under "Literature"

## Auto Italia Pix

Ed McDonough
9 Green Lane
Wooton, Northants NN4 6LH England
TEL: +44-1604-761813
FAX: +44-1604-761813
Email: Ed.McDonough@nene.ac.uk

Auto Italia Pix buys & sells motor racing pictures from the early 1950s to 1975. We are interested in prints or negatives, & welcome collections. Currently searching for pics of the Rodriguez brothers. We can help you find what you are looking for.

## C.S.P. Calendars

See our main listing under "Specialized Automobilia"

## Cadillac Motorbooks

See our main listing under "Books"

## Castle Concepts

See our main listing under "Racing Artifacts"

## Chelsea Motoring Literature

See our main listing under "Literature"

## Fast Art

See our main listing under "Art, Prints & Posters"

## Gregory Gibson

See our main listing under "License Plates, Tags, etc."

## Pablo Gudino

PO Box 21003 PABT
New York, NY 10129-0009 USA
TEL: 212-535-2357
FAX: 212-535-2357

The most beautiful sports cars & prototypes, at their best angles. Postcards, prints, photomagnets. Ferrari, Corvette, Porsche, Jaguar, Datsun, Viper, Mustang, Camaro, Mitsubishi...

*Other categories: Cards, Postal; Art, Prints & Posters; Mixed Automobilia*

## Himes Museum of Motor Racing
See our main listing under "Museum"

## Alan J. Isselhard
See our main listing under "Racing Artifacts"

## Anthony Jackson
See our main listing under "Art, Prints & Posters"

## David M. King Automotive Books
See our main listing under "Books"

## The Klemantaski Collection
Peter G. Sachs
65 High Ridge Rd. #219
Stamford, CT 06905 USA
TEL: 203-968-2970
FAX: 203-968-2970
Email: klemcoll@aol.com
Motor racing photos from 1936-1987. GP racing a specialty. We serve collectors, publishers, authors, & enthusiasts. Our archive has over 300,000 images by Louis Klemantaski, Nigel Snowdon, & Edward Eves. Contact us by fax, phone, or mail for our free brochure.
*Other categories: Racing Artifacts; Art, Original; Specialized Automobilia*

## Ric Kruse
See our main listing under "Literature"

## Larry Machacek
See our main listing under "License Plates, Tags, etc."

## Pacific Communications
See our main listing under "Rt. 66 & Roadside"

## PL8MAN
See our main listing under "License Plates, Tags, etc."

## Paul Politis Automotive Literature
See our main listing under "Literature"

## Port Jefferson Historical Automobile Research Institute
See our main listing under "Literature"

## Arthur Price
See our main listing under "Racing Artifacts"

## Rare Sportsfilms Inc.
See our main listing under "Racing Artifacts"

## Richard T. Rosenthal
4718 Springfield Ave.
Philadelphia, PA 19143 USA
TEL: 215-726-5493
FAX: 215-726-5926
Email: rtrphoto@philly.infi.net
I deal in rare photographs & tend to have a number of automobile-related items in stock at any particular time. I also collect auto racing photographs.

## Tavares Motorsport
See our main listing under "Specialized Automobilia"

## Viewfinders
See our main listing under "General Interest"

## VW Collector
See our main listing under "Marque Specific"

# PROMOS

## Tom Adams
See our main listing under "Literature"

## William Adorjan
See our main listing under "Toys, Truck"

## Auto Literature & Collectibles
See our main listing under "Literature"

## Bart Cars
Barry Marbo
817 Densmore Rd.
Philadelphia, PA 19116 USA
TEL: 215-676-7240
Specialize in dealer promos from 1940s to present. Buy, sell, trade. Complete collections purchased. Also have some early car kits & various trucks, including plastic gasoline, diecast, steel for sale.
*Other categories: Models, Kits; Petroliana, Other; Toys, Truck*

## Bob's Promotional Cars
Bob Reck
484 Bottesford Ct.
Severna Park, MD 21146 USA
TEL: 410-647-1849
FAX: 202-482-0719
Email: robert_reck@ita.doc.gov
Large selection of Johan reissue promos. Sebrings, '97 Vettes, Indy 500 & Brickyard pace cars, Neons, Auroras, Tahoes, '54 Corvette reissue, '97 Camaro set, Viper 3 & 4 car collector sets, '97 F150s, Chrysler Atlantics, Stratus, Cirrus, Monte Carlos, Prowlers, Trans Ams, last ZR-1. Also buy collections. LSASE for list.
*Other categories: Models, Precision; Toys, General; Toys, Truck*

## Bill Brisbane
See our main listing under "Toys, General"

## Brookfield Collectors Guild
See our main listing under "Models, Precision"

## Bill Carlisle
See our main listing under "Toys, Truck"

## Carney Plastics Inc.
See our main listing under "Displays/Fixtures"

## Cliff Douglas
See our main listing under "License Plates, Tags, etc."

## GM Studios, Inc.
See our main listing under "Jewelry"

## Paul Garnand Sales
See our main listing under "Models, Kits"

## Holliday Canopies
See our main listing under "Displays/Fixtures"

## Peter E. Hoyt
See our main listing under "Models, Kits"

## J & T Collectibles

See our main listing under "Toys, Truck"

## John's Scale Autos

John Mellon
260 Walk Circle
Santa Cruz, CA 95060-5945 USA
TEL: 408-423-9612

Collector-dealer sells, buys, trades dealer promotional models, model kits, & other transportation promotional models or toys & automobilia advertising. I want to buy for my collection any promotional models for any FoMoCo product, especially metal cars or trucks made by Banthrico, Master Caster, & National Products.

*Other categories: Models, Kits; Toys, Truck; Toys, General*

## Jim Jones

See our main listing under "Cards, Postal"

## Lincolnia

Charlie Berry
13375 Havelock Trail
Apple Valley, MN 55124 USA
TEL: 612-431-3255
FAX: 612-431-3255

Lincoln specialist. Selling/collecting Lincoln literature. Send SASE, your year for list. Top dollar paid for Lincoln promos. Collecting car care chemicals 1940s-1960s. Search your shelves for green/yellow Lincoln cans & boxes.

*Other categories: Literature; Models, Kits; Toys, General*

## Merchandising Incentives Corp.

Customer Service
352 Oliver
Troy, MI 48084 USA
TEL: 800-345-1445
FAX: 810-362-1535

Specialize in Ford, GM, & Chrysler plastic promotional scale models. Prior to this year, availability of these collectibles was fairly limited to car dealer distribution. Now the thousands of collectors can purchase directly from the Ertl/MIC outlet. Call our customer service for availability & prices.

*Other categories: Toys, General; Toys, Truck; Models, Kits*

## Mike & Bob's Promos

Michael J. Sullivan
80 Shagbark Way
Fairport, NY 14450 USA
TEL: 716-223-5626

Specializing in promotional cars & trucks. Buy, sell, trade. Normally we have 200 cars listed each month. Call 7-9pm EST. Send SASE for lists.

*Other categories: Specialized Automobilia; Toys, General*

## Milestone Motorcars

See our main listing under "Models, Precision"

## Milwaukee Miniature Motors

See our main listing under "Models, Kits"

## Model Car Journal

See our main listing under "Publications, Current"

## Model Kit Hobbies

See our main listing under "Models, Kits"

## NASCAR Novelties

See our main listing under "Motoring Accessories"

## Bob Neubauer

See our main listing under "Models, Kits"

## Jim Newhall Automobilia

Jim Newhall
2039 Maple Rd.
Stow, OH 44224 USA
TEL: 330-688-5258

Interested in promos, car kits, 1/24 diecast, sales literature, & Firestone advertising memorabilia. Buy, sell, trade. Now have available a list of misc. paper collectibles (catalogs, manuals, photos, magazines, Firestone memorabilia, much more). Send $1 & SASE.

*Other categories: Models, Kits; Literature; Toys, Truck*

## Wayne Noller

N5517 County K
Fond du Lac, WI 54935 USA
TEL: 414-923-1735

Toy cars & trucks: promos, kits, Matchbox. Also books, postcards, dealer brochures, other automobilia. Send SASE for list.

*Other categories: Models, Kits; Literature; Toys, General*

## Nylint Collector

See our main listing under "Toys, Truck"

## Dan O'Neill Precision Models

See our main listing under "Manufacturer"

## Port Jefferson Historical Automobile Research Institute

See our main listing under "Literature"

## The Printer's Stone, Ltd.

See our main listing under "Art, Other"

## Pro Drop

See our main listing under "Mixed Automobilia"

## Route 66 Decanters

See our main listing under "Specialized Automobilia"

## San Remo Hobby and Toy

Greg Plonski
93 Beaver Drive
Kings Park, NY 11754-2209 USA
TEL: 516-724-5722

Specializing in all the latest promotional model cars & model car kits. Also Johnny Lightning collector editions in the correct colors & automobile trading cards. Send an SASE & request a list. Phone hours 10 to 10 EST.

*Other categories: Models, Kits; Hot Wheels; Cards, Trading*

## Smith Automotive Group

See our main listing under "Hot Rod Memorabilia"

## Tiger Automotive

Jay D. Szaras
3450 Sahara Springs Blvd.
Pompano Beach, FL 33069 USA
TEL: 954-973-1997

Promotional model cars & trucks, bought, sold, & traded. These were sold, & also given away, at new car dealers during the 1950s & 60s. Appraisal service also offered. Call today! Cash waiting!

*Other categories: Toys, General; Models, Precision; Appraisal Service*

## Edward Tilley Automotive Collectibles

Ed Tilley
PO Box 4233
Cary, NC 27519 USA
TEL: 919-460-8262
Email: edandsusan@aol.com

Buying & selling fine automobilia by mail since 1979. Large selection of promos, out-of-print books, toys, & literature. For all marques. Specialize in Ford Motor Co., Henry Ford. We always offer one-of-a-kind artifacts of our automotive heritage. Send long SASE, 64 cents postage, for current list.

*Other categories: Books; Toys, General; Mixed Automobilia*

## Vintage American Classics

See our main listing under "Models, Kits"

## Ted & Nelda Weems

See our main listing under "Literature"

## Winner's Circle Racing Collectibles

See our main listing under "Hot Wheels"

## Winross Company

See our main listing under "Manufacturer"

# PUBLICATIONS, CURRENT

## AMWP

Scott Means
Box 17107
Little Rock, AR 72222 USA
TEL: 800-994-9268
FAX: 501-868-8858
Email: amwc1@aol.com

America's most wanted to buy bi-monthly magazine packed with over 60 pages of "wanted to buy" ads.

*Other categories: General Interest; Books; Club/Organization*

## Auto Epoch

Robert Brady
PO Box 2377
San Jose, CA 95109-2377 USA
TEL: 888-729-2198
FAX: 408-729-7919
Email: rbrady7191@aol.com

Publisher of the *Auto Epoch Forum*. Features stories, articles, the Automotive Almanac, full-color feature photos, shows & events listing, car repair trouble-shooting tips, & classified. Also available: luggage sets, folding picnic tables, tools, & motoring accessories. Call or write for a free trial subscription.

*Other categories: Luggage/Picnic Sets; Tools; Motoring Accessories*

## Automobile Quarterly

Jonathan A. Stein
15076 Kutztown Rd., PO Box 348
Kutztown, PA 19530 USA
TEL: 610-683-3169
FAX: 610-683-3287

*Automobile Quarterly* is the definitive magazine of automotive history & is totally free of advertising. AQ also publishes books & posters, which are available through the Quatrefoil catalog. Call toll-free 800-523-0236 for more information.

*Other categories: Books; Art, Prints & Posters*

## Autophile Car Books

See our main listing under "Books"

## Milford L. Barley

See our main listing under "Toys, Truck"

## Barry Power Graphic Design

See our main listing under "General Interest"

## C.S.P. Calendars

See our main listing under "Specialized Automobilia"

## Cadillac Motorbooks

See our main listing under "Books"

## Car Collector Magazine

Jeff Broadus
1241 Canton St.
Roswell, GA 30075 USA
TEL: 770-643-1905
FAX: 770-643-2815
Email: dcarguy@atl.mindspring.com

Beautifully illustrated color articles on antique, classic, postwar, special interest, sports, & future collectible cars. Related fields: economics of car collecting, event & auction calendars, miniature cars, automotive art, automobilia, & internat'l collector car events. Q & A from professional concours-quality restorer. Website at http://www.carcollector.com

## Cole Motor Car Club

See our main listing under "Club/Organization"

## Convertible Magazine

Tony Leopardo
PO Box 1011
San Mateo, CA 94403 USA
TEL: 415-340-8669
FAX: 415-340-9473

*Convertible Magazine* tracks the convertible market! Each issue covers new & collectible convertibles, parts, auctions, & accessories. Our buyers' guide lists hundreds of convertibles for sale, as well as upcoming collector car auctions & events. Subscription rates are $24 for 12 issues. Visa & MasterCard accepted. Fax/mail your subscription in today!

## Bob Crisler

See our main listing under "License Plates, Tags, etc."

## Diecast Toy Collectors Association

See our main listing under "Club/Organization"

## Gregory Gibson

See our main listing under "License Plates, Tags, etc."

## Hemmings Motor News

Terry Ehrich, Publisher
PO Box 256 - 222 Main St.
Bennington, VT 05201 USA
TEL: 800-CAR-HERE
FAX: 802-447-9631
Email: http://www.hmn.com

Monthly "bible" of the collector-car hobby. Averaging over 800 pages, including antiques, vintage, muscle, & special interest collector vehicles, plus parts, literature, services, automobilia, etc. without limitations. One-year subscription $26.95 US only. (Foreign & Canadian please call for rates.) Visitors welcome also at Hemmings Sunoco Filling Station & Retail Store.

*Other categories: Retail Store; General Interest; Mixed Automobilia*

## Horseless Carriage Club of America

See our main listing under "Club/Organization"

## Indy Car Racing Magazine

Tom Ceretto
1933 South West Ave.
Waukesha, WI 53186 USA
TEL: 800-432-4639
FAX: 414-896-9203
Email: icr@icr.com

The only magazine devoted exclusively to Indy Car racing.

## Jaguar Automobilia Collector

See our main listing under "Marque Specific"

## Tony Marchitto

See our main listing under "Slot Cars"

## Mobilia

Eric H. Killorin
PO Box 575
Middlebury, VT 05753 USA
TEL: 802-388-3071
FAX: 802-388-2215
Email: mobilia@aol.com

*MOBILIA* is the collectibles magazine for car lovers. Each monthly issue offers features & news on all your favorite automobilia: auto toys, car models, petroliana, mascots, plates, books & literature, & lots more. Great classified ad

section. 100 pages monthly. The only publication devoted to automobilia. 12-issue subscription only $29.

*Other categories: Mixed Automobilia; Specialized Automobilia; General Interest*

## Model A Ford Cabriolet Club

See our main listing under "Club/Organization"

## Model Car Journal

Dennis Doty, Editor
PO Box 154135
Irving, TX 75015-4135 USA
TEL: 972-790-5346
FAX: 972-790-5346

Bringing the hobby into focus since 1974. From static kits, promos, diecast, hand-builts, MCJ covers it all. Reviews of current models & model car histories are features in every issue. Free subscriber ads. Bimonthly, a six-issue sub is $16 in the US. (Outside the US, write us for rates.)

*Other categories: Models, Kits; Models, Precision; Promos*

## Pedal Car News

See our main listing under "Pedal Cars"

## TMC Publications

See our main listing under "Literature"

## Toy Farmer Magazine

Gary Nelson, Mg. Editor
7496 106 Ave. SE
LaMoure, ND 58458-9404 USA
TEL: 701-883-5206
Email: zekesez@aol.com

Favorite farm toy collecting magazine. Each month 100 pages featuring new products, pedal tractors, custom-built projects, extensive farm toy show calendar, classified ads, stories & columns by people who know farm toys. Our 20th year.

*Other category: Toys, Tractor*

## Toy Trucker & Contractor Magazine

Gary Nelson, Mg. Editor
7496 106 Ave. SE
LaMoure, ND 58458-9404 USA
TEL: 701-883-5206
Email: zekesez@aol.com

Monthly magazine specializing in new & old toy trucks & construction toys, fire engines, custom-built projects, new products, classified ads, upcoming show calendar, columns & stories by people who know toys. Our 15th year.

*Other category: Toys, Truck*

## Wheel Goods Trader Magazine

See our main listing under "Pedal Cars"

## Yesterday's Highways Newsletter

Nancy & Bob Neiger
49 Church St.
Weaverville, NC 28787 USA
TEL: 704-645-9045
FAX: 704-645-4045
Email: oldroads@aol.com

Publish a 28-page newsletter six times yearly, exploring US highways & history without Interstate travel. Each issue explores four routes; includes maps, photos, cartoons, book & product reviews, & route-specific advertising. One-year subscription $18.95 US; sample issue is free; gift subscriptions available.

*Other categories: Rt. 66 & Roadside; General Interest; Motoring Accessories*

# RACING ARTIFACTS

## David T. Alexander

See our main listing under "Literature"

## Mats Alfvag

See our main listing under "Art, Prints & Posters"

## American Eagle Racing

See our main listing under "Hot Rod Memorabilia"

## Auto Racing

John Lengenfelder
129 Locust Ave.
Trenton, NJ 08610 USA
TEL: 609-581-0231

Collector of auto racing memorabilia. Especially Trenton, Langhorne, Indy, NJ racetracks. Also collect board games, postcards, photos, movies, Indy driver cards, pennants, toy Indy sprint & midget cars in any scale, material. Also Mercers, Chaparrals. Anything AJ Foyt. Have similar items for sale or trade. Call after 5pm EST.

*Other categories: Cards, Postal; Models, Kits; Toys, General*

## Auto-Ideas

See our main listing under "Specialized Automobilia"

## Autographics

See our main listing under "Books"

## Automobilia Cycles Trucks (ACT)

See our main listing under "Specialized Automobilia"

## Barnett Design Inc.

See our main listing under "Models, Precision"

## Bill Behlman

1014 Bowen St.
Oshkosh, WI 54901 USA
TEL: 414-233-2262
FAX: 414-231-9414

Indy 500 pit badges, ticket stubs, program books, trading cards, anything related to the Indy 500 or Brickyard 400 races.

*Other categories: Cards, Trading; Models, Kits*

## Bill's Garage

See our main listing under "Models, Kits"

## Gabriel Bogdonoff

See our main listing under "Gas-Powered Racers"

## Dennis Brilla

See our main listing under "Mixed Automobilia"

## The British Garage

See our main listing under "Specialized Automobilia"

## British Only Motorcycles & Parts, Inc.

See our main listing under "Motorcycle Collectibles"

## Car Crazy

See our main listing under "Hot Rod Memorabilia"

## Castle Concepts

PO Box 2030
Redondo Beach, CA 90278 USA
TEL: 310-793-0129
Email: aw992@lafn.org

Collector of vintage rally equipment. Heuer stopwatches, Master Time, Auto Rallye, Sebring, Monte Carlo, Super Autavia, Autavia, etc. Also Abercrombie & Fitch Inc. Halda Twinmaster, Tripmaster, Speedpilot, Curta calculator, trophies, plaques, photos, posters, movies.

*Other categories: Specialized Automobilia; Mixed Automobilia; Photographs*

## Classic Performance

See our main listing under "Hot Rod Memorabilia"

## Collector's Studio Motorsport Gallery

Morry Barmak
136 Yorkville Ave.
Toronto, Ontario M5R 1C2 Canada
TEL: 416-975-5442
Email: cstudio@io.org

We offer original signed Formula 1 & Indy Car memorabilia: helmets, uniforms, gloves, visors, paintings, photos, prints, etc.; from Senna, Schumacher, Villeneuve, Fittipaldi, Andretti, & others. Also commissioned Ferrari & Porsche models, artwork & glass etchings. Worldwide shipping & Internet service. WWW page http://www.io.org/cstudio

*Other categories: Art, Prints & Posters; Specialized Automobilia; Models, Precision*

## Robert Covarrubias Studios

See our main listing under "Specialized Automobilia"

## Crazy Irishman Collectibles

See our main listing under "Mixed Automobilia"

## Demarest Motorbooks

See our main listing under "Books"

## Doo-Wop Props

See our main listing under "Hot Rod Memorabilia"

## EWJ Marketing

Eric Jungnickel
PO Box 4674
Naperville, IL 60567-4674 USA
TEL: 630-983-8339

Indy 500 memorabilia wanted, felt pennants (dated) depicting IMS or other auto races to purchase or trade. Other memorabilia also wanted: auto race games (Wilber Shaw), early Indy artifacts, race car bobbin' heads. Anything Indy!

*Other categories: Games; Toys, General; Slot Cars*

## Early Racing Classics

See our main listing under "Models, Precision"

## Fast Art

See our main listing under "Art, Prints & Posters"

## Fast Toys, Inc.

See our main listing under "Marque Specific"

## Flashback

David J. Forsyth
PO Box 309, 301 Riley
Easton, KS 66020 USA
TEL: 913-773-5550

Specialize in hi-performance dealer-installed parts, cross-rams, tri-powers, tachs, radio deletes, etc. Buy, sell, trade. Also collect gas-powered toys, cast-iron toys, & pedal cars/tractors. Full-service retail trading card store specializing in WOTC Magic the Gathering gaming cards. Trade across hobbies. Open 4pm CST.

*Other categories: Toys, General; Gas-Powered Racers; Cards, Trading*

## Rick Hale

See our main listing under "Books"

## Half-Pint Motors

See our main listing under "Pedal Cars"

## Haven Books & Collectibles

See our main listing under "Retail Store"

## Himes Museum of Motor Racing

See our main listing under "Museum"

## Hot Rods

See our main listing under "Hot Rod Memorabilia"

## ICPM Automotive Books

See our main listing under "Books"

## Alan J. Isselhard

16336 Church St.
Holley, NY 14470 USA
TEL: 716-638-6994

Dealing in posters, programs, photos, postcards, tickets, trophies, & metal race toys & trucks. Especially interested in Indy, Watkins Glen & NYS racing items. Send $2 cash for current list – refundable with purchase. Call between 6 & 10pm EST for items to buy or sell. Interested in anything racing!

*Other categories: Photographs; Art, Prints & Posters; Mixed Automobilia*

## Anthony Jackson

See our main listing under "Art, Prints & Posters"

## The Klemantaski Collection

See our main listing under "Photographs"

## Ted Knorr

PO Box 24594
Speedway, IN 46224 USA
TEL: 317-387-9668

Specialize in auto racing memorabilia: Indy, NASCAR, vintage open wheel & early stock car. Collecting related toys, souvenirs, programs, tickets, model/slot kits, gas race cars, early 1950s racing papers (illustrated speedway news pictorial sections). Appraisals for insurance, donations, estates. 35 years of collecting experience.

*Other categories: Toys, General; Models, Kits; Appraisal Service*

## George Koyt

8 Lenora Ave
Morrisville, PA 19067 USA
TEL: 215-295-4908

Longtime collector of auto racing memorabilia looking for any type of auto racing items from any era. Will purchase one piece or complete collections.

*Other categories: Cards, Postal; Games; Gas-Powered Racers*

## Mike Martin

1100 Beach Ave.
Marysville, WA 98270 USA
TEL: 360-653-4736
FAX: 360-658-5232

Specializing in race programs: Grand Prix, Can-Am, F5000, Indy Cars, Trans-Am, & various European races. Buy, sell, trade. Always looking for USRRC programs & photos. Send SASE for current list.

*Other categories: Books; Mixed Automobilia*

## McCoy's Memorabilia

William A. McCoy
35583 N 1830 E
Rossville, IL 60963 USA
TEL: 217-748-6513

Buy, sell, trade. Indy 500 & other auto race programs, yearbooks, memorabilia. 22-page list available. Also have over 6,000 vintage auto magazines 1930s-1990s cataloged on computer by content. Can do search for tech info, specific car, driver, etc.

## Mega-Zines

See our main listing under "General Interest"

## Model Kit Hobbies

See our main listing under "Models, Kits"

## Tim Moe

1876 Defoor Ave.
Atlanta, GA 30318 USA
TEL: 404-355-5936
FAX: 404-355-6428

Indy Car racing collectibles. Diecast, posters, team uniforms, programs, yearbooks, badges, body parts. Buy, sell, trade. Always buying Indy car owner's, driver's, crew chief's, & crew rings.

*Other categories: Hot Rod Memorabilia; Clothing; Specialized Automobilia*

## MotoMedia

See our main listing under "Books"

## Moviecraft Inc.

See our main listing under "Manufacturer"

## Muffler Time Exhaust & Memorabilia

See our main listing under "Hot Rod Memorabilia"

## Palmer Motor Racing

See our main listing under "Models, Precision"

## Pastimes

See our main listing under "Specialized Automobilia"

## Peachstate

See our main listing under "Models, Precision"

## Pirelli Collector

See our main listing under "Specialized Automobilia"

## Arthur Price

144 Ross St. Ext.
Auburn, NY 13021 USA
TEL: 315-253-7402

Specializing in racing memorabilia, autographs, posters, prints, programs, old & recent photographs, rare of Gilles Villeneuve, Senna, Prost. Buy, sell, or trade. Racing memorabilia & whole collections bought. F1 official for 15 years. Appraisal service available on collections & separate items.

*Other categories: Art, Prints & Posters; Photographs; Appraisal Service*

## Race Place Collectables

See our main listing under "Retail Store"

## Rare Sportsfilms Inc.

Doak Ewing
1126 Tennyson Lane
Naperville, IL 60540 USA
TEL: 630-527-8890
FAX: 630-527-9095

Old-time stock car & Indianapolis races 1946-1979 are now available in beautiful color on ultra high-quality home video! Largest selection anywhere! Call us for free listing of all 51 different tapes! Also buying & trading old 16mm racing films. Model builders welcome!

*Other categories: Photographs; Models, Kits; Manufacturer*

## Revell-Monogram, Inc.

Bruce Thompson
8601 Waukegan Rd.
Morton Grove, IL 60053 USA
TEL: 847-966-3500
FAX: 847-966-9802

Revell-Monogram is the world's leading manufacturer of plastic model kits & diecast replicas. Revell has been miniaturizing cars for over 50 years. Our leadership position is based on our acute attention to authentic & detailed replication of real objects.

*Other categories: Manufacturer; Models, Kits*

## Richard's

See our main listing under "Personalities"

## John Snowberger

See our main listing under "Models, Precision"

## SpeedWay MotorBooks

See our main listing under "Books"

## George Spruce

33 Washington St.
Sayville, NY 11782 USA
TEL: 516-563-4211

Vanderbilt Cup & other early auto racing memorabilia wanted. Pennants, posters, programs, trophies, pins, ribbons, photos, anything. Serious & fair buyer.

## Spyder Enterprises

See our main listing under "Specialized Automobilia"

## Mark Suozzi

See our main listing under "Motoring Accessories"

## T and D Toy & Hobby

See our main listing under "Retail Store"

## Tavares Motorsport

See our main listing under "Specialized Automobilia"

## Victory Lane

See our main listing under "Toys, General"

## Vintage Motorbooks

See our main listing under "Books"

## West Coast Replicas

See our main listing under "Toys, Truck"

## Kirk F. White

See our main listing under "Gas-Powered Racers"

## Walt Wimer, Jr.

See our main listing under "Petroliana, Other"

## Winner's Circle Racing Collectibles

See our main listing under "Hot Wheels"

## Wizard's

David C. Sassman
PO Box 24072
Indianapolis, IN 46224 USA
TEL: 317-630-0111
Email: dsassman@aol.com

Indy 500 programs, pit badges, yearbooks, most anything connected to this world-class event. Also team uniforms from open wheel racing. Send want list. Willing to trade or buy mentioned items.

*Other categories: Mixed Automobilia; Clothing; Art, Prints & Posters*

## Michael Wojtowicz

563 Fairview Ave
Glen Ellyn, IL 60137 USA
TEL: 630-858-6059

Collect Indy 500 tickets, passes, badges, pins, & misc. race items. Also race car toys, including Indy slot cars. Like standard-size Indy 500 postcards. Have misc. Indy & racing stuff for sale or trade. Send wants for list. Calls after 7pm CST.

*Other categories: Toys, General; Slot Cars; Cards, Postal*

## The XR-1000 Nut

See our main listing under "Motorcycle Collectibles"

# RESTORATION

## Ablaze Enterprises Inc.

See our main listing under "Mixed Automobilia"

## Blast from the Past

See our main listing under "Neon"

## Chuck's Collectibles

Chuck Egbert
PO Box 648
Claremont, NH 03743 USA
TEL: 603-542-8344

Buy, sell, trade. Coca-Cola & other soda machines & coolers, gas pumps, globes, oil lubesters, air meters & other automobilia, pedal cars. Restorations, parts, service. For quality restorations, give me a call.

*Other categories: Petroliana, Pumps & Globes; Pedal Cars; General Interest*

## Clapper Restorations

See our main listing under "Petroliana, Pumps & Globes"

## Classic Transportation

See our main listing under "Pedal Cars"

## Doney Enterprises

See our main listing under "Mixed Automobilia"

## East Coast Classics

See our main listing under "Petroliana, Pumps & Globes"

## Electric Dreams

See our main listing under "Slot Cars"

## Emblemagic Co.

See our main listing under "Mascots/Badges/Emblems"

## Full Serve

See our main listing under "Petroliana, Pumps & Globes"

## Gasoline Alley

See our main listing under "Mixed Automobilia"

## Bob Gerrity

28048 13th Ave. So.
Kent, WA 98032 USA
TEL: 206-941-6055
FAX: 206-941-9123

Oil co. brand decals, vintage gas-related collectibles, badge & emblem repair & restoration. Toy restoration – oils, decals. Service pin & badge restoration, paint & enamel. Vintage automobilia appraisal service. Dealing in Japanese Mobil tin toys 1940s, 50s, 60s vintage. Texaco, Buddy L tanker decals & grilles for restoration.

*Other categories: Mascots/Badges/Emblems; Petroliana, Other; Toys, General*

## Hi-Tec Customs

Tony Gruppuso
PO Box 141
Medford, NY 11763 USA
TEL: 516-289-4331
FAX: 516-289-4331

Specialize in museum-quality restoration of gas pumps, air meters, signs, pedal cars, vending machines, coolers, & pressed-steel toys. Our attention to detail & oven-baked finish will return your prized collectible to new condition once again for years of enjoyment. Call or write for information.

*Other categories: Petroliana, Other; Signs; Pedal Cars*

## J. Hubbard Classic Cycles & Collectibles

See our main listing under "Motorcycle Collectibles"

## Jake's Mustang Dismantling

Kenneth Cardin
793A Energy Way
Chula Vista, CA 91911 USA
TEL: 619-482-7011
Email: JakesMust@aol.com

Jake's Mustangs sell used, original, & NOS parts for all model Mustangs & early model Ford & Mercurys.

*Other categories: Specialized Automobilia; General Interest*

## Henry Jay Classics, Inc.

Henry Jay
PO Box 1323
Lethbridge, Alberta T1K 4E1 Canada
TEL: 403-328-HJAY
FAX: 403-380-2040

Classic Chevy 5-6-7 car & street rods restoration. Sale of 5-6-7 Chevys & street rods. Chevy auto parts 5-6-7. Overseas classic Chevy sales. We restore classic 1955-6-7 Chevy cars & resell them.

## Kid Stuff

Larry Machacek
PO Box 515
Porter, TX 77365 USA
TEL: 281-429-2505

Specialize in any stage of restoration & repair of 1928-31 Model A Fords. Original used parts available for purchase.

*Other categories: Marque Specific; General Interest; Retail Store*

## Monday's

See our main listing under "General Interest"

## Paul Mote

See our main listing under "Petroliana, Other"

## New Era Toys

Marv Silverstein
PO Box 10
Lambertville, NJ 08530 USA
TEL: 609-397-2113

New Era Toys, first & finest in pressed-steel restoration of Buddy L, Keystone, & alike. Also pedal cars from 1920s to 1960s. Custom built vehicles on request. Call for quote, 9-5 EST.

*Other categories: Toys, Truck; Pedal Cars; Appraisal Service*

## Past Gas

Michael D. Clem
455 7th St.
Penrose, CO 81240 USA
TEL: 719-372-3128

Restoration of older gas pumps & lubesters. Buy, sell, trade same. Also collect gasoline-related items & most anything automobilia. Send SASE for current list. Call 9-6 MST.

*Other categories: Petroliana, Pumps & Globes; Petroliana, Other; Mixed Automobilia*

## Perma Coatings

Jeff Cleere
923 N. Main St.
Hattiesburg, MS 39401 USA
TEL: 800-898-6097

Rust ruining your valuable projects? POR-15 rust preventive will permanently stop rust! POR-15 can be primed, painted, or bonded over. When restoring that gas pump, pedal car, toy, or want to stop the rust on that sign. Free catalog. Automotive oil, gas, misc. advertising bought, sold, traded.

*Other categories: Petroliana, Pumps & Globes; Pedal Cars; Toys, Truck*

## Petrolitis

See our main listing under "Petroliana, Other"

## Prime Pumps

See our main listing under "Petroliana, Pumps & Globes"

## Purveyor of Petroleum Paraphernalia

See our main listing under "Petroliana, Pumps & Globes"

## Rick's Restorations/Custom Toys

George Rickert
Rt 538 Box 219C
Mullica Hill, NJ 08062 USA
TEL: 609-478-4674

Professional pressed steel restoration. We can restore any pressed-steel toy. Custom sheet metal toy fabrication is our specialty. Paint is polyurethane, toys are accepted in trade in rough to good condition. We buy, sell, & trade old toys. Also restore pedal cars/gas pumps.

*Other categories: Toys, Truck; Pedal Cars; Toys, General*

## Road Race Replicas

See our main listing under "Slot Cars"

## Roadkill Decorators Supply Company

See our main listing under "Signs"

## Ron's Relics

See our main listing under "Pedal Cars"

## S & H Chrome Plating & Powder Coating, Inc.

Sam Robinson
817 Madison Ind. Rd.
Madison, TN 37115 USA
TEL: 615-865-0100
FAX: 615-865-6500

Specializing in restoration chrome plating of automobile, motorcycle parts, & more. All work guaranteed. Powder coating offered in many colors. Excellent for gas pumps, motorcycle & auto frames. Anywhere you would use a wet paint, but much more durable.

*Other category: Manufacturer*

## Shriver Auto Mall

See our main listing under "Toys, Truck"

## Steve's Antiques & Restoration

Steve Verhoeven
5609 South 4300 West
Hooper, UT 84315 USA
TEL: 801-776-4835

Gas pumps restored plus parts & supplies. Soda pop machines restored plus parts, supplies, restored machines for sale. Collectible bicycles bought, sold, traded, restored, parts, supplies. 1950s & 1960s automobile restoration & related items. Misc. porcelain, tin, & advertising signs as available.

*Other categories: Petroliana, Other; Specialized Automobilia*

## Valenti Classics, Inc.

Don Valenti
355 S. Hwy 41
Caledonia, WI 53108 USA
TEL: 414-835-2070
FAX: 414-835-2575

Sales & restoration of classic & collectible automobiles. We also buy, sell, & trade auto & gas-related memorabilia. Lots of signs, oil cans, promos, gas pumps in stock. We are always looking to buy quality collectibles. Will also consign larger collections.

*Other categories: Petroliana, Pumps & Globes; Petroliana, Other; Signs*

## Vic's Place

See our main listing under "Petroliana, Other"

## Vintage America

Box 45
Mason, MI 48854 USA
TEL: 517-676-0407
FAX: 517-676-0407
Email: vintageam@aol.com

Quality restorations for pedal cars, riding toys, pressed-steel toys, gas pumps, & related. Buying unrestored pedal cars, riding toys, pressed-steel toys, gas-oil related. Any condition 1920s-early 60s.

*Other categories: Pedal Cars; Toys, General; Petroliana, Pumps & Globes*

## Bill Walls

See our main listing under "Pedal Cars"

## John W. Webster

See our main listing under "Mascots/Badges/Emblems"

## Greg Wheeler

See our main listing under "Petroliana, Other"

## Wright's Custom Repair, Inc.

See our main listing under "Petroliana, Pumps & Globes"

# RETAIL STORE

## The Auto Collectibles Co.

Rob Fariss
3390-D Rasmont Rd.
Roanoke, VA 24018 USA
TEL: 540-989-9656

Specializing in diecast, promos, Hot Wheels, & anything with wheels. Dealer of Ertl, Mattel, Solido, Franklin & Danbury mints, Racing Champions, Bburago, Matchbox, Revell, Maisto, Mira, all scales: 1/18, 1/24, 1/43, 1/64. Hundreds of diecast & plastic models, posters, & everything automotive. Happy's Flea Market, Roanoke, Virginia.

*Other categories: Hot Wheels; Models, Precision; Toys, Truck*

## Automobilia

James Aretakis
PO Box 547
Morrison, CO 80465 USA
TEL: 303-697-0750
Email: gearhead7@aol.com

Located in historic Morrison, Colorado, in an antiquated gas station near Red Rocks Park, Automobilia is a gathering place to swap stories & fill up on unique gifts, antique toys, porcelain signs, pedal cars, classic literature, original artwork, vintage gas pumps, gas station memorabilia, & a "truckful" of nostalgia.

*Other categories: Petroliana, Other; Toys, General; Art, Prints & Posters*

## Blast from the Past, Inc.

Shawn Bauerschmidt
1895 Mt. Hope Ave.
Rochester, NY 14620 USA
TEL: 716-256-4690
Email: info@blastpast.com

Specialize in original gas & oil signage, gas pumps, Coke machines, soda fountain collectibles, diner memorabilia, jukeboxes, & literature. Buying any Mobil gas station memorabilia. If you are looking for anything in particular, don't hesitate to give us a call. Send SASE for current inventory list or call during business hours.

*Other categories: Petroliana, Other; Diner Memorabilia; Signs*

## Canada's All Canadian Service Station Museum

See our main listing under "Museum"

## Car Crazy, Inc.

Richard S. Tabas
723 Montgomery Ave.
Narberth, PA 19072 USA
TEL: 610-667-4333
FAX: 610-667-5726
Email: carcrazy@erols.com

Car Crazy is a most unique store: we specialize in just about anything the autophile could desire! Automotive artwork in original, litho & poster form, videos, books, hand built miniatures as well as diecasts in all scales. We also have a great selection of automotive appearance products as well as great gifts & unusual accessories!

*Other categories: Art, Prints & Posters; Online Service; General Interest*

## Dan's Classic Auto Parts

See our main listing under "Mixed Automobilia"

## G & L Collectibles

See our main listing under "Toys, Truck"

## Gasoline Alley

See our main listing under "Mixed Automobilia"

## Get It On Paper

Gary Weickart
185 Maple Street
Islip, NY 11751 USA
TEL: 516-581-3897

A retail automobilia store that offers original literature for most old cars. Also a great selection of vintage model kits, promos, toys, & other wonderful things from your past. Open every Saturday & Sunday 12-5. I need to buy more car & aircraft models immediately! Send your list or visit.

*Other categories: Literature; Models, Kits; Mixed Automobilia*

## Haven Books & Collectibles

Kenneth E. Sears
5682 Cypress Gardens Blvd.
Winter Haven, FL 33884 USA
TEL: 941-326-9491
FAX: 941-326-9518

General used & antiquarian bookstore specializing in automobilia of all kinds. Fine auto books, literature, original service & owner's manuals, race programs & posters, toy & model cars, & radiator mascots bought & sold. Estates purchased. Also, large inventory of aviation, nautical, & sports books. SASE for response to specific wants.

*Other categories: Books; Literature; Racing Artifacts*

## Hemmings Motor News

See our main listing under "Publications, Current"

## Holliday Canopies

See our main listing under "Displays/Fixtures"

## Keith's Hobby Shop

See our main listing under "Models, Kits"

## Kid Stuff

See our main listing under "Restoration Service"

## Marvelous Auto Miniatures

See our main listing under "Models, Precision"

## Meow

See our main listing under "Clothing"

## Walter Miller

See our main listing under "Literature"

## The Museum of Automobile History

See our main listing under "Museum"

## National Automotive & Truck Model & Toy Museum of the United States

See our main listing under "Museum"

## National Automotive & Truck Museum of the United States (NATMUS)

See our main listing under "Museum"

## Paul Garnand Sales

See our main listing under "Models, Kits"

## Race Place Collectables

Mark Elms
6813 E. Reno
Midwest City, OK 73110 USA
TEL: 405-737-5100

The Race Place Collectibles – Oklahoma's largest NASCAR racing collectibles dealer. Diecast, Hot Wheels, dragsters, funny cars, sprint cars, & apparel. Call for hot, new items arriving daily from Racing Champions, RCCA, Revell, T-shirts, hats, & flags. In Heritage Park Mall.

*Other categories: Hot Wheels; Racing Artifacts; Mixed Automobilia*

## Rader's Relics

Bob Rader
2601 W. Fairbanks Ave.
Winter Park, FL 32789 USA
TEL: 407-647-1940
FAX: 407-647-1930

An antique auto dealer for the last 20 years. Right on I-4, just 20 miles from Walt Disney World. Buying, selling, & appraising cars. Pedal cars, prints, signs, automobilia are a sideline.

*Other categories: Mixed Automobilia; Pedal Cars; Signs*

## Shriver Auto Mall

See our main listing under "Toys, Truck"

## Silver Creek Antiques

Bob Burns
614 N. Bullard
Silver City, NM 88061 USA
TEL: 505-538-8705

Too cool store featuring a great selection of gas, oil, auto signs, pumps, 50s, old cars, weird bikes, toys, & much more. Located in an old Nash, Ply-DeSoto dealership. Owned by ex-drag racer. Check it out!

*Other categories: General Interest; Petroliana, Other; Signs*

## T and D Toy & Hobby

Tom & Dianne Mathews
116 S. Chicago Ave.
Freeport, IL 61032 USA
TEL: 815-232-1419

Full-line hobby shop, model kits, racing collectibles, R/C cars, & more. Dealer for GMP, Action, & Revell Collection Racing. Selected subject program model kits available. Open six days a week, closed Sunday. We mail order & accept Visa, MC.

*Other categories: Racing Artifacts; Models, Kits; Toys, General*

## Tee-Pee Model Toy Collectibles

See our main listing under "Toys, General"

## Thunder Road

Bill Morin
1018 Portion Rd.
Lake Ronkokoma, NY 11779 USA
TEL: 516-732-3877
FAX: 516-732-0753

Thunder Road, Long Island's premier store for automotive memorabilia & collectibles, model cars, diecasts, nostalgic signs, key chains, hats, T-shirts, hat pins, nostalgic decals, promos, books, Harley-Davidson stuff, Johnny Lightning, Hot Wheels, photos, & much much more. Something for everyone. We ship worldwide. Call for details.

*Other categories: Models, Kits; Signs; Clothing*

## Transportation Station

Roger Hurley
120 Broad St.
Kingsport, TN 37660 USA
TEL: 423-245-1601
FAX: 423-245-1601

Ertl banks, Hot Wheels, Matchbox, all types of toy cars. Buy, sell, trade. Open six days a week. Shipping available.

*Other categories: Toys, General; Hot Wheels; Toys, Truck*

## Weber's Nostalgia Supermarket

See our main listing under "Petroliana, Pumps & Globes"

## Keith Wendt

See our main listing under "Toys, General"

## Westchester Collectibles

See our main listing under "Toys, Truck"

## Wizzy's Collector Car Parts

See our main listing under "Mixed Automobilia"

# RT. 66 & ROADSIDE

## Bob Lichty Enterprises

See our main listing under "Shows & Events"

## Canton Classic Car Museum

See our main listing under "Museum"

## City Classics

See our main listing under "Models, Kits"

## Lost Highway Art Co.

Dick Schneider
PO Box 164
Bedford Hills, NY 10507 USA
TEL: 914-234-6016
FAX: 914-234-6016

The source for vintage roadside souvenir decals from the 1940s-1960s. These are original water-transfer decals, not repro stickers. States, cities, parks, & attractions coast to coast. Many styles are available, but quantities are limited for most. For color catalog & a free sample decal, send $3 (credited to order).

*Other categories: Art, Other; Specialized Automobilia*

## Miniatures by Jack

See our main listing under "Models, Precision"

## Monday's

See our main listing under "General Interest"

## Nighthorse Inc.

See our main listing under "Motorcycle Collectibles"

## The Old Road

See our main listing under "Signs"

## Pacific Communications

Matt Haugh
1801 East Fourth Ave.
Olympia, WA 98506 USA
TEL: 360-754-7211
FAX: 360-786-6695
Email: pacificvid@aol.com

Get your kicks on Rt. 66! This award-winning documentary transports you from Chicago to Los Angeles, & from yesterday's Dust Bowl to today's active revival. With archival footage & car commercials, this video road trip was rightfully called "the ultimate tribute to the Mother Road" by *Route 66 Magazine*.

*Other categories: Museum; Photographs; General Interest*

## Russell S. Rein

522 Maulbetsch
Ypsilanti, MI 48197 USA
TEL: 313-434-2968
Email: ypsi-slim@juno.com

Collect, buy, sell, trade memorabilia regarding Lincoln Hwy., Dixie Hwy., National Hwy., Rt. 66, etc. Books, postcards, road maps, travel brochures, route guides, early auto travel narratives, blue books, green books, WPA guides, photos, souvenirs. Topics include auto travel, petroliana, restaurants, diners, drive-ins, highway history, travel trailers, anything roadside America.

*Other categories: Cards, Postal; Books; Diner Memorabilia*

## Road Maps Etc.

See our main listing under "Literature"

## Route 66 Accessories Co.

Dave "Buz" Kirkel
PO Box 145
Western Springs, IL 60558 USA
TEL: 708-246-1543
FAX: 708-246-1085

World's largest selection of Route 66 merchandise. Includes signs, clothes, models, glassware, books, videos, automobilia, petroliana, Burma Shave, plus more. Always something new! Dealer inquiries invited.

*Other categories: Mixed Automobilia; Models, Precision; Petroliana, Other*

**Shelley's Foreign Auto**
See our main listing under "Specialized Automobilia"

**Te Amo J**
See our main listing under "Lamps"

**Ron Throckmorton**
See our main listing under "Petroliana, Other"

**Vanished Roadside America Art**
See our main listing under "Art, Prints & Posters"

**Viewfinders**
See our main listing under "General Interest"

**Walt Wimer, Jr.**
See our main listing under "Petroliana, Other"

**Yesterday's Highways Newsletter**
See our main listing under "Publications, Current"

## SHOWROOM ITEMS

**S. Adams Inc.**
See our main listing under "Specialized Automobilia"

**Auto Literature & Collectibles**
See our main listing under "Literature"

**Blaser's Auto**
See our main listing under "Specialized Automobilia"

**Checker USA**
See our main listing under "Literature"

**Craco Showcase Sales Gallery**
See our main listing under "Displays/Fixtures"

**Le Cramer**
2014 E Lincoln
Royal Oak, MI 48067 USA
TEL: 810-545-9018

FORD SVO MUSTANG 1984-1986 collector, owner, enthusiast. Buy, sell, trade.
*Other categories: Literature; Cards, Postal*

**DKC & Company**
See our main listing under "Models, Precision"

**4 Tek**
See our main listing under "Displays/Fixtures"

**Gus Garton Auto**
See our main listing under "Literature"

**William Goetzmann**
See our main listing under "Motorcycle Collectibles"

**Stan Hurd Auto Literature**
See our main listing under "Literature"

**L. Robert Hurwitz**
See our main listing under "Literature"

**Michael Knittel**
See our main listing under "Literature"

**Ric Kruse**
See our main listing under "Literature"

**M&M Automobilia Appraisers**
See our main listing under "Appraisal Service"

**McLellan's Automotive History**
See our main listing under "Literature"

**Walter Miller**
See our main listing under "Literature"

**Motorpress**
See our main listing under "Literature"

**Original Auto Literature**
See our main listing under "Literature"

**Port Jefferson Historical Automobile Research Institute**
See our main listing under "Literature"

**Rick Radtke**
See our main listing under "Literature"

**Saab Stories**
See our main listing under "Marque Specific"

**James T. Sandoro**
See our main listing under "Appraisal Service"

**Time Passages, Ltd.**
See our main listing under "Petroliana, Pumps & Globes"

**TMC Publications**
See our main listing under "Literature"

**Douglas Vogel**
See our main listing under "Literature"

**Willys/Jeep Collectibles**
See our main listing under "Specialized Automobilia"

**Woody's Garage**
See our main listing under "License Plates, Tags, etc."

**Wright's Custom Repair, Inc.**
See our main listing under "Petroliana, Pumps & Globes"

## SHOWS & EVENTS

**Capitol Miniature Auto Collectors Club**
See our main listing under "Club/Organization"

**The Classic Car Sale**
Tony Leopardo
PO Box 1011
San Mateo, CA 94403 USA
TEL: 415-349-8452
FAX: 415-340-9473

The Classic Car Sale is held every four months just south of San Francisco, California. Approx 150-200 collector cars, trucks, & motorcycles are offered to the public in a car show-like setting with all cars priced. If you are interested in buying or selling a collector car, just call us!

**Finger Lakes Diecast**
See our main listing under "Models, Precision"

**Greater Dakota Classics**
See our main listing under "Club/Organization"

## Gulf Oil Collector

See our main listing under "Petroliana, Other"

## Holliday Canopies

See our main listing under "Displays/Fixtures"

## Horseless Carriage Club of America

See our main listing under "Club/Organization"

## Dan Kruse Classic Car Productions

See our main listing under "Auction Firm"

## Bob Lichty Enterprises

Bob Lichty
1330 Fulton Rd. NW
Canton, OH 44703 USA
TEL: 330-456-7869
FAX: 330-456-7883

Event promoter & event consultant. Co-producer of Annual Gilmore Heritage Auto Show at LA Farmers Market each June. Collector of Gilmore petroliana, F & F Cereal cars, travel memorabilia, especially Lincoln Highway.

*Other categories: Mixed Automobilia; Rt. 66 & Roadside; Toys, General*

## Mid-State Collectibles

See our main listing under "Petroliana, Other"

## Northwest Hot Rod & Custom Car Council

See our main listing under "Club/Organization"

## Pate Museum of Transportation

Jim Peel
PO Box 711
Fort Worth, TX 76101 USA
TEL: 817-332-1161
FAX: 817-336-8441

Pate Swap Meet. Every April at the Pate Museum on US 377 near Cresson, Texas. Third largest swap meet in the US. 7,000 spaces.

## SRE Industries

See our main listing under "Mascots/Badges/Emblems"

## South Shore Auto Sports

Ron Richardson
620 Park Ave., Suite 216
Rochester, NY 14607-2943 USA
TEL: 716-425-2490
FAX: 716-442-3079

Travel to several Carlisle events, Hershey, & other events by motorcoach. Late Friday departures from Buffalo, Rochester, Syracuse, & several other New York State cities. Return 24 hours later! Call for more information.

*Other categories: General Interest; Mixed Automobilia; Toys, Truck*

# SIGNS

## Ablaze Enterprises Inc.

See our main listing under "Mixed Automobilia"

## Allen Oil Sales

See our main listing under "Petroliana, Other"

## Auto Air & Audio

See our main listing under "Mixed Automobilia"

## Big T's Gas Trash

See our main listing under "Petroliana, Other"

## Blast from the Past

See our main listing under "Neon"

## Blast from the Past, Inc.

See our main listing under "Retail Store"

## Bob's Trucks

See our main listing under "Toys, Truck"

## Greg Bowden

See our main listing under "Motorcycle Collectibles"

## Clapper Restorations

See our main listing under "Petroliana, Pumps & Globes"

## Clark's Historic Rt. 99 General Store

See our main listing under "Mixed Automobilia"

## Classic Services

See our main listing under "Specialized Automobilia"

## Collector Auto Appraisal Co.

See our main listing under "Appraisal Service"

## Curtis Equipment Co.

See our main listing under "Appraisal Service"

## DXR Automotive

Dan Reidy
4729 Ramus St., Ste. G
Houston, TX 77092 USA
TEL: 713-956-5223
FAX: 713-956-5241
Email: dxrinc@hal-pc.org

DXR 3D/X-ray Viper GTS wall sign is a very high resolution image that has been lithoed onto a sculptured, vacuum-formed Bakelite mold to produce a very dramatic commercial art wall piece. The Viper literally blasts off the wall when plugged in! Don't be left out – order this soon-to-be collectors item of the most talked-about car in twenty years! Viper GTS by Dodge.

*Other categories: Art, Original; Specialized Automobilia*

## Dave's Signs & Collectibles

See our main listing under "Petroliana, Other"

## Dooley & Sons

Dooley Cameron
1311 Houston St.
Levelland, TX 79336 USA
TEL: 806-894-3321
FAX: 806-894-9272

We buy, sell, trade dealership & oil & gas signs. Mostly auto & truck dealership porcelain signs. Also toy trucks.

*Other categories: Toys, Truck; Pedal Cars; Petroliana, Pumps & Globes*

## Dunbar's Gallery

See our main listing under "Motorcycle Collectibles"

## Bob English

216 Spring St.
Marshfield, MA 02050 USA
TEL: 617-837-0111

Specialize in early (1900-1940) automotive porcelain or tin signs: advertising products, auto clubs, road-directional, tourists, bus, taxi. Also enamel badges of early US auto clubs & auto radiator emblems, Massachusetts chauffeur & taxi items, & New England porcelain license plates. Low numbers, first issues, odd categories. Buy, trade.

*Other categories: Mascots/Badges/Emblems; Chauffeur/Taxi Items; License Plates, Tags, etc.*

## Enterprise Cars

Tom Beary
Dock Road
Limerick, Ireland
TEL: +353-61-301301
FAX: +353-61-301340

European collector will buy, sell shop signs, globes, posters, prints, toys, cans. Travels worldwide. Visits USA every 6 months.

*Other categories: Petroliana, Other; Mixed Automobilia; Art, Prints & Posters*

## Fineline Car Co.

See our main listing under "General Interest"

## Formula 1 World

See our main listing under "Mixed Automobilia"

## Frank's Toys & Adv. Memorabilia

See our main listing under "Mixed Automobilia"

## Full Serve

See our main listing under "Petroliana, Pumps & Globes"

## Paul Furlinger

See our main listing under "Petroliana, Other"

## Bob Gajewski

See our main listing under "Mixed Automobilia"

## Gus Garton Auto

See our main listing under "Literature"

## Gasoline Alley

See our main listing under "Motorcycle Collectibles"

## Gregory Gibson

See our main listing under "License Plates, Tags, etc."

## Philip R. Goldberg

See our main listing under "Mascots/Badges/Emblems"

## Gulf Oil Collector

See our main listing under "Petroliana, Other"

## Robert J. Harrington

See our main listing under "Spark Plugs"

## Hi-Tec Customs

See our main listing under "Restoration Service"

## Richard Hurlburt

See our main listing under "License Plates, Tags, etc."

## Iowa Gas Swap Meet & Auctions

See our main listing under "Petroliana, Other"

## Jim Jalosky

See our main listing under "Petroliana, Pumps & Globes"

## Jim & Connie's Collectibles

See our main listing under "Specialized Automobilia"

## Brad Kellogg

See our main listing under "Pedal Cars"

## Key Telephone Co.

Paul Engelice
23399 Rio Del Mar Dr.
Boca Raton, FL 33486-8504 USA
TEL: 561-338-3332

Wanted: Porcelain signs, prefer 16 in. or smaller. Gas, oil, pump, lubester-related. Buy, sell, trade.

*Other categories: Petroliana, Other; Petroliana, Pumps & Globes*

## License Plates, Etc.

See our main listing under "License Plates, Tags, etc."

## John Mancino's Garage

See our main listing under "Petroliana, Other"

## Ron & Carol Martinelli

See our main listing under "Petroliana, Other"

## Max Neon Design Group

See our main listing under "Manufacturer"

## Metropolitan & British Triumph

See our main listing under "Toys, General"

## Mid-State Collectibles

See our main listing under "Petroliana, Other"

## Mobil Maniacs

See our main listing under "Petroliana, Other"

## Paul Mote

See our main listing under "Petroliana, Other"

## Motorcycles & Memorabilia

See our main listing under "Motorcycle Collectibles"

## Motoring Memories

See our main listing under "License Plates, Tags, etc."

## Thomas Novinsky

See our main listing under "Petroliana, Other"

## The Old Road

PO Box 2030
Redondo Beach, CA 90278 USA
TEL: 310-793-0129
Email: aw992@lafn.org

Neon signs & clocks, originals & limited edition replicas of some of your favorite signs. Neon clocks customized with your family or company name. Porcelain limited production signs: interested in Buster Brown, Poll Parrot, Pup n Suds.

*Other categories: Rt. 66 & Roadside; Petroliana, Other; Diner Memorabilia*

## Oniell's Collectibles

See our main listing under "Petroliana, Other"

## Rick Pease

See our main listing under "Petroliana, Other"

## Petrolitis

See our main listing under "Petroliana, Other"

## Portell Restorations

See our main listing under "Pedal Cars"

## Production Plus Graphics Inc.

Kevin Sulzer
1616 E. Roosevelt Rd. #1
Wheaton, IL 60187 USA
TEL: 630-588-1948
FAX: 630-588-1848

Create your own graphic decals from your computer with the S2 Graphics Modeler. Type in text or customize a graphic, then click "cut," & the S2 Modeler will cut out the letters & graphics on a wide variety of colors. Simply peel & stick! Includes software & model cutter. Only $675.

*Other categories: Specialized Automobilia; Toys, Truck*

## Pumping Iron

See our main listing under "Petroliana, Other"

## Rader's Relics

See our main listing under "Retail Store"

## Frank R. Righetti

2075 E. Main St.
Peekskill, NY 10566 USA
TEL: 914-737-7772
FAX: 914-737-7773

3 tons of original porcelain signs for sale. Dealer, gasoline, tire, battery, truck, & related items. Buy, sell, trade. Complete collections purchased. Appraisals for estate settlement. Large display at Peekskill, New York. Call for personal appointment.

*Other categories: License Plates, Tags, etc.; Appraisal Service; General Interest*

## Roadkill Decorators Supply Company

David Webb
293 Chase Ave.
Manson, WA 98831 USA
TEL: 509-687-3879
Email: oldneon@kozi.com

Purveyors of fine American roadside art & souvenirs from the 20th century. Buy, sell, trade. Specializing in porcelain/neon signs such as auto, truck, bus, motorcycle, gas, paint, soda, ice cream, etc. Collecting all light-up advertising signs, clocks, arcade games, vintage televisions, vending machines, Veltex, Seaside, Mohawk, Webb oil.

*Other categories: Petroliana, Other; Restoration Service; Art, Other*

## Thomas Rootlieb

See our main listing under "Petroliana, Pumps & Globes"

## SMB Designs

Jack Blair
3005 Mesa Rd.
Willow Park, TX 76087 USA
TEL: 817-441-7805
FAX: 817-441-7805
Email: jblairjr@imagin.net

Nostalgic tin & porcelain signs, thermometers, refrigerator magnets. From 27 different manufacturers worldwide. Widest selection in the nation! New signs coming out every month! These signs are the newest decorating craze for businesses, homes, dorms, clubs, etc. Send $1 (refundable) for catalog.

*Other categories: Mixed Automobilia; Mascots/Badges/Emblems*

## SAAB Stuff

See our main listing under "Marque Specific"

## Sign of the Times

John Aschenbrenner
969 Wallace Drive
San Jose, CA 95120 USA
TEL: 408-268-1564

Specialize in advertising signs. Everything original, no reproductions. Gasoline, soft drinks, tobacco, automotive/petroleum, & 1950s collectibles. Buy, sell, trade. Looking for Mobil gas collectibles. Send for list or call after 4pm PST.

*Other categories: Mixed Automobilia; Diner Memorabilia; Petroliana, Other*

## Silver Creek Antiques

See our main listing under "Retail Store"

## Al Simonenko

217 S. Evangeline
Dearborn Heights, MI 48125 USA
TEL: 313-730-8742
FAX: 313-730-1035

Porcelain & tin petro-related signs for sale from private collection. All items grade 8-1/2 or better. Also: gas pumps, globes, light-up clocks, 1930s cigarette mach., oil cans, Polarine porc. thermometer, light-up "Penn-Eaton" 1930s sign, automobilia signs, miscellaneous petro-related containers, NOS "Pennzoil" oil can rack, etc.

*Other categories: Mixed Automobilia; Petroliana, Other; Petroliana, Pumps & Globes*

## Dan Smith

See our main listing under "Mascots/Badges/Emblems"

## David C. Start

Rt 4 Box 1177
Cleveland, TX 77327 USA
TEL: 281-592-3250

Signs, auto memorabilia, & other junk.

*Other category: Mixed Automobilia*

## Dennis C. Stauffer

See our main listing under "Petroliana, Other"

## Steve's Antiques

Steve Music
8164 NW 68th Terrace
Tamarac, FL 33321 USA
TEL: 954-726-9071

Buy, sell, trade. Vintage advertising tins & signs picturing early automobiles, Indians, women, blacks. Early auto body & paint shop signs. Graphic auto display cabinets. Excellent condition only. Send pictures & prices.

*Other categories: Petroliana, Pumps & Globes; Mixed Automobilia; Specialized Automobilia*

## Steve's Service Station Stuff

See our main listing under "Petroliana, Other"

## Thunder Road

See our main listing under "Retail Store"

## Time Passages, Ltd.

See our main listing under "Petroliana, Pumps & Globes"

## Toys & Cars

See our main listing under "Petroliana, Other"

## Mike Tyler

See our main listing under "Petroliana, Other"

## Valenti Classics, Inc.

See our main listing under "Restoration Service"

## Robert Van Gilder

See our main listing under "Petroliana, Other"

## Vanished Roadside America Art

See our main listing under "Art, Prints & Posters"

## Weber's Nostalgia Supermarket

See our main listing under "Petroliana, Pumps & Globes"

## Greg Wheeler

See our main listing under "Petroliana, Other"

## Willys/Jeep Collectibles

See our main listing under "Specialized Automobilia"

# SLOT CARS

## Joseph Camp

See our main listing under "Mixed Automobilia"

## Diamond Hobbies

Tom Stumpf
316 Brehaut Ave.
Staten Island, NY 10307 USA
TEL: 718-948-4268

Slot cars, HO, 1/32, 1/24 bought, sold, traded. Drag racing diecast.

## Doc & Jesse's Auto Parts

See our main listing under "Models, Kits"

## EWJ Marketing

See our main listing under "Racing Artifacts"

## Electric Dreams

Philippe de Lespinay
1121 Wakeham Ave. Ste. M
Santa Ana, CA 92705 USA
TEL: 714-547-5382
FAX: 714-547-5382

Buy & sell 1/24, 1/32, HO slot racing cars/kits of the 1960s. We also restore & build cars to your needs. We carry only NOS parts & cars, no reproductions. We make our own line of slot racing-related products, & we can estimate the value of your collection. Our price list is published four times per year & costs $4, refundable.

*Other categories: Models, Kits; Mixed Automobilia; Restoration Service*

## HO Motoring & Racing

Joe Bodnarchuk
62 McKinley Avenue
Kenmore, NY 14217-2414 USA
TEL: 716-873-0264
FAX: 716-873-0264
Email: webmaster@bodnarchuk.com

Atlas HO, 1/32, 1/24 slot car archivists & historians. Seeking the following historically significant material: slot cars, racing sets, kits, store displays, parts displays, salesmen's samples, old hobby shop store stock, boxed track, artwork, buildings, magazines, photographs, commercials, dealer catalogs, accessories, etc. Also looking for Marusan, a Japanese version of Atlas.

*Other categories: Hot Rod Memorabilia; Models, Kits*

## Howard Johansen

5738 So. Redwood Rd. Ste. 263
Salt Lake City, UT 84123-5395 USA
TEL: 801-967-6454
FAX: 801-562-2831
Email: howardj@inconnect.com

*HO Slot Car & Accessories Value Guide #4.* Features include: manufacturers, part numbers, car & color descriptions, cross references, & dollar values. Covers over 75 manufacturers' products! $21.95 plus S&H $4 US, $5 Europe.

*Other category: Books*

## Tony Marchitto

2061 Oak Springs Road
Oakville, Ontario L6H 5P9 Canada
TEL: 905-842-8916
FAX: 905-338-7244

Specializing in 1/32, 1/24, & HO slot cars. Buy, sell, trade. From the early 1960s to the most present Scalextric, Eldon, Ninco, SCX, Fly, Strombecker, Cox, Revell, Monogram, K & B, Dynamic, Aurora, etc. Parts, accessories. Also collecting books, catalogs, magazines, singles or complete collections purchased. Call after 7pm, send SASE, or fax.

*Other categories: Books; Art, Prints & Posters; Publications, Current*

## Pacific Restoration

Rick Stevens
9312 E. Heaney Circle
Santee, CA 92071 USA
TEL: 619-562-1295
FAX: 619-562-6755
Email: jasinc.santee@worldnet.att.net

Models, diecast, & slot cars. Restoration of cars & construction of kit cars.

*Other categories: Models, Kits; Gas-Powered Racers*

## Road Race Replicas

Phil Pignon
7184 Hwy A
Strafford, MO 65757 USA
TEL: 417-736-2494
Email: Tjet Parts@aol.com

HO slot car restoration parts, chassis & even bodies for Aurora Vibrators, Thunderjets, AFX, & Tyco slot cars. We have replacement chrome bumpers, glass, boots, booms, drivers, & bodies for nearly 70 different slot cars! Road Race Replicas is a complete service house with thousands of parts & bodies in stock.

*Other categories: Restoration Service; Manufacturer; Models, Kits*

## Wee Wheels Restoration

See our main listing under "Pedal Cars"

## Wheels of Fun, Inc.

David Burtch
P.O. Box 1153
Polson, MT 50860 USA
TEL: 406-883-2278
FAX: 406-883-4449
Email: wheels@servco.com

Western Montana's fun spot! Largest go-cart & slot car tracks around. We sell diecast, models, rockets, car pictures, NASCAR items, & more. Check our web page at
http://www.inetco.net/~wheels/

*Other categories: Hot Wheels; Mixed Automobilia; Models, Kits*

## Kirk F. White

See our main listing under "Gas-Powered Racers"

## Michael Wojtowicz

See our main listing under "Racing Artifacts"

# SPARK PLUGS

## Robert J. Harrington

6 Village Road
Milford, CT 06460 USA
TEL: 203-878-8013
FAX: 203-878-2013

Wanted: old & unusual spark plugs as follows: odd names, sizes, features,

primer cups, coil tops. Tin & porcelain signs. Cabinets, cleaning machines, literature, paper & cloth banners. Paperweights, pins, & buttons. Also salesmen's samples, cutaways. Also salesmen's sample cases. Please no Champion or AC items.

*Other categories: Specialized Automobilia; Signs; Manufacturer*

## Clyde Hensley

See our main listing under "Motorcycle Collectibles"

## Bob Lint Motor Shop

See our main listing under "Mixed Automobilia"

## Kirk Monson

719 Farmington
Derby, KS 67037 USA
TEL: 316-788-1667

Collector of old, odd, & unusual spark plugs. Buy, sell, & some for trade. Have lots of obsolete NOS plugs for old cars, trucks, & engines. Interested in anything spark plug-related. Need spark plug application literature printed prior to 1950. Gasoline collectibles, including oil & antifreeze change tags.

*Other category: Petroliana, Other*

## RJN Automobilia

See our main listing under "Marque Specific"

## Seebee Enterprises

See our main listing under "Displays/Fixtures"

## Spark Plug Collectors of America

Chad Windham, President
3401 NE Riverside
Pendleton, OR 97801-3431 USA
TEL: 541-276-4069

Spark plugs – collect, trade, sell plugs & any related signs, displays, etc. For information on Spark Plug Collectors of America, call or write.

# SPECIALIZED AUTOMOBILIA

## AAA Small Car World

See our main listing under "Marque Specific"

## S. Adams Inc.

Stan Adams
9359 SE Dundee Dr.
Portland, OR 97266 USA
TEL: 503-238-7999

Museum setting of collector cars, gas pumps, signs, cans, extensive petroliana, neon, toys, pedal cars, soda signs & machines, picnic coolers. Various original & restored items for sale. Also, strong buyer of above items in mint condition.

*Other categories: Petroliana, Other; Pedal Cars; Showroom Items*

## Alex & Phil's Filling Station

See our main listing under "Petroliana, Other"

## American Arrow

See our main listing under "Mascots/Badges/Emblems"

## American Eagle Racing

See our main listing under "Hot Rod Memorabilia"

## Art's Automobilia

See our main listing under "Toys, General"

## Auto-Ideas

Tim Pawl
4960 Arrowhead
West Bloomfield, MI 48323 USA
TEL: 810-682-2007
FAX: 810-682-2043
Email: pawl@earthlink.com

Specializing in all items related to Cadillac cars, parts, toys, etc. All pace car items & Indy 500, particularly interested in low production volume vehicles, show cars, accessories, autographs, literature. Buy, sell, trade. Call with your needs & leads.

*Other categories: Marque Specific; Racing Artifacts; Motoring Accessories*

## Autographics

See our main listing under "Books"

## Automobilia Auctions, Inc.

See our main listing under "Auction Firm"

## Automobilia Cycles Trucks (ACT)

Randy House
7903 W. Layton Ave. Suite 411
Greenfield, WI 53220 USA
TEL: 414-281-9012
FAX: 414-281-9014

We specialize in diecast autos, pace cars, & race cars. All scales, motorcycles, beverage trucks, beer & soda, gas & oil. All scales, all logos. Also automotive art lithographs, prints, posters, all forms of racing art, NASCAR, Indy Car, NHRA, motorcycles. Also petroleum, nostalgia cars, & hot rod art & books.

*Other categories: Toys, Truck; Art, Prints & Posters; Racing Artifacts*

## Automotive Magazines

See our main listing under "Literature"

## BJM

See our main listing under "Mascots/Badges/Emblems"

## Back In Time Toys

See our main listing under "Models, Precision"

## Bergen Distributors

See our main listing under "Petroliana, Other"

## Andy Bernstein

See our main listing under "License Plates, Tags, etc."

## Blaser's Auto

Stewart or Steven Blaser
3200 48th Ave.
Moline, IL 61265 USA
TEL: 309-764-3571
FAX: 309-764-1155
Email: blazauto@sprynet.com

We specialize in Nash Rambler & AMC NOS replacement parts. We also have many showroom & sales-related items for sale. Large inventory of dealer service letters, owner's manuals, literature,

& original service books for repair by owners. Please call Monday - Friday, 9 to 5 CST.

*Other categories: General Interest; Showroom Items; Books*

## The British Garage

John Jennings
91 Palmer Ave.
Tenafly, NJ 07670 USA
TEL: 201-894-0091

Specializing in automobilia of British motoring history prior to 1969. Buy & sell art, prints, posters, service station collectibles, racing memorabilia, & motoring accessories, all British. Interested in anything British auto-related prior to 1969. Also deal in all kinds of rally paraphernalia. Call any evening, EST.

*Other categories: Racing Artifacts; Motoring Accessories; Mixed Automobilia*

## Brooklin Models, Ltd.

See our main listing under "Models, Precision"

## Harry Burnstine

56860 State Rd. 15 So.
Bristol, IN 46507 USA
TEL: 219-848-7702
FAX: 219-522-0827

Specialize in Porsche-related items only. These include literature, posters, toys, signs, & all dealer-related items. Buy, sell, trade. Dealers – I have large quantities of several items available.

*Other categories: Literature; Toys, General; Art, Prints & Posters*

## C.S.P. Calendars

Larry & Alice Richter
300 Parkway Lane
Coos Bay, OR 97420 USA
TEL: 541-269-1815
FAX: 541-269-1815

Specialize in the photography of original, award-winning Corvettes from 1953 to the current year. Beautiful scenery & Corvette trivia are included each month. Prints can be bought of any car in the calendar. Old calendars, license plates, & bumper stickers are available. Send for free information.

*Other categories: Photographs; Publications, Current; Art, Prints & Posters*

## The Can Man
See our main listing under "Petroliana, Other"

## Car Crazy
See our main listing under "Hot Rod Memorabilia"

## Castle Concepts
See our main listing under "Racing Artifacts"

## Check the Oil! Magazine
See our main listing under "Petroliana, Other"

## Christie's
See our main listing under "Auction Firm"

## Classic Services
Reg Morrison
PO Box 280
Bismarck, ND 58502 USA
TEL: 701-258-8661

Auto, truck, tractor, gasoline, & misc. collectibles & gifts. Handcrafted clocks, thermometers, pen sets, buckles. Also sketches, note cards, & porcelain signs. Send SASE for list.

*Other categories: Art, Other; Jewelry; Signs*

## Collector's Studio Motorsport Gallery
See our main listing under "Racing Artifacts"

## Robert Covarrubias Studios
Robert Covarrubias
330 W. Hwy. 246 #59
Buellton, CA 93427 USA
TEL: 805-688-5529

A true classic returns. Cast from the original work of art, a dirt track racer desktop humidor bonded in bronze. Limited edition of 500.

*Other categories: Petroliana, Other; Mixed Automobilia; Racing Artifacts*

## Curtis Equipment Co.
See our main listing under "Appraisal Service"

## Christopher R. Custer Inc.
Christopher R. Custer
7315 Parkview Dr.
Frederick, MD 21702 USA
TEL: 301-473-7988

Wanted: Custer car information, parts cars, wheelchairs, electric motors, gasoline engines, etc. I will trade copies of anything that I have for any copies of anything you may have collected. C'mon you enthusiasts out there. Let's get enough info to put a small book about our critters on the shelves.

## DXR Automotive
See our main listing under "Signs"

## Dave's Tag Barn
See our main listing under "License Plates, Tags, etc."

## Doo-Wop Props
See our main listing under "Hot Rod Memorabilia"

## Ed Jacobowitz Cadillac & LaSalle
See our main listing under "Marque Specific"

## Elegant Accessories
Roy Lassen
29 Betty Dr.
Santa Barbara, CA 93105 USA
TEL: 805-569-7160

Specialize 1920s-1950s auto-motorcycle accessories, dealer options, & quality aftermarket offerings. Examples: fog lights, spotlights, cow lights, fender lights, taillights, musical horns, windwings, trunks, trunk racks, sidemount covers, mirrors, clocks, compasses, record players, tissue dispensers, radios, heaters, vanities, robe rails, footrests, steering mounts, fan turn signals, flashlights, holders, suitcases. Buy, sell, trade.

*Other categories: Mixed Automobilia; Motoring Accessories; Luggage/Picnic Sets*

## Eureka Antique & Collectibles
See our main listing under "Marque Specific"

## Fairlane Automotive Specialties
See our main listing under "Pedal Cars"

## Fast Times Automobilia
See our main listing under "Art, Prints & Posters"

## Formula 1 World
See our main listing under "Mixed Automobilia"

## Robert J. Harrington
See our main listing under "Spark Plugs"

## Harvey Racing Engines
Jim Harvey
1 Toll Lane
Levittown, NY 11756 USA
TEL: 516-796-9179
FAX: 516-796-9179
Email: jim@hre.com

Custom racing engines. Restoration of vintage race engines, specialized machining services. Small-block Chevrolet specialists. Hilborn & Enderle fuel injection specialists.

*Other categories: Manufacturer; Tools*

## Hayes Associates
See our main listing under "Petroliana, Pumps & Globes"

## Himes Museum of Motor Racing
See our main listing under "Museum"

## Holly's Miniatures
Mark & Holly Thorson
1303 Panorama Drive
Decorah, IA 52101 USA
TEL: 319-382-0075
FAX: 319-387-0685

Specialty custom-built miniature wooden gas stations & automobile dealerships 1/12 or 1/24 scale. Incredible detail, including lighting, fixtures, gas pumps, pop machines, signs, tools, etc. Will build according to your specifications. Prices commensurate with detail. Color pictures $4 refundable with order. Inquiries welcomed.

*Other categories: Displays/Fixtures; Toys, General; General Interest*

## Hot Rod Art

See our main listing under "Art, Prints & Posters"

## Hudson Motor Car Company Memorabilia

Ken Poynter
19638 Huntington
Harper Woods, MI 48225 USA
TEL: 313-886-9292

Serious collector of anything pertaining to Hudson, Essex, & Terraplane cars & trucks. If it pertains to the Hudson Motor Car Company, I'm interested! Looking for items such as factory badges, pins, signs, dealer displays, model cars, watch fobs, jewelry, accessories, banners, posters, trophies, awards, emblems, watches, anything!

*Other categories: Mixed Automobilia; General Interest; Appraisal Service*

## L. Robert Hurwitz

See our main listing under "Literature"

## Italian Cars & Related Stuff

See our main listing under "Marque Specific"

## J & E Spindizzie

See our main listing under "Gas-Powered Racers"

## S.L. Jaffe, Inc.

See our main listing under "Appraisal Service"

## Jake's Mustang Dismantling

See our main listing under "Restoration Service"

## Jim & Connie's Collectibles

Jim Harris
16743 39th Ave NE
Seattle, WA 98155 USA
TEL: 206-364-6637

Specialize in Mopar automobilia. Buy, sell, trade. Shop manuals, brochures, parts books, Road Runner, & *Dukes of Hazzard*. Also dealing in tin-litho & pressed-steel toys, gas station automobilia.

*Other categories: Mixed Automobilia; Signs; Toys, General*

## Ron Johnson

See our main listing under "General Interest"

## Jim Jones

See our main listing under "Cards, Postal"

## Robert Kegler

See our main listing under "Mascots/Badges/Emblems"

## The Klemantaski Collection

See our main listing under "Photographs"

## Lights Up

Ray W. Bryant
14862 E 45th Ave.
Denver, CO 80239 USA
TEL: 303-371-0306

Specializing in cigarette lighters, pocket & table models. Buy, sell, trade. Wanted: Zippos, Ronson, Evans, Dunhill with advertising of the following: oil & gas company, autos, trucks, motorcycles, airplanes. Highest price paid for old Zippos, any lighter with watch or clock, lighter for race cars or track. Please send SASE.

*Other categories: Petroliana, Other; Jewelry; General Interest*

## Lost Highway Art Co.

See our main listing under "Rt. 66 & Roadside"

## Ron & Carol Martinelli

See our main listing under "Petroliana, Other"

## Bob McClernan

See our main listing under "Petroliana, Other"

## Jamie McGuire

RD 2, Box 273, Frenchtown
Towanda, PA 18848 USA
TEL: 717-265-2614

Pennsylvania inspection stickers, most years. Buy, sell, trade for ones I don't have.

*Other category: License Plates, Tags, etc.*

## McLong Tags & Ads

See our main listing under "License Plates, Tags, etc."

## Mike & Bob's Promos

See our main listing under "Promos"

## Milestone Motorcars

See our main listing under "Models, Precision"

## Miniatures by Jack

See our main listing under "Models, Precision"

## Edward E. Moberg, Jr.

See our main listing under "Art, Original"

## Mobil Maniacs

See our main listing under "Petroliana, Other"

## Mobil & Morgans

See our main listing under "Petroliana, Other"

## Mobilia

See our main listing under "Publications, Current"

## The Model Shop

See our main listing under "Models, Kits"

## Tim Moe

See our main listing under "Racing Artifacts"

## Motorcycles & Memorabilia

See our main listing under "Motorcycle Collectibles"

## Motorpress

See our main listing under "Literature"

## Muffler Time Exhaust & Memorabilia

See our main listing under "Hot Rod Memorabilia"

## Mustang Restorations

Herb Brown
Box 326
East Taxes, PA 18046 USA
TEL: 610-398-2176
FAX: 610-266-4736

AC Cobra & Cord memorabilia wanted. Literature, advertising items, models, dealer displays, anything you have, I'm interested. Please state condition & price.

*Other categories: Literature; Toys, General; General Interest*

## NASCAR Collectibles

Steve Baun
25 Winding Hill Dr.
Etters, PA 17319 USA
TEL: 717-932-1284
FAX: 717-932-1284

NASCAR collectible & souvenirs, autograph items from top NASCAR drivers. Items include diecast, clothing, signs, sheet metal, photos.

## Original Auto Literature

See our main listing under "Literature"

## Palmer Motor Racing

See our main listing under "Models, Precision"

## Pastimes

James M. Jones III
880 Montclair Rd. 1st Floor
Birmingham, AL 35213 USA
TEL: 205-599-3500
FAX: 205-599-3569
Email: jjones9572@aol.com

NASCAR programs & yearbooks. Serious collector; will buy, sell, or trade. Also primary interest is NASCAR Winston Cup pre-1972. Also Busch Grand National, modified & truck programs. Indy Car programs collected.

*Other categories: Racing Artifacts; Literature*

## People Kars

See our main listing under "Toys, General"

## Pirelli Collector

David W. Reed
17 Middle Brook Pond Rd.
Redding, CT 06896 USA
TEL: 203-938-3836
FAX: 203-938-8087

Specialize in Pirelli Tire Co. items. Buy, sell, trade. Porcelain signs, sales literature, tire ashtrays, calendars, display items, lapel pins, letter openers, dishes, plant badges, paper clips, banners, tire holders, posters, painted signs, promo-

tional items, tin signs. Hershey spaces CG97-102. "If it's Pirelli, I collect it."

*Other categories: Marque Specific; Mixed Automobilia; Racing Artifacts*

## Prime Pumps

See our main listing under "Petroliana, Pumps & Globes"

## The Printer's Stone, Ltd.

See our main listing under "Art, Other"

## Production Plus Graphics Inc.

See our main listing under "Signs"

## Rick Radtke

See our main listing under "Literature"

## Stephen J. Raiche

See our main listing under "License Plates, Tags, etc."

## Railfan Specialties

M. DeRosa
PO Box 10245
Wilmington, NC 28405 USA
TEL: 910-686-2820

Museum gift shop supplier of quality flashing LED buttons. All feature classic cars that light up with LEDs. Unique & very popular. Call for dealer price list & artwork. Also available: police cars, school buses, fire trucks, & ambulances. Will be adding muscle & antique cars over the next few months.

*Other categories: Clothing; Jewelry; License Plates, Tags, etc.*

## Rally Enterprises

See our main listing under "Models, Kits"

## Remember Woodward, Inc.

See our main listing under "Mixed Automobilia"

## Route 66 Decanters

Gary Vass
2279 E. Kearney Blvd.
Springfield, MO 65803 USA
TEL: 417-865-9500

Liquor decanters by Route 66 – transporation-related decanters are our specialty. We re-create many Jim Beam auto decanters in special colors, also Texaco trucks & Route 66 cars & trucks.

Any decanter available. We buy, sell, trade decanters.

*Other categories: Mixed Automobilia; Promos; General Interest*

## Royal Coach

Charles B. Wotring
911 Conley Drive
Mechanicsburg, PA 17055-5159 USA
TEL: 717-691-1147
FAX: 717-691-6623

Bus industry memorabilia bought & sold, limited to North American vintage through current. Manufacturers' brochures, photos, operator & maintenance manuals, postcards, promotional items, timetables, model & toy buses. For current general catalog listing, send $2.

*Other categories: Toys, General; Models, Precision*

## Saab Stories

See our main listing under "Marque Specific"

## SAAB Stuff

See our main listing under "Marque Specific"

## James T. Sandoro

See our main listing under "Appraisal Service"

## Charles Schalebaum

See our main listing under "Art, Original"

## Shelley's Foreign Auto

Roy Shelley
RD #3
Sewickley, PA 15143 USA
TEL: 412-266-7707
FAX: 412-266-2259

Specializing in Maserati, Ferrari, Alfa Romeo, Fiat autos & parts, signs, dealer-related articles & European & British gas & oil, parts suppliers, etc. Buy, sell, trade. Also Rt. 66, 40, 30-related items.

*Other categories: Mixed Automobilia; Petroliana, Other; Rt. 66 & Roadside*

## Dan Smith

See our main listing under "Mascots/Badges/Emblems"

## Sotheby's

See our main listing under "Auction Firm"

## Spyder Enterprises

Everett "Tony" Singer
RFD 1682
Laurel Hollow, NY 11791-9644 USA
TEL: 516-367-3293
FAX: 516-367-3260

Porsche (356/Spyder), Ferrari, Formula 1 & 2 of 1950s/60s era: memorabilia, literature, posters, dealer or display presentation items, photos, programs, books, models, signs, advertising items, etc. Very active worldwide buyer; glad to trade or sell. Please phone 6-10pm EST or weekends; 24-hour fax; send SASE for current list.

*Other categories: Art, Prints & Posters; Literature; Racing Artifacts*

## Steve's Antiques

See our main listing under "Signs"

## Steve's Antiques & Restoration

See our main listing under "Restoration Service"

## Mark Suozzi

See our main listing under "Motoring Accessories"

## Supercar Collectibles

See our main listing under "Toys, General"

## Tavares Motorsport

Mat Tavares
PO Box 165
Carlisle, MA 01741 USA
TEL: 508-369-0801
FAX: 508-369-8076

We specialize in vintage & historic automobilia, including racing ephemera – autographs, programs, photographs, postcards, original art & prints – & rare & out-of-print books on racing, makes & marques, & biographies.

*Other categories: Racing Artifacts; Books; Photographs*

## Te Amo J

See our main listing under "Lamps"

## Ron Throckmorton

See our main listing under "Petroliana, Other"

## Turtle Creek Scale Models

See our main listing under "Models, Precision"

## US Toy Collector Magazine

See our main listing under "Toys, Truck"

## Robert Van Gilder

See our main listing under "Petroliana, Other"

## Victory Lane

See our main listing under "Toys, General"

## Viewfinders

See our main listing under "General Interest"

## VW Collector

See our main listing under "Marque Specific"

## John W. Webster

See our main listing under "Mascots/Badges/Emblems"

## Willys/Jeep Collectibles

Ed Paige Jr.
1284 North Main St.
Raynham, MA 02767 USA
TEL: 508-824-2479

Wanted: all Jeep-related items, including signs (porcelain, tin, backlit, Masonite), posters, clocks, banners, toys, dealer showroom items, etc. from the 1946 to 1986 era (Willys-Kaiser-AMC). Also collect unusual advertising clocks & want porcelain GMC Trucks sign, Chevrolet super service sign 30-42 ins., priced reasonably.

*Other categories: Signs; Showroom Items; Mixed Automobilia*

## Henry Winningham

3205 S. Morgan St.
Chicago, IL 60608 USA
TEL: 773-847-1672

Taxicab stuff. Wanted – everything & anything pre-1950.

## Woody's Garage

See our main listing under "License Plates, Tags, etc."

## Workbench

See our main listing under "Mascots/Badges/Emblems"

## Wyckoff Auto

See our main listing under "Mixed Automobilia"

## John J. Zolomij, Inc.

See our main listing under "Appraisal Service"

# TOOLS

## Adams Flea Market

See our main listing under "Mixed Automobilia"

## Auto Epoch

See our main listing under "Publications, Current"

## Classic Restoration

Roy A. Judd
2416 Hermosa Ave.
Hermosa Beach, CA 90254 USA
TEL: 310-379-3914

Tools wanted. Auto tools (non-Ford) for collector. Send details.

*Other categories: General Interest; Mixed Automobilia; Motoring Accessories*

## Harvey Racing Engines

See our main listing under "Specialized Automobilia"

## The Model Shop

See our main listing under "Models, Kits"

## Western Industrial

See our main listing under "Toys, Tractor"

# TOYS, GENERAL

## Abbott & Hast Ltd. Auto Promos & Kits

See our main listing under "Models, Kits"

## Adams Flea Market

See our main listing under "Mixed Automobilia"

## William Adorjan

See our main listing under "Toys, Truck"

## Antique Toys

See our main listing under "Motorcycle Collectibles"

## Antique Toys

Frank A. Najbart
2736 Bee Tree Lane
St. Louis, MO 63129-5610 USA
TEL: 314-846-2444

Specialize in buying antique transportation toys for personal collection. Serious collector looking to acquire nice examples of any superior toys from cast iron to Japanese tin. Call or write with description, photo, & price.

*Other categories: Toys, Truck; Gas-Powered Racers*

## Antiques Warehouse of Cape Cod

See our main listing under "Toys, Truck"

## Art's Automobilia

Arthur McFadyen
15 Cross St.
Stoughton, MA 02072 USA
TEL: 617-344-6272
FAX: 617-341-1727

Specialize in diecast banks, cars, & trucks from all major companies. Buy, sell, trade, consignment, great source for hard-to-find items. Major wholesale supplier of miniature replica gas pumps to automotive museums & gasoline stations. Also buy, sell, collect gas station memorabilia. Accept credit cards, call anytime.

*Other categories: Petroliana, Other; Mixed Automobilia; Specialized Automobilia*

## Auto Futura

See our main listing under "Hot Wheels"

## Auto Racing

See our main listing under "Racing Artifacts"

## Automobilia

See our main listing under "Retail Store"

## Autophile Car Books

See our main listing under "Books"

## Autopia Advertising Auctions

See our main listing under "Auction Firm"

## B.A.S.I.C.

See our main listing under "Mixed Automobilia"

## Bob Baker

See our main listing under "Toys, Truck"

## Barkin' Frog Collectible Co.

John Cammisa
350 College Hwy.
Southwick, MA 01077 USA
TEL: 413-569-3291

Dealer in toys since 1978. Including but not limited to cast iron, pressed steel, & pedal cars. Actively buying, selling, & collecting automobilia, gasoline collectibles, & most auto & motorcycle-related items.

*Other categories: Petroliana, Other; Mixed Automobilia; Motorcycle Collectibles*

## Milford L. Barley

See our main listing under "Toys, Truck"

## Bob Barnes

See our main listing under "Toys, Truck"

## Big T's Gas Trash

See our main listing under "Petroliana, Other"

## Bill's Garage

See our main listing under "Models, Kits"

## Bob's British Car Parts

See our main listing under "Marque Specific"

## Bob's Promotional Cars

See our main listing under "Promos"

## Gabriel Bogdonoff

See our main listing under "Gas-Powered Racers"

## Bowers Collectable Toys

See our main listing under "Mixed Automobilia"

## Bill Brisbane

4515 Willard Ave. #23115
Chevy Chase, MD 20815 USA
TEL: 301-907-6951
Email: williambr@iadb.org

Specialize in obsolete (only) miniature vehicles of all types from the 1940s through 70s. Buy, sell, trade. Reasonable prices. Updated monthly list sent to regular customers. Send one loose 55-cent stamp.

*Other categories: Models, Precision; Toys, Truck; Promos*

## Harry Burnstine

See our main listing under "Specialized Automobilia"

## C & C Creations

See our main listing under "Mixed Automobilia"

## C & M Enterprises

Marty Kirkham
5614 65 Ave. SE
Rochester, MN 55904 USA
TEL: 507-288-0219

Specialize in 1/18 diecast cars & trucks, Ertl, Mira, Revell, Road Tough, Road Legends. Airplane, car, & truck banks by Ertl, Spec-Cast, First Gear, & scale models. Also have farm toys, model kits, old trucks, & construction toys. NASCAR dragsters, funny cars in several sizes & makes.

*Other categories: Toys, Tractor; Toys, Truck; General Interest*

## Caribbean Sun Gold

See our main listing under "Models, Precision"

## Kenneth R. Chane

9755 Independence Ave.
Chatsworth, CA 91311 USA
TEL: 818-407-0855
FAX: 818-407-0850
Email: kschane@msn.com

Toys: ice cream vendors, baggage carts with figures, porters, buses & trolleys, graffiti cars. Mercedes literature & art. Hans Liska materials. Carlo Demand, Walter Gotscke, & Nicholas Watts art.

*Other categories: Art, Prints & Posters; Literature; Art, Original*

## Cotton Candy Classics

See our main listing under "Hot Rod Memorabilia"

## Craco Showcase Sales Gallery

See our main listing under "Displays/Fixtures"

## Davison Street Garage

See our main listing under "General Interest"

## Diecast Toy Collectors Association

See our main listing under "Club/Organization"

## Doc & Jesse's Auto Parts

See our main listing under "Models, Kits"

## Doo-Wop Props

See our main listing under "Hot Rod Memorabilia"

## EWJ Marketing

See our main listing under "Racing Artifacts"

## Edward Tilley Automotive Collectibles

See our main listing under "Promos"

## EinSteins

See our main listing under "Gas-Powered Racers"

## Elevenparts AG

See our main listing under "Literature"

## Finger Lakes Diecast

See our main listing under "Models, Precision"

## Flashback

See our main listing under "Racing Artifacts"

## Wm. P. Fornwalt, Jr.

See our main listing under "Models, Precision"

## G & L Collectibles

See our main listing under "Toys, Truck"

## Genuine Collectibles

See our main listing under "Toys, Truck"

## Bob Gerrity

See our main listing under "Restoration Service"

## Charles Gilbert

1103 Camelot Ct.
Johnstown, PA 15909 USA
TEL: 814-269-3634
FAX: 814-269-3634

Buying, selling, & trading quality toy cars, trucks, & tin windup toys, 1870 to 1970. We buy one toy or large collections.

*Other category: Toys, Truck*

## Great Planes Model Distributors

See our main listing under "General Interest"

## Greater Seattle Toy Show

Todd Aicher
7803 156th St. S.E.
Snomomish, WA 98290
TEL: 360-668-7144

Hertz Rent a Racer 1996 GT 350H Shelby Mustang models.

## Clyde Hensley

See our main listing under "Motorcycle Collectibles"

## Joseph Herr

903 S. 32nd Pl.
Renton, WA 98055 USA
TEL: 206-915-3096
FAX: 206-637-8671
Email: cuervojose@aol.com

Buy, sell, trade. Collect pressed-steel toys, especially fire-related Matchbox trucks/fire engines. Also collect, trade the following: coin-op countertop machines of all types, smoking-related items, pinup items, tabletop marble pinball games.

*Other categories: Toys, Truck; Mixed Automobilia; Displays/Fixtures*

## Hiway 79 Classic Collectibles

See our main listing under "Mixed Automobilia"

## Holly's Miniatures

See our main listing under "Specialized Automobilia"

## Hot Rods

See our main listing under "Hot Rod Memorabilia"

## Hot Stuff By Tri-C

See our main listing under "Hot Wheels"

## J. Hubbard Classic Cycles & Collectibles

See our main listing under "Motorcycle Collectibles"

## Richard Hurlburt

See our main listing under "License Plates, Tags, etc."

## The Hunt

Jim Larimer
25W151 Fairmeadow Ln.
Naperville, IL 60563 USA
TEL: 630-955-0633

Collectible toys for sale: Hot Wheels, Matchbox, Corgi, Tootsietoys, & others. Designate type of cars of interest when you send for list. Send SASE.

*Other categories: Hot Wheels; Toys, Tractor; Toys, Truck*

## Imperial Palace Auto Collection

See our main listing under "Museum"

## Inside Only

Scot Marechaux
6234 Glosser Rd.
Belmont, NY 14813 USA
TEL: 716-268-5582
FAX: 716-268-5533

Antique toys wanted 1880, 1970 Dinkys, airplanes, trucks, helicopters, diecast, cast iron, windup, Tootsies, Hubley, Arcade, Japanese, etc. Call or write.

*Other categories: Hot Rod Memorabilia; Motorcycle Collectibles; Pedal Cars*

## J & J Models

John D. Marshall
8573 La Baya Ave.
Fountain Valley, CA 92708 USA
TEL: 714-842-3483
FAX: 714-842-3483
Email:
105417.3705@compuserve.com

I collect Dinky toys, both French & English, also Corgi toys & the catalogs that came with these three makes. I buy, sell, & trade these makes & also have some early Lledo & other miscellaneous diecast toys to sell or trade. I can appraise the above also.

*Other categories: Appraisal Service; Toys, Truck; Books*

## J & T Collectibles

See our main listing under "Toys, Truck"

## Jim & Connie's Collectibles

See our main listing under "Specialized Automobilia"

## Jimmy Lightning

See our main listing under "Hot Wheels"

## John's Scale Autos

See our main listing under "Promos"

## Juvenile Automobiles

See our main listing under "Pedal Cars"

## K & K Old Time Toy Store

Kim Kimmel
RR 1 Box 36
Magnolia, MN 56158 USA
TEL: 507-967-2109

Buy, sell, trade. Old cars, gas engines, tractors, toys, old cast-iron cars, trucks, toy tractors, airplanes, pedal tractors & cars, gas pumps & signs & tin windup toys, etc. Restore & collect & sell anything old & auto or gas-related! Spark plugs, pressed-steel toys, & East Coast brand gas globes.

*Other category: Petroliana, Other*

## Kirk's Ghetto Garage

See our main listing under "Mixed Automobilia"

## Kneipp's Toy & Collectibles

Charlie Kneipp
6263 Price Rd.
Loveland, OH 45140-6924 USA
TEL: 513-683-0054

Large selection of old toys, cars, trucks, boats, planes, trains, Tootsie, Dinky, pressed-steel Marx, Hubley, Structo, Tonka, Midge, Buddy L, Courtland, Doepke; tin Auburn, Sun, Wyandotte; toys, pedal cars, Murray, AMF Garton badges, DAV tags, tire ashtrays, locks, keys, BB/cap guns, misc. toys & automobilia.

*Other categories: Pedal Cars; Mascots/Badges/Emblems; Mixed Automobilia*

## Ted Knorr

See our main listing under "Racing Artifacts"

## L'art et l'automobile

See our main listing under "Art, Prints & Posters"

## Dave Leopard

2507 Feather Run Trail
West Columbia, SC 29169 USA
TEL: 803-791-9400

Buy, sell, trade old toy vehicles from the 1920s to 60s. Small scale preferred, any material. Author of *Rubber Toy Vehicles*, the only real sourcebook on rubber toys. Contains many photos, old catalogs, & price guide. Available directly from author at $26.95 postpaid.

*Other categories: Toys, Truck; Books; Mixed Automobilia*

## Bob Lichty Enterprises

See our main listing under "Shows & Events"

## Lincolnia

See our main listing under "Promos"

## Lust Auction Services

See our main listing under "Auction Firm"

## Marchbanks Ltd.

See our main listing under "Pedal Cars"

## Marvelous Auto Miniatures

See our main listing under "Models, Precision"

## Charles McCabe

See our main listing under "Toys, Tractor"

## Memory Lane Collectibles

Art Hernandez
2011 Johnson St.
Hollywood, FL 33020 USA
TEL: 954-927-0025
FAX: 954-921-2211

Old toys, toys general, automobilia, gas pump, plastic toys, general plastic toys, Buddy L, Keystones, etc.

*Other categories: Pedal Cars; Toys, Truck; Mixed Automobilia*

## Merchandising Incentives Corp.

See our main listing under "Promos"

## Metropolitan & British Triumph

Pete Groh
957 Frederick Rd.
Ellicott City, MD 21042-3647 USA
TEL: 410-750-2352

British automobilia, buys, sells: toys, NOS parts, signs, tool kits, literature. Also wanted: British auto dealership-related items, including LUCAS & Girlings items. Key-cutting service, Wilmot Breeden. Need numbers. Any inquiries, SASE with your phone number. Call evenings EST.

*Other categories: Mixed Automobilia; Signs*

## Mike & Bob's Promos

See our main listing under "Promos"

## Milestone Motorcars

See our main listing under "Models, Precision"

## Moonlight Peddler

See our main listing under "Pedal Cars"

## Morris Manor Collectables

Lori & Stephen Newby
5306 181 Ave. Court East
Sumner, WA 98390-8952 USA
TEL: 206-891-2775
FAX: 206-891-2775
Email: morriscoll@aol.com

Classic/race car miniatures, pewter, coal, resin, & diecast models, greeting cards, & more. All imported from Britain. Automotive artwork by the Turners, Fearnley, Warwick, Watts, & paper sculptor Jonathan Milne. Something for everyone. Mail order available.

*Other categories: Art, Prints & Posters; Mixed Automobilia; Cards, Postal*

## Motoring Goodies
See our main listing under "Mixed Automobilia"

## Mustang Restorations
See our main listing under "Specialized Automobilia"

## National Automotive & Truck Model & Toy Museum of the United States
See our main listing under "Museum"

## National Automotive & Truck Museum of the United States (NATMUS)
See our main listing under "Museum"

## NAV, Inc.
See our main listing under "Models, Precision"

## Bob Neubauer
See our main listing under "Models, Kits"

## Wayne Noller
See our main listing under "Promos"

## Nylint Collector
See our main listing under "Toys, Truck"

## Donroy Ober
901 Dirk Dr.
Richmond, VA 23227 USA
TEL: 804-262-1532

Specialize in 1/43, 1/25-scale toy cars & trucks, mainly Ertl, Liberty Classic, Dinky, Rio, Solido. Also collect license plates, car books, auto postcards.

*Other categories: Toys, Truck; Books*

## Palmer Motor Racing
See our main listing under "Models, Precision"

## Pat's Part
See our main listing under "General Interest"

## Peachstate
See our main listing under "Models, Precision"

## Pedal Car News
See our main listing under "Pedal Cars"

## People Kars

Frank Konisky
290 Third Avenue Ext.
Rensselaer, NY 12144 USA
TEL: 518-465-0477
FAX: 518-465-0477

Mail order & shows. Specializing in toys, models, & collectibles for all years of Volkswagens. People Kars features VW models from Vitesse, Minichamps, Siku, & more, plus an extensive collection of older discontinued models, toys, & promotional pieces, all with the VW enthusiast in mind. Please write for current catalog.

*Other categories: Models, Precision; Marque Specific; Specialized Automobilia*

## Rick's Restorations/Custom Toys

See our main listing under "Restoration Service"

## Allan Rosenblum

PO Box 022181
Brooklyn, NY 11202 USA
TEL: 212-673-4370

Seeking Buddy L toys from the 1920s & 1930s. Prefer original Juniors, water towers, buses, trains, & construction equipment. Mint pieces appreciated. Have cash or will consider trading. I may have a few pieces for sale. Please send SASE. Will return all calls or mail. Accessories sought.

*Other category: Toys, Truck*

## Royal Coach

See our main listing under "Specialized Automobilia"

## SABAR International

See our main listing under "Motoring Accessories"

## San Francisco Bay Brooklin Club

See our main listing under "Models, Precision"

## Bill Sandy

See our main listing under "Marque Specific"

## Charles Schalebaum

See our main listing under "Art, Original"

## Snyder's Oil & Gas Collectibles

See our main listing under "Mixed Automobilia"

## Philip Stellmacher

3535 E. Calle del Prado
Tucson, AZ 85716 USA

Lots of diverse items: model kits, toys, automobilia, bus items, gasoline items, collectibles, advertising. Buy, sell, trade. Trucks, cars, planes, paper items, motorcycle items, transportation items in general. Send your lists, I'll send mine.

*Other categories: Mixed Automobilia; Models, Kits; Petroliana, Other*

## Mark Suozzi

See our main listing under "Motoring Accessories"

## Supercar Collectibles

Jim Thoren
508 - 81st Ave. No.
Minneapolis, MN 55444 USA
TEL: 612-425-6020

Distributor of Ertl 1/18-scale diecast. Original source for the Yenko, Copo, & ZL-1 Camaros. Limited to 2,500 pieces each. We deal in retail & wholesale, & take Visa/MC. Call for newest limited editions available. These are not just "color" changes, but very accurate replicas with casting "changes" done.

*Other categories: Models, Kits; Specialized Automobilia; Hot Rod Memorabilia*

## T and D Toy & Hobby

See our main listing under "Retail Store"

## Taxi Toys & Memorabilia

See our main listing under "Chauffeur/Taxi Items"

## Tee-Pee Model Toy Collectibles

Patrick Bickel
230 So. Cypress Rd.
Pompano Beach, FL 33060 USA
TEL: 954-941-3707
FAX: 954-941-4438

Selling quality diecast collectibles for over 12 years. Cars, airplanes, banks, trucks, buses, construction models, tow trucks, racing models, oil & gasoline-related models, old auto-related magazines, old Indy 500 books, buy, sell. Free list on request.

*Other categories: Retail Store; Mixed Automobilia; General Interest*

## Thomas Toys, Inc.

Julian Thomas
Box 405
Fenton, MI 48430 USA
TEL: 810-629-8707

3000+ parts, tires for antique, collector toys in 50s & 60s. 1997 catalog available $7 postpaid. We collect old toys, cast iron to Tonkas. Always looking to add quality toys, especially postwar Buddy L's 1957-1960 GMC trucks.

*Other categories: Pedal Cars; Toys, Truck; Toys, Tractor*

## Tiger Automotive

See our main listing under "Promos"

## Tompkins Collectible Toys

Wayne S. Tompkins
7156 Hardscrabble Rd.
Addison, NY 14801 USA
TEL: 607-359-4304

Retired, private collector will sell, trade, or buy model cars, trucks, tractors, banks, Hallmark, auto & truck sales literature, Franklin Mint, Danbury Mint, 1st Gear, promos, Precision Classics, foreign farm, Hess, & like, kit built, construction, 1/18 diecast, 1/64 tractor trailers, NASCAR, old large metal toys, pedal tractors, etc.

*Other categories: Models, Precision; Toys, Tractor; Toys, Truck*

## Transportation Station

See our main listing under "Retail Store"

## Victory Lane

Suzanne Nelson
369 Broadway
Ulster Park, NY 12487 USA
TEL: 914-331-1851
FAX: 914-331-1851
Email: escolect@mindspring.com

NASCAR diecast novelties & much more! Corgi, Ertl, Revell, Action Racing Champions, Matchbox, & many more! Storefront coming to Kingston, New York, area soon! We mail order. Give us a call, or check us out on the Internet!

*Other categories: Online Service; Specialized Automobilia; Racing Artifacts*

## Vintage America

See our main listing under "Restoration Service"

## Vintage Autos & Automobilia

See our main listing under "Mixed Automobilia"

## VIP Ltd.

See our main listing under "Models, Kits"

## Bill Walls

See our main listing under "Pedal Cars"

## David Wasserman

See our main listing under "Motorcycle Collectibles"

## Keith Wendt

2633 - 150 St
Traer, IA 50675 USA
TEL: 319-478-2249

Buy, sell, trade. Cast-iron & pressed-steel trucks, cars, tractors prior to 1950. Do nickel plating on cast iron, men wheels, etc.

*Other categories: Toys, Truck; Retail Store; Pedal Cars*

## West Coast Replicas

See our main listing under "Toys, Truck"

## Westchester Collectibles

See our main listing under "Toys, Truck"

## Wheel Goods Trader Magazine

See our main listing under "Pedal Cars"

## Michael Wojtowicz

See our main listing under "Racing Artifacts"

## Yankee Trader

Mike Thompson
4000 Tennyson St.
Denver, CO 80212 USA
TEL: 303-480-1132

Largest antique & collectible toy dealer in the Rocky Mountain region. We also carry motoring memorabilia. Open 7 days a week, M-Sat 10-5:30, Sun 11-5. Be sure to visit us when you're in the Denver area.

*Other categories: Toys, Truck; Motorcycle Collectibles; Games*

# TOYS, TRACTOR

## C & M Enterprises

See our main listing under "Toys, General"

## The Hunt

See our main listing under "Toys, General"

## Charles McCabe

122 Algonquin Dr.
Wallingford, CT 06492 USA
TEL: 203-269-5424

Farm & construction toys, tractors, trucks, pedal tractors. Specializing in lawn & garden tractors. We also deal with literature & memorabilia related to farm & construction items. We are always looking to buy pedal tractors & other related items. Call Chuck or Mike.

*Other categories: Toys, Truck; Toys, General; Literature*

## Clifford D. Stubbs

See our main listing under "Hot Wheels"

## Thomas Toys, Inc.

See our main listing under "Toys, General"

## Tompkins Collectible Toys

See our main listing under "Toys, General"

## Toy Farmer Magazine

See our main listing under "Publications, Current"

## Western Industrial

Ed Short
1341 E. Orchid Ln.
Phoenix, AZ 85020 USA
TEL: 602-944-1212

Collector of toys. Farm toys, pedal tractors, old tools. Buy, sell, trade, restore, & collect.

*Other categories: Toys, Truck; Tools; Pedal Cars*

# TOYS, TRUCK

## William Adorjan

1667 Winnetka Rd.
Glenview, IL 60025 USA
TEL: 847-657-8502

Specialize in 1/43 diecast Tootsietoys, Dinky, Corgi, pre & postwar. Complete collections purchased. Also Tootsie, LaSalle, & Graham replicas. Send SASE for complete list of over 300 automotive toys for sale. Also buying tin & pressed-steel truck & autos, French tin buses & cars.

*Other categories: Toys, General; Promos*

## Antique Toys

See our main listing under "Toys, General"

## Antiques Warehouse of Cape Cod

Michael J. Welch
3700 Rt. 6 RR 2
Eastham, MA 02642 USA
TEL: 508-255-1437

Antique toys. Buy, sell, trade. Pressed steel, pedal cars, balloon-tire bikes, automobilia, petroliana, nostalgia, & much, much more. Open daily or winters by appointment. Now open at Atlantic Oaks camp.

*Other categories: Toys, General; Pedal Cars; Mixed Automobilia*

## The Auto Collectibles Co.

See our main listing under "Retail Store"

## Automobilia Cycles Trucks (ACT)

See our main listing under "Specialized Automobilia"

## Back In Time Toys

See our main listing under "Models, Precision"

## Bob Baker

200 Cathy Ann Lane
Marietta, GA 30064 USA
TEL: 770-427-1932

Hess toy trucks mint in box, Texaco banks. Hess '89 $80, Hess '90 $65, Hess '91 $45, Hess '92 $55, Hess '93 $35, Hess '94 $30, Hess '95 $55, Hess '96 $35. Texaco Airplane #1 $225, #2 $100, #3 $75, #4 $50. Other Hess & Texaco – write! No collect calls, please.

*Other categories: Toys, General; Petroliana, Other; General Interest*

## Milford L. Barley

1146 Bodine Rd.
Chester Springs, PA 19425-2005 USA

Toys sale. Wanted: Ertl, Tonka, Nylint, Smith-Miller, MIC, Tootsietoy, Hubley, etc. Mail only – parts for many pressed steel & diecast, tin, plastic toys.

*Other categories: Toys, General; Publications, Current*

## Bob Barnes

43 Via Alicia
Santa Barbara, CA 93108 USA
TEL: 805-962-9559
FAX: 805-962-9559

Specialize in automotive toys from 1920-1960: pressed steel, Smith-Millers, Tonkas, race cars, Japanese tin.

*Other categories: Toys, General; Gas-Powered Racers*

## Bart Cars

See our main listing under "Promos"

## Bob's Promotional Cars

See our main listing under "Promos"

## Bob's Trucks

R.E. (Bob) Golladay
11033 Woodside Ave.
Santee, CA 92071-3255 USA
TEL: 619-448-2627

Specialize in 1946 through 1964 toy trucks: Tonka, Smith-Miller, Doepke, Buddy L, Wyandotte, True-Scale, All American, Nylint, & plastic models. Also signs: auto, beer, & soda. Swap spaces at Fall Indy, Carlisle, & Hershey. Also most Pomonas, Feb. Big 3 San Diego, & Spring Pate. Call weekday mornings, PST.

*Other categories: Signs; Marque Specific*

## Bill Brisbane

See our main listing under "Toys, General"

## Brookfield Collectors Guild

See our main listing under "Models, Precision"

## C & M Enterprises

See our main listing under "Toys, General"

## Capitol Miniature Auto Collectors Club

See our main listing under "Club/Organization"

## Caribbean Sun Gold

See our main listing under "Models, Precision"

## Bill Carlisle

5505 Medhurst
Solon, OH 44139 USA
TEL: 800-989-6644
FAX: 216-641-1333

First Gear diecast trucks. Specializing in trucks for the beer, pop, & dairy industries.

*Other category: Promos*

## Carney Plastics Inc.

See our main listing under "Displays/Fixtures"

## Crazy Irishman Collectibles

See our main listing under "Mixed Automobilia"

## Crown Premiums

See our main listing under "Manufacturer"

## Davison Street Garage

See our main listing under "General Interest"

## Dooley & Sons

See our main listing under "Signs"

## Finger Lakes Diecast

See our main listing under "Models, Precision"

## Frank's Toys & Adv. Memorabilia

See our main listing under "Mixed Automobilia"

## Frontier Group

See our main listing under "Petroliana, Other"

## Frost International Enterprises

See our main listing under "Literature"

## G & L Collectibles

George Peterson
332 N. Citrus Ave.
Covina, CA 91723 USA
TEL: 818-966-6829
FAX: 818-336-3773

Specialize in pressed-steel trucks. Smith Miller, All-American, Hubley, Structo, Steelcraft, Tonka, & Wyandotte. Also buy & sell pedal cars & pedal tractors. Sales of furniture, crystal, etc. Retail store located in Old Town, Covina, California.

*Other categories: Pedal Cars; Toys, General; Retail Store*

Scale Model Truck Sales

Miniature Truck Collector
**JOE GOLABIEWSKI**
P.O. Box 28
Fork, MD 21051  (410) 592-5854

Winross     Ertl     First Gear

## Genuine Collectibles

Patrick Paldino
599 Fermery Dr.
New Milford, NJ 07646 USA
TEL: 201-384-8159
FAX: 201-384-3645

Specialize in oil company diecast & plastic promotional toy trucks. Buy, sell, trade. Also road maps, magazine advertisements, & other oil company collectibles. Mail order only. Send LSASE for current list. Call 10-6 EST.

*Other categories: Petroliana, Other; Toys, General; General Interest*

## Charles Gilbert

See our main listing under "Toys, General"

## Joseph R. Golabiewski

12317 Harford Rd.
Kingsville, MD 21087 USA
TEL: 410-592-5854

Scale model trucks. First Gear, Ertl, & many Winross. My merchandise is all mint in original boxes. I will not be undersold. Look for me at toy shows, fall Hershey, & ATCA at Macungie in June 1997. Mail order. Send SASE for lists. Call after 6pm EST.

*Other categories: Models, Precision; Hot Wheels*

## Joseph Herr

See our main listing under "Toys, General"

## Peter E. Hoyt

See our main listing under "Models, Kits"

## The Hunt

See our main listing under "Toys, General"

## J & J Models

See our main listing under "Toys, General"

## J & T Collectibles

Jim Balzano
3 Radnor Ct.
Belle Mead, NJ 08502 USA
TEL: 908-359-4205
Email: balzaja@churchdwight.com

Specialize in Hess promotionals, including: trucks, signs, pump-toppers, buttons, etc. Always buying & selling. Also have other gas station promos. Especially interested in pre-1979 mint-in-box trucks. Call after 5pm EST.

*Other categories: Toys, General; Promos; General Interest*

## Jamar Company

See our main listing under "Displays/Fixtures"

## John's Scale Autos

See our main listing under "Promos"

## Juvenile Automobiles

See our main listing under "Pedal Cars"

## Dave Leopard

See our main listing under "Toys, General"

## Lilliput Motor Car Co.

See our main listing under "Models, Precision"

## Magazine Man

See our main listing under "Books"

## Charles McCabe

See our main listing under "Toys, Tractor"

## Bob McClernan

See our main listing under "Petroliana, Other"

## Memory Lane Collectibles

See our main listing under "Toys, General"

## Merchandising Incentives Corp.

See our main listing under "Promos"

## New Era Toys

See our main listing under "Restoration Service"

## Jim Newhall Automobilia

See our main listing under "Promos"

## Nylint Collector

Jonathan Walker
910 Coolidge
Pekin, IL 61554 USA
TEL: 309-346-9626

Nylint trucks. I'm looking for Ford trucks & vans made by Nylint during the 1960s. They made toy versions of the cab-over, F100 pickups, Econoline trucks & vans, Broncos. I buy near mint to mint & boxed examples. Private labels such as Holiday Inn, Penneys, U-Haul, others especially wanted!

*Other categories: Promos; Toys, General; Manufacturer*

## Donroy Ober

See our main listing under "Toys, General"

## Dan O'Neill Precision Models

See our main listing under "Manufacturer"

## Pedal Car News

See our main listing under "Pedal Cars"

## Perma Coatings

See our main listing under "Restoration Service"

## Portell Restorations

See our main listing under "Pedal Cars"

## Production Plus Graphics Inc.

See our main listing under "Signs"

## Rick's Restorations/Custom Toys

See our main listing under "Restoration Service"

## Allan Rosenblum

See our main listing under "Toys, General"

## Shriver Auto Mall

Robert Shriver
W4498 Cty Hwy BZ
Rio, WI 53960 USA
TEL: 414-992-3218

Tonkas, Buddy Ls, Smith Millers, Structo, Hubley Trucks, 1940s through 60s. Gasoline collectibles & auto literature, street rod quality restorations available for toy trucks, gas pumps & pedal cars. Buy, sell, & take consignments.

*Other categories: Retail Store; Restoration Service*

## Ed Smith
See our main listing under "Petroliana, Other"

## South Shore Auto Sports
See our main listing under "Shows & Events"

## Squat Rods
See our main listing under "Pedal Cars"

## T&T Collectables
Thomas Davidson
243 Pleasant Ave.
Johnstown, NY 12095 USA
TEL: 518-762-1012

Wanted – old pressed-steel trucks. Buddy L, Keystone, Sonny, Smith Miller, Kelmet, Steelcraft, MIC of Calif., Turner, Chein, Buffalo Toys, Kingsbury, Metalcraft, Sturditoy.

## Thomas Toys, Inc.
See our main listing under "Toys, General"

## Tompkins Collectible Toys
See our main listing under "Toys, General"

## Toy Trucker & Contractor Magazine
See our main listing under "Publications, Current"

## Transportation Station
See our main listing under "Retail Store"

## Turtle Creek Scale Models
See our main listing under "Models, Precision"

## US Toy Collector Magazine
Gordon Rice
PO Box 4244
Missoula, MT 59806-4244 USA
TEL: 406-549-3175

America's largest toy vehicle photomarketplace. Hundreds of toy trucks, cars, construction toys for sale each month in photo ads. Tonka, Buddy L,

Structo, Marx, Wyandotte, Hubley, Tootsietoy, Matchbox, Dinky, Sturditoy, etc. Sample $3. Yearly $21.

*Other categories: Specialized Automobilia; Pedal Cars; Gas-Powered Racers*

## Bill Walls
See our main listing under "Pedal Cars"

## Keith Wendt
See our main listing under "Toys, General"

## West Coast Replicas
Bruce W. Risley
11317 Folsom Blvd.
Rancho Cordova, CA 95742 USA
TEL: 916-464-1310
FAX: 916-464-1309

Producers of quality limited edition diecast replicas of trucks & cars. Custom imprint specialist. Wholesale/retail dealer inquiries invited, USA & overseas. WCR presently holds licensing approval from several major corporations.

*Other categories: Toys, General; Petroliana, Other; Racing Artifacts*

## Westchester Collectibles
Barry Matthews
600 North Broadway
White Plains, NY 10603 USA
TEL: 914-684-6951
FAX: 914-684-6952

A producing First Gear dealer. We operate a mail order & retail store. We also handle Corgi Classics, Ertl, Matchbox, Solido, Joal diecast collectibles. As a producing First Gear dealer we can offer many first releases of new models. When in New York visit our retail store.

*Other categories: Toys, General; Retail Store*

## Western Industrial
See our main listing under "Toys, Tractor"

## Winross Company
See our main listing under "Manufacturer"

## Winross-By-Mail
Larry V. Warfel
PO Box 38
Palmyra, NY 14522-0038 USA
TEL: 800-227-2060
FAX: 315-986-3849

Manufacturer of 1/64-scale diecast tractor trailer models.

## Yankee Trader
See our main listing under "Toys, General"

# GENERAL INTEREST

## AMWP
See our main listing under "Publications, Current"

## C. Sherman Allen, Auctioneer & Associates
See our main listing under "Auction Firm"

## American Eagle Racing
See our main listing under "Hot Rod Memorabilia"

## Auto Futura
See our main listing under "Hot Wheels"

## The Automobile Art Studio
See our main listing under "Art, Original"

## Automobile Sportswear Inc.
See our main listing under "Clothing"

## BJM
See our main listing under "Mascots/Badges/Emblems"

## Baja Cantina Grill & Filling Station
Pat Phinny
7166 Carmel Valley Road
Carmel Valley, CA 93923 USA
TEL: 408-625-BAJA
FAX: 408-625-2279
Email: bkbill@earthlink.net

This watering hole is dedicated to the preservation of racing automoblies, automobilia, etc. All items in the restaurant are originals. (Including the owner, Pat Phinny.) Located just minutes from Laguna Seca Raceway.

## Bob Baker

See our main listing under "Toys, Truck"

## Bare Necessities

Tom Benke
804 E. High St.
Jefferson City, MO 65101 USA
TEL: 573-636-5509

Buying any transportation-related memorabilia. Postcards, Cracker Jack prizes, old photos, badges, magazines, displays, letters, autographs, etc.

*Other categories: Books; Cards, Postal; Petroliana, Other*

## Bergen Distributors

See our main listing under "Petroliana, Other"

## Blaser's Auto

See our main listing under "Specialized Automobilia"

## C & M Enterprises

See our main listing under "Toys, General"

## Car Crazy, Inc.

See our main listing under "Retail Store"

## Check the Oil! Magazine

See our main listing under "Petroliana, Other"

## Chuck's Collectibles

See our main listing under "Restoration Service"

## City Classics

See our main listing under "Models, Kits"

## Classic Restoration

See our main listing under "Tools"

## Collectors Auction Services

See our main listing under "Auction Firm"

## Cosdel International Co. Inc.

Martin E. Button
55 New Montgomery Street, #400
San Francisco, CA 94105 USA
TEL: 415-777-2000
FAX: 415-543-5112
Email: info@cosdel.com

We are an international shipping company specializing in the international movements of collector cars & associated automobilia. We are always happy to assist with imports & exports anywhere, especially when temporary importation for trade show sales or car meets is involved.

## Dan's Classic Auto Parts

See our main listing under "Mixed Automobilia"

## Davison Street Garage

Dave Thiel
415 S. Davison St.
Davison, MI 48423 USA
TEL: 810-653-1871

Always interested in buying, selling, or trading oil cans, road maps, Hess trucks, tow trucks, tankers, pressed-steel cars & trucks, Tootsie Toys, slush cast. Especially interested in cars & trucks to restore.

*Other categories: Toys, Truck; Petroliana, Other; Toys, General*

## David Ellnor

See our main listing under "Books"

## Fineline Car Co.

Tim Kinderknecht
1836 110 Ave.
Ellis, KS 67637 USA
TEL: 913-726-3511

Locating automobilia/petroliana central US auctions, flea markets. Ship worldwide. Call with your needs or interests. Dealer of antique & classic cars also.

*Other categories: Signs; Pedal Cars*

## GameRoomAntiques

See our main listing under "Games"

## Genuine Collectibles

See our main listing under "Toys, Truck"

## Dwayne L. Gordon

See our main listing under "Mixed Automobilia"

## Great Planes Model Distributors

PO Box 9021
Champaign, IL 61821-9021 USA
TEL: 217-398-8970
FAX: 217-398-1104

Wholesale distributor of high-quality radio-control model cars & accessories, all scales of diecast car & truck models, plastic model kits & accessories, slot car sets, etc. Exclusive distributor of Kyosho radio-control models. Dealer inquiries welcome. Call for a dealer information packet.

*Other categories: Models, Precision; Toys, General; Models, Kits*

## Robert N. Haldeman

12050 S. Bay Dr.
Fredericktown, OH 43019 USA
TEL: 614-694-5326

Buy & sell items in the categories of gasoline, automobilia, motorcycle & all other categories.

*Other categories: Petroliana, Other; Mixed Automobilia; Motorcycle Collectibles*

## Hemmings Motor News

See our main listing under "Publications, Current"

## Hiway 79 Classic Collectibles

See our main listing under "Mixed Automobilia"

## The Hobby Shop

See our main listing under "Manufacturer"

## Holly's Miniatures

See our main listing under "Specialized Automobilia"

## Hubcap Mike

Michael Collins
26242 Dimension Dr. Ste. 150
Lake Forest, CA 92630 USA
TEL: 714-597-8120
FAX: 714-597-8123

Hubcaps, wheel covers, trim rings, 1930 to present. 25,000 in stock. We ship anywhere. Customer satisfaction guaranteed.

## Hudson Motor Car Company Memorabilia

See our main listing under "Specialized Automobilia"

## Imperial Palace Auto Collection

See our main listing under "Museum"

## J. Hubbard Classic Cycles & Collectibles

See our main listing under "Motorcycle Collectibles"

## J & T Collectibles

See our main listing under "Toys, Truck"

## Jake's Mustang Dismantling

See our main listing under "Restoration Service"

## Jamar Company

See our main listing under "Displays/Fixtures"

## Ron Johnson

613 South C St.
La Harpe, IL 61450 USA
TEL: 217-659-7667

Wanted: Any item pertaining to Dick Harrell, Fred Gibb, Don Yenko, Dana, Berger, Baldwin-Motion, Shay Nichols, Grady Bryant, ZL-1 Camaro, Book: *The Edsel Affair.*

*Other categories: Personalities; Mixed Automobilia; Specialized Automobilia*

## Jim Jones

See our main listing under "Cards, Postal"

## Robert Kegler

See our main listing under "Mascots/Badges/Emblems"

## Kid Stuff

See our main listing under "Restoration Service"

## Dale Klee

See our main listing under "Art, Prints & Posters"

## Lights Up

See our main listing under "Specialized Automobilia"

## Lust Auction Services

See our main listing under "Auction Firm"

## Larry Machacek

See our main listing under "License Plates, Tags, etc."

## Marvelous Auto Miniatures

See our main listing under "Models, Precision"

## McLong Tags & Ads

See our main listing under "License Plates, Tags, etc."

## Mega-Zines

C.A. Mansfield
2708 Thornbridge Rd. E.
York, PA 17404 USA
TEL: 717-767-4262
FAX: 717-767-4262

Source for out-of-print automotive magazines & a research service for their contents. Topics include hot-rodding, racing, road tests & performance reports, personalities, etc. Other services include original magazine advertisements, programs, paint chips, club & organization publications, & manuals. Send SASE or fax us with requests.

*Other categories: Hot Rod Memorabilia; Racing Artifacts; Literature*

## Ken Miller Specialties

See our main listing under "Literature"

## Mobilia

See our main listing under "Publications, Current"

## Mobilia South Africa

See our main listing under "Petroliana, Other"

## Model A Ford Cabriolet Club

See our main listing under "Club/Organization"

## Monday's

Fred & Denise Monday
3665 Canelli Ct.
Pleasanton, CA 94566 USA
TEL: 510-846-6096
FAX: 510-846-6096

Specialize in quality restoration of gas-related items, soda machines, pedal

cars; also design new clocks for diners, game rooms, & automobilia collectors. Buy, sell, trade signs of all kinds. Also broker for nationwide shipping of all above items plus any coin-op items at a 25% discount off regular charge.

*Other categories: Restoration Service; Petroliana, Other; Rt. 66 & Roadside*

## Motordrive

See our main listing under "Motorcycle Collectibles"

## Motoring Memories

Donald A. Bartlett
115 18 Ave. SE
St. Petersburg, FL 33705 USA
TEL: 813-894-5690

Dealer in general automobilia with emphasis on posters (art & movie), prints, & auto postage stamps. Buying & selling.

*Other categories: Art, Prints & Posters; Art, Other; Mixed Automobilia*

## Moviecraft Inc.

See our main listing under "Manufacturer"

## The Museum of Automobile History

See our main listing under "Museum"

## Mustang Restorations

See our main listing under "Specialized Automobilia"

## Mystic Motorcar Museum

See our main listing under "Museum"

## NASCAR Novelties

See our main listing under "Motoring Accessories"

## Pacific Communications

See our main listing under "Rt. 66 & Roadside"

## Pat's Parts

Pat Martin
57 Cramton Ave.
Rutland, VT 05701-2606 USA
TEL: 802-775-6608

Anything auto-related. Buy, sell, trade. Specialize in Vermont license plates,

DAV tags, also have others including NY pairs. Many quality toys. Buddy L, Tonka, Marx Steelcraft, Doepke Metalcraft, Dinky, Corgi, Lledo, Japanese tin, others. Much auto literature, books, manuals, ads. Send wants or call before 8pm EST.

*Other categories: Toys, General; License Plates, Tags, etc.; Literature*

## Barry Power Graphic Design

Barry Power
3921 19th St.
San Francisco, CA 94114 USA
TEL: 415-863-5085
FAX: 415-863-5085

Logo design, letterhead, business card, display ad, image search, etc. for your auto-related business. Automobile themes my passion! Vroom.

*Other category: Publications, Current*

## R & G Automobiles & Collectables

See our main listing under "Mixed Automobilia"

## Stephen J. Raiche

See our main listing under "License Plates, Tags, etc."

## Frank R. Righetti

See our main listing under "Signs"

## RJN Automobilia

See our main listing under "Marque Specific"

## Route 66 Decanters

See our main listing under "Specialized Automobilia"

## San Francisco Bay Brooklin Club

See our main listing under "Models, Precision"

## Ed Schwartz

See our main listing under "Petroliana, Other"

## Silver Creek Antiques

See our main listing under "Retail Store"

## Skyline Design

See our main listing under "Art, Prints & Posters"

## South Shore Auto Sports

See our main listing under "Shows & Events"

## SpeedArt Enterprises

See our main listing under "Mascots/Badges/Emblems"

## The Strong Collection

See our main listing under "Mixed Automobilia"

## Tee-Pee Model Toy Collectibles

See our main listing under "Toys, General"

## Unocal 76 Products

See our main listing under "Petroliana, Other"

## Marnix Verkest

Tasscheweg 11A
Roeselare, Belgium 8800
TEL: +32-51225828
FAX: +32-51225828

Specializing in early Belgian cars & motorcycles & American 4-cylinder motorcycles. Buy & trade original parts, literature, & posters. Write or fax.

*Other categories: Art, Prints & Posters; Literature; Motorcycle Collectibles*

## Viewfinders

Pete Smith
PO Box 913
Lemon Grove, CA 91946 USA
TEL: 619-463-7292

Have camera will travel. Photograph your collection or event. Complete photographic service.

*Other categories: Rt. 66 & Roadside; Specialized Automobilia; Photographs*

## Wizzy's Collector Car Parts

See our main listing under "Mixed Automobilia"

## Woody's Garage

See our main listing under "License Plates, Tags, etc."

## Workbench

See our main listing under "Mascots/Badges/Emblems"

## Wyckoff Auto

See our main listing under "Mixed Automobilia"

## Yesterday's Highways Newsletter

See our main listing under "Publications, Current"

## Yosemite Sam's Auto Art

See our main listing under "Art, Original"

# INDEX: All Main Listings by Collecting Category
### (Cross listings appear in text but not in this index)

# Don't Be Left Out!

**If you're an automobilia specialist and would like to appear in the second edition of the *MOBILIA Sourcebook*, here's what you can do:**

*Complete and mail the Free Listing form appearing on pp. 142-143 in its entirety—<u>Deadline is November 30, 1997</u>;*

*OR,*

*Complete and mail the Free Listing Request form below—<u>Deadline is October 31, 1997</u>.*

# Thank you.

**MOBILIA Sourcebook Free Listing Request Form**
<u>Send to:</u> **MOBILIA Sourcebook, P.O. Box 575, Middlebury, VT 05753 • USA**
**FAX: 802-388-2215**

I want to be included in the second edition of the MOBILIA Sourcebook! Here's my name and address—please send me a Free Listing Form:

_____
Business Name

_____
Individual Name

_____
Address

_____
City

_____
State                        Zip

_____
TEL

_____
FAX

_____
E-Mail

# List Frequently Used Contacts Here

| Business Name | Area of Specialty | Page No. | Remarks |
|---------------|-------------------|----------|---------|
|  |  |  |  |
|  |  |  |  |
|  |  |  |  |
|  |  |  |  |
|  |  |  |  |
|  |  |  |  |
|  |  |  |  |
|  |  |  |  |
|  |  |  |  |
|  |  |  |  |
|  |  |  |  |
|  |  |  |  |
|  |  |  |  |
|  |  |  |  |
|  |  |  |  |
|  |  |  |  |
|  |  |  |  |
|  |  |  |  |
|  |  |  |  |
|  |  |  |  |
|  |  |  |  |
|  |  |  |  |
|  |  |  |  |
|  |  |  |  |
|  |  |  |  |
|  |  |  |  |

# Don't be left out!

If you're an automobilia specialist, then you need to be in the second edition of the *MOBILIA Sourcebook*.

## INSTRUCTIONS

- Your listing will appear under one main category, and up to three additional cross-referenced categories.
- Form must be filled out in its entirety. Kindly write in block letters, or type.
- One form per lister.
- We reserve the right to reject any listing considered unsuitable.

**Second Edition
MOBILIA
Sourcebook**

# Free Listing Form

**Response Deadline:**
November 30, 1997

# Sample

Main Listing

Up to three additional cross-referenced listings.

**I**

**Automobilia Grand**
Steven Riley
149 Monogram Way
Middlebury, VT 05753 USA
TEL: 802-388-3071
FAX: 802-388-2215
email: AG@aol.com

Specialize in early model kits. Buy, sell, trade. Also collect cast-iron and pressed-steel toys, and East Coast brand gas globes. Complete collections purchased or for consignment. Appraisals for insurance or estate settlement. Mail-order, or Iowa Gas and Fall Hershey. Send SASE for current list. Call after 5 pm.

**MODELS, KITS**
Toys, General
Petroliana, Pumps & Globes
Appraisel

*Models, Kits*

**Automobilia Grand**
See our main listing under "Models, Kits"
**Toys, General** **A**

**Automobilia Grand**
See our main listing under "Models, Kits"
**Petroliana, Pumps & Globes** **B**

**Automobilia Grand**
See our main listing under "Models, Kits"
**Appraisal** **C**

# Begin here

*Form must be completed in __full__ for us to process your listing.*

## 1. Categories

Your free listing will appear in one main category, plus up to three additional categories.

Pick from the following list. The list combines activity-oriented categories (i.e. "Museum") and subject-oriented categories (i.e. "Pedal Cars"). You can mix and match—it's up to you.

Use "1" to indicate your Main Listing. Use "A", "B", and "C" to indicate up to three additional cross-referenced listings. *In the example above, Automobilia Grand chose the main category "Models, Kits" (1), and three cross-referenced categories of "Toys, General" (A), "Petroliana, Pumps & Globes" (B), and "Appraisal" (C).*

____ Appraisal Service
____ Art, Original
____ Art, Prints & Posters
____ Art, Other
____ Auction Firm
____ Books
____ Cards, Postal
____ Cards, Trading
____ Chauffeur/Taxi Items
____ Clothing
____ Club/Organization
____ Diner Memorabilia
____ Displays/Fixtures
____ Games
____ Gas-Powered Racers
____ Horns
____ Hot Rod Memorabilia
____ Hot Wheels
____ Jewelry

____ Lamps
____ Legal Service
____ License Plates, Tags, etc.
____ Literature
____ Luggage/Picnic Sets
____ Manufacturer
____ Marque Specific
____ Mascots/Badges/Emblems
____ Mixed Automobilia
____ Models, Kits
____ Models, Precision
____ Motorcycle Collectibles
____ Motoring Accessories
____ Museum
____ Neon
____ Online Service
____ Pedal Cars
____ Personalities
____ Petroliana, Pumps & Globes

____ Petroliana, Other
____ Photographs
____ Promos
____ Publication, Current
____ Racing Artifacts
____ Restoration Service
____ Retail Store
____ Rt. 66 & Roadside
____ Showroom Items
____ Shows & Events
____ Signs
____ Slot Cars
____ Spark Plugs
____ Specialized Automobilia
____ Tools
____ Toys, Tractor
____ Toys, Truck
____ Toys, Other
____ *General Interest*

## 2. Main Listing

This information will appear in your main listing. Short declarative sentences will be the most effective in describing your automobilia activity. Listing space is limited to 50 words. What you write is <u>exactly</u> what will appear in the *Sourcebook*. (We reserve the right to edit for grammar, consistency, space, etc.)

### Contact Information

Business Name
_____

Individual Name
_____

Address
_____

City
_____

State _____ Zip _____

TEL
_____

FAX
_____

E-Mail
_____

Signature (required for us to print your listing)

### Listing

*Please use block letters, or type.*

___ ___ ___ ___ ___
___ ___ ___ ___ ___
___ ___ ___ ___ ___
___ ___ ___ ___ ___
___ ___ ___ ___ ___
___ ___ ___ ___ ___
___ ___ ___ ___ ___
___ ___ ___ ___ ___
___ ___ ___ ___ ___
___ ___ ___ ___ ___

**50 max.**

## 3. Get Noticed!

☐ **Yes! Send me details on value-priced *Sourcebook* display ads.**

## 4. Mail or FAX Your Completed Form
### <u>Deadline</u>: November 30, 1997

# MOBILIA
# Sourcebook ™

**P.O. Box 575, Middlebury, VT 05753 • USA**
**FAX 802-388-2215**